Derek and Julia Parker are familiar nam
in astrology. Since 1970 their many books have introduced
innumerable readers to the subject, many of whom started to
study astrology by using them, and have subsequently become
professionals. Julia started life as an art teacher and dancer,
Derek as a journalist and broadcaster; they became interested in
astrology in the 1960s, and besides their numerous books on the
subject (including *The Compleat Astrologer* and *Parkers'
Astrology*) they have also written books on dream interpretation,
mythology, magic, the theatre, and travel. Julia has written two
novels, and Derek a number of biographies.

PARKERS'
ENCYCLOPEDIA
OF ASTROLOGY

DEREK AND JULIA PARKER

WATKINS PUBLISHING

LONDON

Distributed in the United States and Canada by Sterling Publishing Co., Inc.
387 Park Avenue South, New York, NY 10016-8810

This edition first published in the UK and USA 2009 by
Watkins Publishing, Sixth Floor, Castle House,
75–76 Wells Street, London W1T 3QH

1 3 5 7 9 10 8 6 4 2

Designed by Jerry Goldie

Typeset by Dorchester Typesetting Group Ltd, Dorset, England

Printed and bound in Great Britain

Library of Congress Cataloging-in-Publication data available

ISBN: 978-1-905857-85-2

www.watkinspublishing.co.uk

For information about custom editions, special sales, premium and
corporate purchases, please contact Sterling Special Sales
Department at 800-805-5489 or specialsales@sterlingpub.com

To Chester Kemp and Angela Priestman,
with love and gratitude.

INTRODUCTION

This is a book for everyone who is interested in astrology – for those who are attracted to it but have never studied it; and for those who may be expert in calculating and interpreting a chart, but have never thought about the long and fascinating history of the subject.

Anyone simply interested in their 'star signs' will find the subject easily explained here, without any jargon – just what it means to have the Sun in a zodiac sign – but also how you have a rising-sign, a Midheaven, and the Moon and planets also scattered about your birth-chart. You can check whether it's really true that Scorpios are mad for sex while Virgos aren't in the least interested.

But the encyclopedia contains much more than the usual book aimed at laymen, because if you want to look further you can discover here what it means when a planet has a *trine aspect* to another; what a trine aspect *is*, and how it works. What is a *polar sign*? What is *precession*? – a *critical degree*? – a *planetary hour*? Almost every question you can ask about astrology is answered here – so the book will be useful, too, to the student astrologer who needs quickly to find what *orb* is allowed a *sesquiquadrate aspect* or in what sign Mars is *exalted*.

There is in these pages much to fascinate those who are not in the least interested in how (or even whether) astrology works – here you can trace the history of the subject over the past 2,000 years and more. You can read how Nostradamus wrote his famous predictions, how the astrologer Thrasyllus ruled Rome under the Emperor Tiberius, how and when Ptolemy wrote the first great astrological textbook – and how 1,500 years later William Lilly wrote the first one to be published in English. On one page Jean-Baptiste Morin is hiding behind the bed-curtains to note down the precise moment when the Dauphin of France consummates his marriage, on another Simon Forman is busy calculating the charts of his female clients – not only to help them, but to find out whether he'll be successful in seducing them. In one century Pope

Paul III sets up a university of astrologers and employs Luca Gaurico to work out the most propitious moment to lay the foundation stones of his churches, and centuries later here is Cardinal Wolsey employing an astrologer to read the mind of his employer, King Henry VIII.

The spread of astrology through the world can be followed here, too – from Greece to Rome via an astrology school on the island of Kos; from the East to the West as the textbooks of Albumasar are translated into English by Adelard of Bath; how astrology travelled to the new lands of North America, and how after the invention of printing the burgeoning astrological almanacs brought the subject to the ordinary people – for many years, the two books most commonly to be found in every home were the Bible and the current almanac.

Then there is the long association between astrology and medicine – for centuries it was improper and usually illegal to practise medicine unless you had studied astrology. And, just to annoy the sceptics, the equally long association between astrology and astronomy – how for a millennia one word described both professions, and how even the great Kepler kept his 'horoscope book' and published annual almanacs.

After two centuries in the doldrums, some aspects of astrology are now once more being taken seriously; courses in its history are being taught in universities, biographers have looked at the lives of Lilly, Simon Forman, John Dee and others, and work has at last begun on examining and codifying the countless astrological manuscripts in European libraries which throw an often extraordinarily new and illuminating light on social and intellectual history. Can anyone afford to ignore all this with a disdainful sniff? Or is it worth at least dipping one foot into the fascinating sea which this book surveys?

Derek and Julia Parker
Sydney, 2007

– A –

Abano, Pietro d' (ca.1250–ca.1317) Italian astrologer, philosopher and
doctor who studied philosophy and medicine in Paris before opening a
practice in Padua. Admired by REGIOMONTANUS, he was described as 'a
great master' of astrology and astronomy, and published translations of
ABENEZRA. He was summoned twice to appear before the Inquisition
accused of magical practices, was acquitted the first time, but died before
the second trial ended. He was found guilty – but since he was dead,
escaped the stake. His body was ordered to be exhumed and burned, but
friends had removed it from the grave and it escaped that ignominy.

Abenezra *see* ABRAHAM BEN MEIR IBN EZRA

Abiathar Crescas (fl.15th c.) Court astrologer to King John I of Aragon
(1350–95). He was also a surgeon, and restored the King's eyesight.

Abraham bar Ḥiyya ha-Nasi (1070–1136) Also known as Savasorda.
A Spanish Jewish astronomer and philosopher with a keen interest in
astrology who in his *Megillat ha-Megalleh* claimed to have calculated
from scripture the exact time for the advent of the Messiah.

Abraham ben Meir ibn Ezra (1093–1167) Also known as Abenezra.
An enormously well-respected Jewish literary critic and commentator on
biblical texts, philosopher, and writer on astronomy and astrology who
travelled widely in Europe and the Middle East. He published an introduction to the subject as well as an extremely thorough exegesis on
contemporary Arabic astrology. Among his published works are *Keli ha-
Nehoshet* (a treatise on the ASTROLABE), *Sefer Ha'te'amim* or *The Book of
Reasons*, a survey of Arabic astrology, and *Reshith Hochma*, or *The
Beginning of Wisdom*, an introduction to astrology.

Abraham Zacuto (ca.1450–ca.1510) A Jewish rabbi, astrologer, astronomer and mathematician, for some time Royal Astronomer to King John of Portugal. He taught at the University of Salamanca and elsewhere. He published several books on astrology, but his main achievement was the development of the ASTROLABE.

Abū Ma'shar al-Balkhī (787–886) Also known as Albumasar, an Afghan astrologer, astronomer and mathematician, much of whose work consisted of Latin translations of the writings of ARISTOTLE, which thus became available for the first time to Europeans. His treatise on astrology, translated by Adelard of Bath, was a particularly important text for Western astrologers. He is said to have been the first to calculate the astrological AGES.

accidental dignity *see* DIGNITY

accidents Significant occurrences in the life of a client – not necessarily damaging or unhappy – used by an astrologer to RECTIFY a chart.

Adams, Evangeline (1868–1932) An extremely popular American astrologer at the turn of the century, Adams worked as a consultant and published a number of books. She was twice arrested in New York and accused of 'fortune-telling', and twice acquitted, since when there have been no further attempts to mount similar prosecutions in the US. Her autobiography, *The Bowl of Heaven*, is short on personal detail, but fascinating in its details of the life of an astrologer at the turn of the century.

Addey, John (1920–82) English astrologer and researcher, whose work on HARMONICS gave birth to serious interest in that subject in the UK. With Charles HARVEY he founded the British Astrological Association.

affinity Certain pairs of planets are said to have an affinity, generally because they both have a bearing on a mutual emotion or state of mind.

affliction A planet is said to be *afflicted* when it is in an unfavourable ASPECT with another planet; formerly it was believed that a planet could be afflicted by a so-called 'evil' or malevolent fixed star.

Age of Aquarius, Age of Pisces, etc. *see* AGES

Ages The astrological Ages are the result of a phenomenon called the PRECESSION of the EQUINOXES. As a revolving top slows down, it begins to wobble. The Earth's axis of rotation wobbles in a similar way, and within about 26,000 years the VERNAL EQUINOX slowly describes a circle backwards through the twelve signs of the zodiac. The phenomenon is chiefly caused by the gravitational effect of the Sun and Moon, and to a lesser extent that of the planets, and was discovered as long ago as the 2nd century BC by the Greek astronomer HIPPARCHUS.

Astrologers take note of the 12 'ages' of rather over 2,000 years each, during which the vernal equinox moves through each sign of the zodiac in turn – but account is also taken of the sign through which the AUTUMNAL EQUINOX is moving, so for instance the Age of Pisces is linked to the sign of Virgo, and astrologers sometimes speak of the 'Age of Pisces-Virgo'. It is impossible to calculate precisely when each age begins or ends, and while some astrologers would suggest that the Age of Aquarius has begun, others are of the opinion that the Age of Pisces has not quite ended.

There has been much discussion, often centred on religion, about the extent to which each 'age' may affect mankind. The Taurean Age has been associated with bull worship in the Middle East, the beginning of the Piscean age with the birth of Christianity (an early symbol of Christianity was the fish found scrawled on the walls of the Christian catacombs in Rome); the Virgin Birth can of course be associated with Virgo. While in St Luke's Gospel Christ tells his disciples to follow a man bearing a pitcher of water, which might be thought to be a clear reference to the symbol of Aquarius, it is more generally thought that that Age, whether it has already begun or not, is likely to be associated with universal brotherhood founded on reason rather than religion – though some astrologers predict the foundation of 'religious science' or 'a scientific religion'.

ages of man There have been several attempts by astrologers to link the planets to particular periods of human life. Popularly, Jacques' speech on the seven ages of man in Shakespeare's *As You Like It* is the most obvious division of life into separate periods – the infant, the schoolboy, the lover, the soldier, the justice, the 'pantaloon' or weak old man, and the descent into second childhood. But this list in itself is derived from other, earlier lists – by HIPPOCRATES, for instance. A medieval list, the original source of which is unknown, divides a typical life of 70 years into 6 periods, with:

- the Moon ruling childhood up to the age of 4;
- Mercury dominating the period into adolescence at of the age of 14;
- Venus then governing the ages between 14 and 24 (the years of the lover, 'when we begin to produce seed');
- the Sun ruling the prime of life, up to 43 ('youth in full vigour');
- Mars presiding over the years between 43 and 58 ('prudence and an active political life');
- Jupiter the remaining years until the age of 70, when we should be preparing for death.

Saturn is left to rule any years that may remain – optimistically for a period of 30 years.

Agrippa von Nettesheim, Heinrich Cornelius (1486–1535) Agrippa (the 'von Nettesheim' and the two other names were assumed) studied in Cologne, set up a laboratory in the hope of making gold, and travelled widely in Europe as an alchemist. In 1520 he began a medical practice and four years later became physician to the queen mother at the court of Francis I at Lyon. His appointment did not last long, and after practising in Antwerp he was banned for lacking a licence. He was several times imprisoned for debt, and died in poverty. Despite this less than reputable career (he was also at times a soldier, professor of law and secret agent) he associated with a number of the prominent humanists of his time including the German Johann Reuchlin (1455–1522) and the English educational pioneer John Colet (1467–1519). In his three-volume *De occulta philosophiae* (1510) he wrote engrossingly of astrology, and particularly astrological magic (he believed that 'upper powers' could be drawn to Earth in that way). His work much influenced the later Giordano BRUNO.

air signs Gemini, Libra and Aquarius are said to be 'air signs' – that is, they are affected by the air ELEMENT or triplicity, which is associated with intellect, thought, communication and unpredictability. Gemini expresses its air characteristic through MUTABILITY, Libra through cardinality and Aquarius through FIXITY, and these characteristics mirror some of the QUALITIES of the signs: Geminian ideas developing in various directions at once, difficult to discipline and channel; Libran ideas well directed and purposeful; Aquarian ideas somewhat static, introverted, possibly developed only with some strain and tension.

Alan, William Frederick (1860–1917) Born to a mother who was a member of the severely puritanical Plymouth Brethren and a father who deserted the family when he was nine, in 1888 Alan became involved with Madame BLAVATSKY's Lodge of the Theosophical Society in London, of which the poet W B Yeats was also, briefly, a member. Changing his name by deed poll to Alan Leo, he started an astrological magazine with his friend and fellow theosophist F W LACEY (Aphorel), and with SEPHARIAL as a contributor. *The Astrologer's Magazine* was extremely successful from its first issue – partly because its editors offered a free horoscope for all subscribers, sending out over a thousand in the first week. Lacey resigned in 1891, and Leo carried on alone, at the same time undertaking several lecture tours. In 1895 he married Ada Elizabeth Murray Phillips, who became known as Bessie Leo (the marriage followed a consultation she had sought with Leo, and the breakdown of her former marriage, when her husband decided to ignore the condition that it should be platonic). The pair worked excellently together, and soon began a postal consultation service, simply bringing together a number of separate sheets each of which dealt with one aspect of the applicant's chart – the Sun- and Moon-signs, the ASCENDANT, the MIDHEAVEN, and so on – and sending them off. These days the same system is used, but with computers taking the place of the separate files in which Leo kept his sheets of paper. No attempt was made to correlate the various elements of the birth-chart, just as no such attempt is made by 21st-century computers. Within three years Alan had sent out 20,000 horoscopes at a shilling a time; many of these resulted in subscriptions to *The Astrologer's Magazine*, and others in requests for more detailed and more expensive work. Other astrologers hastened to copy the system.

In April 1914, Leo was summoned to appear at Mansion House police court to answer the charge that he 'did unlawfully pretend to tell fortunes to deceive and impose upon' a certain Hugh McLean. McLean was a detective, who had written to him for a ten-shilling horoscope. The Lord Mayor dismissed the summons on technical grounds, though he said that he had no doubt that the defendant had attempted to tell the detective's fortune. Leo decided that in future he must refer to the horoscope as showing 'tendencies' within a life, rather than anything more definite. In July of 1914 he and Bessie Leo called a meeting of astrologers and friends, and proposed the start of a new Astrological Lodge of the Theosophical Society, which continues to operate at the date of writing, and has been responsible for teaching many astrologers.

Leo was again prosecuted in 1917, with the famous advocate Travers Humphreys acting for the Director of Public Prosecutions. Leo's defence that he merely dealt in 'tendencies' failed (he was shown at one stage to refer to 'a death in the family', scarcely a 'tendency'). He was found guilty, and fined £5 with £25 costs. He did not appeal. The Vagrancy Act remains on the statute book.

al-Battānī, Abū Abdullāh Muḥammad ibn Jābir ibn Sinān ar-Raqqī al-Ḥarrani aṣ-Ṣabi (ca.850–ca.923) Sometimes known as Albategnius, Albategni or Albatenius, an Arab astronomer and astrologer whose main achievement was the precise calculation of the length of the SOLAR year – at 365 days, 5 hours, 46 minutes and 24 seconds. He also calculated the values for the PRECESSION of the EQUINOXES (at 1° in 66 years) and the inclination of the Earth's axis (at 23° 35'). He worked on the writings of PTOLEMY, and contributed much to the development of mathematics. *See* 'SOLAR TIME'.

Albertus Magnus (1193–1280) Known as St Albert the Great, Albertus was a Dominican friar and the greatest German philosopher and theologian of his time. He worked to reconcile religion and the growing interest in science, the philosophy of ARISTOTLE and that of the Church. His interest in astrology was lifelong, and he argued that a study of the subject could assist mankind to live as Christian morality instructed – after all, God had placed the planets in the sky to instruct mankind of his intentions. His most authoritative book on the subject is his *Speculum astronomiæ* (1260).

Albumasar *see* ABU MA'SHAR

Alchabitius or **Alcabitius** (d. 967) The author of *Introduction to the Art of Judgments of the Stars*, an influential work on JUDICIAL ASTROLOGY, translated several times in the 14th and 15th centuries.

alchabitius house system Similar to PLACIDUS, except that the time it takes the ASCENDANT to reach the MERIDIAN is divided into three equal parts.

alchemy For at least 2,000 years alchemy has been associated with astrology, the interest originating perhaps with the Babylonians and Greeks and the writings of HERMES TRISTMEGISTUS, the alleged Greek and Egyptian god. In the 17th century it was closely associated with the origins of ROSICRUCIANISM. The main astrological theory associated each of the seven planets with a particular metal that they ruled:

the Sun – gold	Mars – iron
the Moon – silver	Jupiter – tin
Mercury – quicksilver	Saturn – lead
Venus – copper	

Of the so-called 'modern' planets Uranus is said to rule uranium, Neptune neptunium and Pluto plutonium. Some ancient astrological writers believed that the metals were actually brought to Earth from their respective planets by angelic forces. The associations were used in the production of TALISMANS, which were made of the metal associated with the sign most important in an individual's HOROSCOPE.

Aldebaran A fixed star, the left eye of the Bull, positioned at 9° 47′ Gemini. One of the four Royal Stars of Persian astrology, it is also associated with the archangel Michael. Said to confer eloquence and integrity, courage and popularity and to bring honours; but also to lead to confrontation and possibly war – depending on the aspects formed.

Alexander the Great (Alexander III of Macedon) (356–323BC)
Though history tells us that Alexander was the son of King Philip II of Macedon, there was a strong tradition during his lifetime that his real father

was a King of Egypt, Nectanebus, who, when it was predicted that his enemies there would defeat him, travelled to Macedon and set up as an astrologer. Entranced by Queen Olympias, he seduced her, disguised as the god Ammon. When her term came, Nectanebus set up a golden ASTROLABE at her bedside, begging her not to give birth until the time was propitious. The result was the birth of the child who became Alexander the Great. Nectanebus is said to have tutored Alexander, using a text by ARISTOTLE entitled *The Secret of Secrets*. His lessons included astrology; but when the boy was 12 he threw Nectanebus over a cliff to prove that he could not foretell his own death. (The story bears a strong resemblance to that of Tiberius's meeting with THRASYLLUS). Though there is a tradition that Alexander made use of astrology during his campaigns, there is no evidence to support the assertion.

Alexandrinus, Paulus (fl. AD350–390) The author of *Eisagogika*, the main source of knowledge of astrology in the Rome of his time. He discussed astrological technique and in particular the phases of the Moon.

Algol A fixed star, the head of Medusa, positioned at 26°10′ Taurus. Traditionally the most malevolent of all stars, 'the Evil One'; it is associated with danger to the throat and neck (thus, beheading), murder and violence, provoking intense, hysterical passion. Hebrew astrologers called it Lilith, and it has been associated with female sexuality at its most basic level.

alien signs *see* DISSOCIATE SIGNS

Alleyn, Thomas (1542–1632) English astrologer and mathematician who, under the patronage of the Earl of Northumberland, became an acquaintance and friend of many notable contemporaries, including John DEE. He was also known to the Earl of Leicester, and was accused of using astrology to support him in his campaign to marry Queen Elizabeth. He made a fine collection of historical, mathematical, and astrological manuscripts, later presented to the Bodleian Library.

Almagest The chief astrological work of PTOLEMY of Alexandria.

almanacs Records of the astronomical and astrological events of a coming year. The earliest of these were 'clog almanacs' made of wood or horn, in which notches and symbols indicated the Moon's cycles, and details of festival and saints' days of the Church. Although almanacs were among the earliest books to be printed – the earliest known published from Gutenberg in 1448 – manuscript almanacs written on vellum persisted for many years. Almanacs were published throughout Europe, most commonly at first in Germany and the Netherlands; in France they remained as popular as fiction until as late as the 19th century – especially at court of Catherine de Medici, where they were enormously influential.

In the most popular almanacs, general predictions were made for the countries and cities where they were issued – of the possibility of famine, war or disease. But the study of astrology and MEDICINE made it essential for every doctor to possess a current almanac (the University of Paris made this obligatory in1437). In England the market for almanacs grew at great speed, and as soon as printed matter became relatively cheap, enormous sales were achieved. Notable astronomical events such as a CONJUNCTION or an ECLIPSE always resulted in increased interest and increased sales.

In Elizabethan and Tudor times almanacs were possessed by every class of society from the monarchs to their meanest subjects, and in the first century of settlement in North America it was said that every home contained two books: the Bible, and the current almanac. During the British and American civil wars almanacs were used on both sides of the question, Royalists and Parliamentarians in England publishing prognostications of success for their own forces. Astrologers such as William LILLY made fortunes by publishing their own almanacs each year – and each publication further increased their income by publicizing their work as consultants.

With the coming of the Age of Enlightenment, while astrology itself suffered from the criticism of scientists, almanacs did much to educate their readers, explaining with simple diagrams such phenomena as eclipses of the Sun and Moon and the appearance of comets, and so quelling the superstitious fears which such events formerly provoked. Tycho BRAHE's discovery of a nova in 1572 was correctly described in the almanacs as a new star. They also often advertised scientific instruments – quadrants and astrolabes – and their uses, and explained such mathematical aids as logarithms.

In the 18th century the reduced intellectual interest in astrology resulted in a change: almanacs began to concentrate more on predicting the possible future patterns of events for readers. They became in every way cheaper, and the trend continued to the present day, when monthly magazines are for the most part aimed at the superstitious who wish to know 'what the future holds', and the attitude of their editors, contributors and publishers remains that of a sentence published on the title page of *Poor Robin's Almanac* in the 1662 edition: 'Every word in this almanac was writ on purpose to get money.'

altitude The elevation of a planet above the horizon, measured by the angular distance from the horizon between 0° and 90°.

Ambjornson, Karl (1914–81) American astrologer and electrical engineer. A devotee of URANIAN ASTROLOGY, which he taught.

Americas, astrology in A kind of astrology was certainly in use in Mexico before Columbus, though based on a system unlike anything in Europe. In Toltec astrology the world was divided into four sections, ruled by the Bull, Lion, Eagle and Man. Later, some tribes of the Peruvians, the Quiché for instance, were used to preparing BIRTH-CHARTS for their children – using techniques brought to America by the Spaniards. Later, just as the invention of printing in Europe almost immediately produced a flow of almanacs, so in America one of the earliest books printed by the Harvard University Press was an *Almanack Calculated for New England*, published in 1639, before the Press was 12 months old. It contained astro-nomical information and a 'ZODIAC MAN' called 'The Man of Signs', illustrating the correspondence between certain zodiac signs and certain areas of the body.

During the next 30 years the number of astrological books published was rivalled only by books of sermons and tracts, and during the next two centuries many more almanacs were published than books of any other kind – well over a thousand between 1639 and 1799. While information about individual astrologers working in America at this time is sparse, we can infer that since almanacs were so popular, astrologers will have had a share in that popularity. There are one or two references to local astrologers at work in their communities, advising on personal matters, and many people constructed their own horoscopes ('hope that my mistress will be kind again', noted William Byrd) and used astrology in particular in agriculture and farming ('nothing has grown… it is my third planet that governs, and I shall not this year amount to a groat', moaned Col. Carter). The Puritans were especially devoted to astrology, and produced such astrologers as Zechariah Brigden, an early 'scientific' astrologer, Samuel Cheever, and a governor of Massachusetts, Joseph Dudley.

Gradually, there was a move to make personal predictions as important as the simple suggestions for good farming practice – such as the best time for planting crops or mating cattle – which were the most useful contents of the early American almanacs. The hold the almanac had on its readers, year after year, was extraordinary, and even in the middle of the 18th century, when the Age of Enlightenment had certainly reached America, *Ames' Almanac*, which concentrated on personal astrology – 'what the stars foretell' – continued to sell up to 60,000 copies a year, and many more almanacs were sold than newspapers. By that time individual astrologers were advising personal clients in every state, and their influence has continued – despite growing criticism both from scientists and members of various religious movements – until the present day. It is probably true to say that in the 1970s much of America, particular on the West Coast, was besotted with astrology. There were, however, many serious astrologers who enlarged technical knowledge of the subject and did much speculative work. *See* ADAMS, BENJAMINE, DIXON, GOODMAN, GRASSHOFF, JILLSON, JONES, OMARR, RIGHTER, RODDEN.

amulet *see* TALISMAN

angels An ancient astrological tradition links the planets and zodiac signs with certain angels. This seems to have been first put into writing by a Syrian monk who forged a number of treatises and published them under the name of Dionysius the Areopagite, said to have been the first Bishop of Athens (but also confused with St Denis of France). The pseudo-Dionysian works were of great importance in the development of the Catholic faith, and the Treatise on the Celestial Hierarchy dealt in detail with the spiritual creatures descending from God to man – among them the Seraphim (concerned with the ordering of the solar system), the Cherubim (which rule the zodiac), the archangels (in charge of the sphere of Mercury) and the angels (linked with the Moon's sphere). Comets were in the care both of Seraphim and Cherubim, the fixed stars were kept in order by the Kyriotetes or Spirits of Wisdom, the Moon by the archangels and the Earth by both angels and men.

The planetary angels are:

- Gabriel – the Moon
- Raphael – Mercury
- Haniel – Venus
- Michael – the Sun
- Camael – Mars
- Zadkiel – Jupiter
- Zaphkiel – Saturn

The association of archangels with the zodiacal signs are:

Aries – Malshidael	Libra – Zuriel
Taurus – Asmodei	Scorpio – Barchiel and Solzol
Gemini – Ambriel	Sagittarius – Adnachiel and Ayil
Cancer – Muriel and Manuel	Capricorn – Hamael
Leo – Vercheil	Aquarius – Cambiel
Virgo – Hamaeliel	Pisces – Barchiel

The archangels Michael, Uriel, Raphael, and Gabriel are responsible for the ELEMENTS, fire, earth, air and water.

angle The word refers to the four angles of a HOROSCOPE which form a cross within it: the ASCENDANT, DESCENDANT, MIDHEAVEN (Medium Coeli) and IMUM COELI (IC).

angles The aspects made to the angles of a HOROSCOPE are vital in its interpretation, especially if an accurate birth time is known. The relationship the planets make to each other, and to other areas of the chart, are known as ASPECTS.

angular A planet is said to be angular when in conjunction with the starting HOUSE CUSPS of one of the ANGULAR HOUSES – the 1st, 4th, 7th, and 10th.

angular houses The 1st, 4th, 7th and 10th houses fall on the ANGLE of the chart, and are said to be the 'strongest;' houses in the horoscope.

animals, astrological The lion, bull, eagle and a winged human figure represent the four FIXED SIGNS of the zodiac, linked to the four ELEMENTS – the lion said to represent emotion, the bull the physical aspect of life, the eagle aspiration, and the winged figure the union of these elements in a human being. In the Old Testament, the creatures are described in Ezekial I, 5–10, and there is a clear association with the four beasts 'full of eyes before and behind' described in Revelations IV, 6–10.

- The lion is related to the sign of Leo, the fire element, the evangelist St Mark and the archangel Michael;
- the bull – to Taurus, earth, St Luke and Uriel;
- the eagle – to Scorpio, water, St John and Gabriel;
- the winged figure – to Aquarius, air, St Matthew and Raphael.

Anoubion (fl.1st c. AD) Egyptian astrologer and poet who wrote a textbook of astrology in elegiacs. FIRMICUS MATERNUS later relied upon it for much of his knowledge of the subject. Anoubion was also praised by RHETORIUS. Among other matters, he speculated on the *thema mundi*, the 'horoscope of the universe', showing the positions of the planets at the moment of the Creation (a subject THRASYLLUS also considered). Only fragments of Anoubion's work are extant.

Antares A 'Royal' fixed star in the body of the Scorpion, associated with adventure, violence and suspicion, obstinacy and stubbornness – and by some astrologers with the probability of several marriages.

Antiochus of Athens (fl.2nd c. AD) The probable author of an influential textbook on astrology, the *Thesaurus*, widely quoted by astrologers from the 3rd to the 7th centuries – particularly Arab astrologers; in it he carefully defines the terms PTOLEMY uses in his *TETRABIBLOS*, and gives the earliest detailed definition of the DECANS. He is credited with devising the system of HOUSE DIVISION later attributed to PORPHYRY.

aphelion The point in a planet's orbit at which it is furthest from the Sun.

apogee The point in a planet's orbit at which it is at its greatest distance from Earth.

apparent motion The Sun and planets only seem to circle the Earth – their motion is *apparent* rather than real.

apparent noon The moment at which the Sun crosses the MERIDIAN.

Aquarius ♒

The eleventh sign of the zodiac. Sun-sign period 21 January–18 February.

> *It should be remembered when reading of the characteristics of the Sun-signs that these will always be affected by the effects of the rising-sign, the planets in various other signs and houses, and the relationships the planets make to each other.*

General characteristics

One person with the Sun in Aquarius may seem to bear very little resemblance to another with the Sun in the same sign, for individuality often seems to be the only hallmark that distinguishes them. They have an enormous need for independence, often illustrated by a highly individual lifestyle which each devises for him- or herself. Extremely private people who it is difficult to know really well, Aquarians are extremely friendly and usually gregarious, but disinclined to share themselves emotionally with other people, with the result that they often have difficulties when establishing or trying to establish a permanent personal relationship. (This of course will be affected by the rising-sign, and by other planets in other signs in the complete HOROSCOPE). Aquarian originality and flair can be shown in any number of ways and in various careers, from 'glamour' industries to science, and perhaps especially in areas related to past and future human history: archaeology and geology on the one hand and the exploration of space on the other.

The growing child

Like Aquarian adults, children with the Sun in this sign will seem 'different' in some way, certainly compared to their non-Aquarian siblings or friends. From the earliest years they will express this in one way or another – often by involving themselves surprisingly early, both at school and in their leisure time, with humanitarian causes of some sort. Their reactions at home may be unpredictable, and they can be extremely stubborn (especially when any attempt is made to dissuade them from something they have decided should be done). Their reaction to discipline will be determined by how sensible they think the rules are. Leisure time will involve the lighter sports such as skating or roller-blading, and there will probably be an interest in the arts – drama and music clubs, for instance. They will be good with younger siblings, expressing all kindness and helpfulness in helping to bring them up and protecting them when they need protection.

Education

The Aquarian child and older student is in a sense not naturally 'good' – he or she for instance will always question school rules, and if they do not seem to be founded on good sense, will probably have no hesitation in disobeying them. A repressive regime, a 'strict' school will not suit them at all – and quite apart from making them unhappy, will not get good educational results. The idiosyncratic Aquarian will want to work in a way which is particular to him or her, and allowed to do so will prosper – particularly perhaps in scientific subjects, in English, and in history. There may be an interest in science fiction – but it will be a serious interest, founded in genuine curiosity and concern about the future.

Friendship, romance and sex

Sun-sign Aquarians are faithful friends, for whom friendship is a lifetime commitment. Even if circumstances keep them apart for long periods of time, the friendship will be renewed with reunion. They will always be ready to come to the aid of a friend, expecting nothing in return – to the extent that unscrupulous people can take advantage of them. Personally, they can be wonderfully attractive, but disinclined to intimacy; once having made a commitment, however, they will be devoted, while finding it difficult to express the devotion as warmly as the subject of it might wish – indeed it may seem sometimes that the love they give is really devoted friendship, with the sexual element rather muffled and less than exciting. In permanent relationship or marriage the Aquarian will be very susceptible to praise and flattery. If he or she has an extramarital affair, it is more likely to be speedily confessed than kept secret; the extent to which this is a problem depends of course on the partner's reaction.

Occupation

Sun-sign Aquarians need to be in contact with their fellow-humans; a job which involves loneliness will be highly unsuitable (although if the work is sufficiently engrossing they will grit their teeth and get on with it). They need to be allowed to get on with their own work without interruption – working in an open-plan office, with chatter and bustle all around them, will be a distraction. They will have their own methods of work, which it is unwise to question – if their motives are examined they are more than likely simply to resign. This may from time to time occur if their superiors do not recognize that their occasional eccentricity has its own values. With their natural kindliness and concern for others, work in the social services is excellent – but there is often a scientific bent, and work in telecommunications, television or radio also suits them well. Work in the field of ecology is engrossing and stimulating for them; they make excellent trades unionists, with real concern for working conditions.

Health

Aquarians react particularly well to holistic medicine, and are not enthusiastic about even medically prescribed drugs or antibiotics. They respond also to chiropractics, acupuncture, acupressure and aromatherapy. This is particularly the case when they suffer from back-ache – and since Leo, Aquarius' POLAR sign, rules the spine this can occasionally be a problem. the RULING PLANET of Aquarius, Uranus, is concerned with the circulatory system, and this is particularly vulnerable, possibly with age bringing problems with varicose veins and hardening of the arteries. These can particularly affect both sexes during cold weather. Like those with the Sun in Capricorn, Aquarians can be prone to rheumatic and arthritis problems. Vigorous exercise can help. The traditional body area for Aquarians is the ankles, and women who are devoted to fashionable shoes can damage these.

Finance

Aquarians find the idea of making a great deal of money out of the labours of others repugnant, and this – consciously or unconsciously – affects their attitude to investment. They will not go about looking for opportunities to make sudden killings on the stock exchange; what money they have will be securely placed in the simplest of bank or building society accounts, and they will be perfectly happy with whatever interest accrues. They may well want to set up special accounts through which they can contribute to a favourite charity. They are not gamblers – yet sometimes can be seized by some demon which persuades them to invest everything they have in one spectacular scheme, winner take – or lose – all. In partnership their attitude to money can tend to be somewhat secretive; there are many things which seem to them to be more important than money, and this can result in funds leaking away almost without them noticing.

Growing older

As they begin to age, Aquarians may gradually become more and more aware that retirement is creeping up on them – and become more and more concerned about it, for they hate to have decisions hanging over them because of necessary delays. The wisest among them devote time to considering what they are to do with their spare hours, and many of them decide that the time will be right to devote them to expressing those aspects of their originality and creative or scientific flair that they have been unable to articulate while at work. From the point of view of health, the tendency to rheumatism or arthritis (*see* above) may show itself, but be fended off by continual exercise – creative rather than repetitive exercise. Walking is especially good for them; though many continue to ski or play other winter sports for as long as possible.

Aquarius as rising-sign

Those with Aquarius rising are likely to be less unpredictable, less 'different', than those with the Sun in that sign. They can also have a tendency to be dogmatic, and a dislike of admitting when they are wrong. Willing to try new, interesting, unusual things they will be attracted to the ideas of younger people, and slow to disapprove of actions which others may find too radical. The powerful humanitarian aspect of Aquarius will show itself strongly, especially when friends or acquaintances need help. The area of personal relationships is less complex than with Sun-sign Aquarians, and is affected by the POLAR sign, Leo – they will be enormously supportive of their partners, but with a tendency to lay down the law in what can be a somewhat too proscriptive way. Their emotional and sex-life should present no problems, though as with the Sun-sign people they will need continual stimulation and (to an extent) change.

Traditional associations

- Ruling Planet – Uranus (formerly, Saturn)
- Triplicity/Element – air
- Quadruplicity/Quality – fixed
- Colour – turquoise
- Gemstone – aquamarine
- Metal – aluminium
- Flower – orchid
- Trees – fruit trees
- Herbs and Spices – those with a sharp or unusual flavour
- Foodstuffs – foods that preserve well; dried fruits
- Animals – large birds with long-flight ability
- Countries – India, Mexico, Sweden
- Cities – Moscow, Salzburg, Hamburg, St Petersburg
- US States – Arizona, Massachusetts, Michigan, Oregon

* * *

Arabic astrology This is a subject which requires an entire book to itself. Medieval astrology borrowed most of its theories from Arabia – a proliferation of information which it took centuries for Western astrologers to systematize and learn how to use. In the 8th and 9th centuries it embraced Hellenistic, Indian and pre-Islamic Sāsānian astrology, with translations from Greek, Sanskrit and Persian texts. Then there was the Neoplatonic idea of the influences of the stars, taught, for instance, by the Harranians – astrologers from the Mesopotamian city of Harran, who saw the planets as gods to whom one could pray for mitigation of their influences (*see* ABU MAS'HAR). The development and importance of this declined after the 13th century, but by then its influence had spread widely in the West.

Aries – Al Hamal	Libra – Al Mizan
Taurus – Al Thawr	Scorpio – Al Aqrab
Gemini – Al Jawza	Sagittarius – Al Qaws
Cancer – As Saratan	Capricorn – Al Jadiyy
Leo – Al Asad	Aquarius – Al Dalw
Virgo – Al Sunbula	Pisces – Al Hut

For those who come across Arab texts and find the difference in nomenclature difficult, the Arabic names of the signs and planets are:

- the Sun – Shams
- the Moon – Qamar (but Badr when full and Hilal when new)
- Mercury – Utarid
- Venus – Zuhra
- Mars – Mirrih
- Jupiter – Mushtari
- Saturn – Zuhal

arc Any part of a circle, measured around its circumference. Thus, an arc of 5° occupies a 5° section of the circle. A zodiac sign occupies 30° of arc – one-twelfth of the circle of 360°. An ORB is expressed as degrees of the zodiac.

archangels *see* ANGELS

Aries ♈

The first sign of the zodiac. Sun-sign period 21 March–20 April.

It should be remembered when reading of the characteristics of the Sun-signs that these will always be affected by the effects of the rising-sign, the planets in various other signs and houses, and the relationships the planets make to each other.

General characteristics

Traditional Aries characteristics are energy, courage, enthusiasm, confidence, dynamism, quick-wittedness and a pioneering spirit; but also selfishness, impulsiveness, impatience, foolhardiness and quickness of temper. There is in general an uncomplicated attitude to life, and an impatience with trivial detail.

Achievement is vital to the Arien personality, and the challenges faced in moving towards any goal are met with great determination. Failure to reach a goal – or achieving it incompletely (perhaps due to impulsiveness, which can result in carelessness) will result in depression – as will a failure to find sexual satisfaction in a partnership. Restlessness and boredom can ensue in both cases. Selfishness can cause problems in almost every area of life – 'me first' is a phrase many astrologers associate with this sign.

In any career freedom of expression will bring the best results, and restriction – to a repetitive, pedestrian physical or mental routine – the worst. Ambition will be a strong motivation; but once achieved there will be no relaxation, for another ambition will immediately present itself. Enterprise linked to a good head for business spells success, provided impetuosity and impatience do not lead to mistakes, and selfishness and a quick temper do not alienate friends and colleagues. Typical careers for Ariens include the armed services, psychiatry, dentistry, engineering, the electronics industry.

Exercise is important to Arien health, and will usually be embraced not merely with enthusiasm but with a degree of compulsion – sometimes to the extent that the constitution to which it is important will actually be damaged by strain or injury due to overenthusiasm. The head (traditionally ruled by Aries) is specially vulnerable to injury, and the Arien tendency to rush thoughtlessly about can in general result in minor injuries. There is usually a liking for traditional rather than 'fancy' food – and also for spicy food, which is not always good for the Arien digestion.

The growing child

Throughout childhood and teenage years, activity, activity, activity will be a necessary theme. Arien children certainly do not lack energy, and learning to walk sooner rather than later will consequently tend to be susceptible to small accidents. Adventurous from a very early age, they are likely to give parents a certain amount of anxiety, for an adventurous spirit and enthusiastic approach to life in general are unlikely to persuade them to stay quietly at home studying – especially since boredom will set in all too easily when school lessons become tedious (as they may too often seem to be). The desire – need – for freedom will sit uneasily with discipline if that is too rigorously or unsympathetically administered. Selfishness may mar relationships with other children, and too often this is especially the case with siblings.

The usual problems which arise at adolescence are likely to be accentuated by Arien stubbornness and short temper; characteristic explosions within the family circle will certainly not be ameliorated by the fact that a youngster has Aries as a Sun-sign. Happily, once the explosion has taken place the pressure is immediately released and the air cleared. Resentment is not an Arien characteristic, and once the current disagreement is over, there will be a period of peace and quiet until the fuse is reignited (which will inevitably happen sooner or later).

Education

Boredom will inevitably be the greatest obstacle during the years of school and further education. Arien high spirits simply refuse to be contained if the mind is not kept as active as the body, and this means that the child and later the student must be kept interested in the subject which is being studied. This is a particular problem if, as too often, the child or young man or woman doesn't have a strong personal interest which can be encouraged and cultivated. There is a distinct possibility that outside interests, and especially sport, may be a distraction from intellectual study, and it will be a talented teacher who can compete with the attractions of the gym or, more desirably, the open air. Rugby football, hockey, wrestling and boxing, all good outlets for excess energy, will be enthusiastically indulged. In the class- or lecture-room the Arien is all too likely to be regarded as a disruptive influence, for hating to work in the peace and quiet of a studious environment, requests for silence are unlikely to be respected. Challenge can be the keynote, in study as well as sport, and given an area in which a competitive interest can be aroused, this will keep the Arien at work, for fear some contemporary will outshine him or her.

Friendship, romance and sex

Ariens like, indeed often require, their friends to be as enthusiastic as themselves, and if possible for the same things – so friendships will often be formed with fellow-members of some club or association. Friends may have to deal with expressions of selfishness – forgotten appointments, for instance – but there will be no lack of generosity, either emotional or financial. A first sexual experience is likely to be the result of a sudden irresistible impulse rather than anything planned, and promiscuity is more likely than not until a possibly permanent partner is found – he or she more likely than not to be a weaker, more dependent type who can be dominated by the stronger Arien personality. But Aries is idealistic as well as passionate, and equally likely to fall suddenly and romantically in love – and to leap too rashly and suddenly into a commitment, before (for instance) discovering whether the prospective partner is as enthusiastic for an exciting and varied sex-life as the Arien; many a partnership has foundered on that particular rock – but there is also danger from Arien self-ishness – a lack of interest in foreplay and a tendency, in men, to premature ejaculation. There is a contrast between Arien men and women: Arien men are attracted by beauty and by helplessness, needing a partner ready to admire and support him; the Arien woman is capable, generous and masterful, and can become self-opinionated and bossy. Both sexes can become violently jealous, and occasionally even violent.

Permanent partnership and family

Despite all their thrusting, positive, ambitious traits, Ariens need support, particularly from a permanent partner – indeed, partners may occasionally feel that this is all that is needed from them, for selfishness is as likely to show itself in a domestic situation as in any other, and the 'me first' attitude all too common with Ariens can lead to thoughtlessness and, at worst, neglect. Reliance on the partner when support is needed is not necessarily balanced by the ability or willingness to offer necessary support in the other direction, especially if it is in an area of life which does not specially interest the Arien. Restlessness can also be a problem, and boredom can arise if the partner is unwilling or unable to meet Arien enthusiasm with equal passion. This will be equally true of children, who will be expected to show enthusiasm for their own interests – these need not necessarily be interests which the Arien shares, but that will not matter as long as they exist. An Arien father or mother will not be particularly patient with their children's failings, and there may be sudden anger, which however will quickly blow over. A pride will be taken in the physical surroundings of the home, but this is likely to take the shape the Arien wishes to impose. The idea of 'give and take' may be too heavily weighted on the latter word.

Occupation

Ariens, like those with any Sun-sign, of course find themselves in any and every occupation, but some are more suited to the Arien temperament than others. The sign and house positions of Mercury and Venus will be of significance in this area of Arien lives – Venus suggesting how the Arien is likely to get on with colleagues, Mars indicating the degree of enthusiasm and vigour which will be directed towards the working life. As in every other area of life, a person with the Sun in Aries will need to be able to direct a great deal of energy towards his or her work, so a job which needs a degree of physical energy is more desirable than one which chains one to an office desk. There should also be room for competitiveness, whether with colleagues or with rivals in other organizations. Typically, one might think of a salesman of some sort, who must push not only himself but some product, some new idea, in competition with others – and preferably who can get out and about in the world to do so. The stronger the competition, the more exercise the physical and mental muscles of the Arien will have, and the healthier and stronger he or she will remain.

Health and exercise

Abundant energy and the need to expend it usually dominate the typical Arien's physical life. It is when movement and exercise are restricted or become impossible that problems will inevitably set in. Ariens usually thoroughly dislike routine, which means that a regular regime at a gym will be difficult to sustain – working out on machines may initially be popular, but will swiftly become boring, as will jogging unless there are several different routes which can be alternated, and unless a group of people is available with whom to exercise, not only providing pleasant company but an element of competition, also dear to the Arien heart. Sport is of course an alternative – and sport in which the Arien has an opportunity to show personal expertise or vigour; somewhat aggressive sport – boxing, martial arts, wrestling – is often popular. Arien enthusiasm means that exercise can be easily overdone, and Arien haste can result in careless accidents. The traditional Arien body area is the head, which is claimed to be especially susceptible both to accidents and to headaches which may be the result of kidney disorders.

Finance

The person with the Sun in Aries is usually enterprising and enjoys making money, but as in other areas of life eagerness to win and a tendency to rush into situations can bedevil the financial life. 'Winning' does not necessarily infer semi-professional gambling, but there will certainly be a desire to make money, and any opportunities which suddenly arise and seem to offer a quick profit will be almost irresistible – to the extent that they may be grasped before they are thoroughly thought through. The Arien usually has a good business sense, which can help keep feet on the ground, and a generally reliable instinct; but the tendency to buy impulsively can show itself just as fatally in the purchase of 'fashionable' shares as in the buying of clothes or household furnishings, and may be equally strongly regretted, at leisure (Ariens enjoy spending money almost as much as making it). The desire for a good income can encourage a second job or business, though after a while the less successful occupation may suffer from neglect as the Arien tendency toward boredom sets in.

Growing older

Retirement is not a concept which is welcome to Ariens. Apart from the fact that a life without structure, without work of some sort, would be insufferably boring, Ariens hate the idea that they must inevitably lose some of that overwhelming drive and vigour, and will work to retain both for as long as possible. The possible danger which arises is of 'overdoing things' – a phrase all too often associated with increasing age, and one which they will do their best to ignore. However, a refusal to moderate an on-going exercise regime can, for instance, have dangerous results as bones grow brittle and falls become dangerous. Apart from physical ageing, however, Arien minds should not suffer with old age – the competitive spirit will be as strong as ever, even if it has to take a slightly different forms.

Aries as rising-sign

The competitiveness and ambition of those with Aries as a rising-sign will be driven not so much by the desire for money or position as by the desire to keep abreast of rivals, and draw ahead of them. They will tend to be ruthless, not so much out of lack of consideration for the feelings of others as by the notion that such consideration may be seen as weakness, and in any event would sap their own energy. The sense of urgency strong in Sun-sign Ariens can be overwhelming in those with an Arien rising-sign, and they will only feel really fulfilled when they have overcome some almost insuperable obstacle or gained some almost unattainable objective. Similarly, they need to burn their physical energy in a positive and satisfying way, which generally means in competition with others.

Traditional associations

- Ruling Planet – Mars
- Triplicity/Element – fire
- Quadruplicity/Quality – cardinal
- Colour – red
- Gemstone – diamond
- Metal – iron
- Flowers – honeysuckle, thistle
- Trees – all thorn-bearing trees
- Herbs and Spices – capers, mustard, cayenne pepper
- Foodstuffs – onions, leeks, hops
- Animals – sheep and rams
- Countries – England, France, Germany

- Cities – Naples, Florence, Krakov, Birmingham (UK), San Francisco
- US States – No traditionally associated signs

* * *

Aries, first point of The first point of Aries marks the ascending intersection of the ECLIPTIC with the EQUATOR – the position of the Sun at the time of the VERNAL EQUINOX, around 21 March.

Arroyo, Stephen (b.1946) American astrologer, teacher and lecturer; originally a mathematician with a master's degree in psychology, he has concentrated largely on exploring one-to-one counselling, with reference to the human energy field. He has lectured widely in America and Europe. Among his publications are *Relationships and Life Cycles* (1979), *Astrology, Psychology and the Four Elements* (1975) and *Person-to-Person Astrology: energy factors in love, sex and compatibility* (2008).

Ascendant, the The degree of the zodiac rising over the eastern horizon at a significant time (the birth-time, or the time of an event or question, in HORARY ASTROLOGY). The ascending degree was originally called *Horoscopos* in Greek astrology, from which the modern term HOROSCOPE is derived. This suggests the importance of the *rising-sign*, as it is sometimes called, and indeed traditionally it was considered to be more important than the Sun-sign, and to show the outward aspects of one's personality. Some astrologers now speculate that since the development of SUN-SIGN ASTROLOGY in the 1930s, so many people have begun to emphasize their Sun-sign characteristics that those of the Ascendant have perhaps come to represent the aspects of a personality which are not obviously apparent to others. However, this begs several questions, and further discussion will no doubt take place on the subject.

ascension, long and short Because the ECLIPTIC and EQUATOR are not parallel, some signs rise over the eastern horizon more quickly than others. In northern latitudes, Capricorn, Aquarius, Pisces, Aries, Taurus and Gemini rise relatively quickly, and are known as signs of *short ascension*. The others are signs of *long ascension*. In southern latitudes, these are reversed.

Ascham, Anthony (fl.1540–60) Astrologer, priest and physician, brother of Roger Ascham, tutor to Queen Elizabeth I. Ascham studied at Cambridge and in 1553 was presented by Edward VI to the vicarage of Burneston, Yorkshire. He first published a small herbal, and then, in 1550, *Anthonie Ascham his Treatise of Astronomie, declaring what Herbs and all Kinde of Medicines are appropriate, and also under the influence of the Planets, Signs, & Constellations* – an early example of an astrological medical textbook. He published several almanacs. Like a number of priest-astrologers of the period he used these to threaten his readers with hell-fire and damnation and to propagate his religious views, which included bitter opposition to the publication of the Bible in English.

Ashmole, Elias (1617–92) Starting life as a solicitor, Ashmore was an enthusiastic Royalist, and during the Civil War joined Charles I at Oxford, where he served under Sir John HEYDON, met George WHARTON, and began to study astrology. After the Restoration he was made Windsor Herald and Comptroller of the Excise, was a founder member of the Royal Society, and steadfastly argued that there need be no barrier between the study of natural philosophy and 'magical' subjects. He employed a number of astrologers, including BOOKER, as clerks in the Excise Office, and counted among his close friends GADBURY, WING and above all LILLY. He built a magnificent library, and collected the manuscripts of Simon FORMAN, Richard NAPIER and Lilly. His books and a number of 'curiosities' formed the basis of the Ashmolean Museum at Oxford. He was himself an astrologer, and was said to be able to calculate and draw a horoscope in between 7 and 15 minutes (a remarkable feat in the days before calculators and computers). He was consulted by a wide selection of the great men of his time, including Charles II. Unlike many contemporaries, including Lilly, he took a fatalistic view of astrology – his own horoscope, printed as a frontispiece to his first book, bears the motto *Astra regunt homines* (man is ruled by the stars).

aspects The angles made by planets to each other and to the ASCENDANT and MEDIUM COELI are known as aspects, and are important in interpretation. To be 'in aspect', planets have to be at a specific angular distance from each other within the HOROSCOPE, and 'in ORB' – that is to say, the angular distance has to be more or less exact. The major aspects are the CONJUNC-

TION, when two planets occupy the same point in the chart, the TRINE (two planets at an angle of 120°), the SEXTILE (60°), the OPPOSITION (180°), the SQUARE (90°), the QUINCUNX (150°), the SESQUARE (135°), the SEMI-SQUARE (45°), the SEMI-SEXTILE (30°), the QUINTILE (72°) and bi-quintile (144°). The trine and sextile are said to be 'positive' aspects, the opposition, square, semi-square and quincunx 'negative', the sesquare and semi-sextile 'weakly negative', and the conjunction – the most powerful of aspects – either positive or negative, according to other influences in the chart. The last two, relatively rarely used, are slightly strenuous. The orbs allowed for the aspects are: for the conjunction and opposition, 8°, but up to 10° when the aspect is to the Sun or Moon; for the trine and square, 8°; for the sextile 6°; for the others, 2°.

asteroids Minor planets – sometimes described as 'planetoids' – of about 1,000km or less in diameter, which orbit the Sun mostly between the orbits of Mars and Jupiter. There are about 50,000 of them – among them CERES, JUNO, PALLAS, and VESTA. A minority of astrologers have been using them since the 1930s, and EPHEMERIDES have been worked out for a few. The American astrologer Zipporah Dobbins has suggested that asteroids 'correspond closely to the characteristics of the goddesses for whom they were named', an assertion which perhaps raises more problems than it solves (are the astronomers who named the asteroids really responsible for asserting their characteristics?). It is now however generally agreed that the use of at least some asteroids can contribute to the knowledge to be gained by a study of the HOROSCOPE. *See* CHIRON, CERES, VESTA, PALLAS ATHENE, JUNO.

Astro*Carto*Graphy Sometimes known as relocation astrology, Astro*Carto*Graphy was devised in the 1970s by the American astrologer Jim LEWIS. It involves relocating a birth-chart and interpreting it as though the subject were born in the new location. It is claimed that this will reveal whether the new locality would be receptive to the subject, whether he or she would prosper and be happy there.

astrolabe A device invented to measure the altitudes of stars. Legend attributes its accidental invention to PTOLEMY: out riding and carrying a brass celestial ball, he dropped it and his horse trampled it flat, producing the first astrolabe. It is also said to have been invented by Hipparchus in the 2nd century BC, in its earliest form as a simple disc whose circumference was marked with the degrees of a circle, and with a pointer along which a heavenly body could be sighted. The first description of an astrolabe dates from the 6th century AD, and the oldest extant astrolabe itself from about 1200. Pope Sylvester II (940–1003) wrote a treatise on its use, and the English poet Geoffrey CHAUCER did the same in 1392. From medieval times it was used by mariners to calculate latitude, until it was replaced by the sextant. Islamic scientists perfected it as an aid to astrologers. Enormous architectural astrolabes were built by some Indian maharajahs – *cf.* the one at Jaipur.

astrological twins Two people born within four minutes of each other at the same location are known as astrological twins, share strong astrological factors, and therefore – it is alleged – though unrelated by blood will share personality traits and in some cases similar patterns of life. When such persons have been discovered, they have been the source of considerable study, though to date it has been inconclusive. Strong anecdotal evidence turns up again and again, often featured in the press – two people who have never met share the same job, have married similar partners in the same year, had the same number of children, share the same tastes – even possess similar cars of the same colour: they turn out to have been born at the same hospital within minutes of each other. Such phenomena deserve more rigorous study than has so far been given them.

astrology The study of the influence of the bodies of the solar system and fixed stars on life on Earth.

astronomical co-ordinates The values used to define a position of a planet or star on the CELESTIAL SPHERE. The three systems used are the ECLIPTIC system, the EQUATORIAL system and the horizon system.

astronomy The study of the physical nature of the universe and the measurement of the positions and movements of stars and planets. It should be remembered that for centuries astronomers were also inevitably astrologers – *astronomia* and *astrologia* were used indiscriminately to describe both sciences. The study of the lives and work of most great astronomers of ancient times readily confirms that scientific astronomy would not have developed so rapidly and so early in man's history had the astronomers not been confident that the planets affected life on Earth.

Athena Starwoman (fl.1980–2004) The wife of an inspirational lecturer, John Demartini, the true name of this extremely popular newspaper and magazine columnist remains unknown. Her Sun-sign columns were syndicated world-wide, especially in women's magazines, and she made a considerable fortune, living in a luxurious house on the Australian Gold Coast, an apartment in the Trump Tower in New York, and on the cruise liner *The World*.

Athenio An overseer in Sicily, ca.100BC, who became the leader of a slave revolt, claiming that his horoscope revealed that he would become King. At first he had considerable success, but was killed before his prediction could be fulfilled.

Augustine, St *see* CHRISTIANITY AND ASTROLOGY

Augustus (63BC–AD14) The first of the Roman emperors, whose success was reputed to have been foretold by the astrologer Theogenes. After he became emperor, Augustus had a number of coins stamped with the symbol of Capricorn, his Sun-sign; various pieces of sculpture have also survived from his reign with the sign carved upon them. The historians Suetonius and Cassius Dio claim that Augustus published his horoscope. He employed astrologers to advise him, and during his reign a large number of astrological texts were published, including 13 volumes by NECHEPSO, in verse, and the first two substantial treatises on the subject, by MANILIUS and VETTIUS VALENS.

autumnal equinox The first point of Libra – one of the points of inter-section between the ECLIPTIC and the CELESTIAL EQUATOR that the Sun meets as it crosses from north to south on or about 23 September. *See also* VERNAL EQUINOX.

– B –

Backhouse, William (1593–1662) Born in Berkshire and educated at Christ Church, Oxford, Backhouse studied astrology and devoted much time to teaching the subject. He was particularly attached to young Elias ASHMOLE, whom he adopted. (Ashmole wrote in his diary for 26 April 1651, 'Mr. William Backhouse… caused me to call him father thenceforward', and two months later, 'Mr. Backhouse told me I must now needs be his son, because he had communicated so many secrets to me'.) He never published, but left a number of manuscripts which Ashmole preserved.

Bacon, Roger (1214–94) An English philosopher, Bacon was one of the earliest men to profess a belief in science and scientific method, though still relying himself on the old traditions which included astrology. Supported by Pope Clement IV, for whom he worked in Rome, he published among other works books on astrology, but was arrested when in 1277, after Clement's death, the Church openly condemned the practice. Bacon returned to England to continue his work. His mind was open and catholic, and he wrote about telescopes, flying machines, the possibility of providing lenses through which short-sighted people could look, and the future of gunpowder. He is said to have invented the magnifying glass. He also speculated on the positions and sizes of the planets, and throughout his life continued to study astrology, believing that it influenced every aspect of life on Earth.

Bailey, E H (1876–1959) British astrologer, physician and publisher, editor of *The British Journal of Astrology*. Author of *The Prenatal Epoch*, which speculated on CONCEPTION charts. Another publication was a book about the use of astrology during the Second World War.

Balbillus, Tiberius Claudius (fl. ca.10BC–ca.79BC) Greek astrologer, the supposed son of THRASYLLUS. During the reign of the Emperor Caligula he fled from Rome to Alexandria, but returned to Rome under Claudius, with whom he had been friendly when they were children and whom he had met at the house of Thrassylus. He accompanied Claudius on his expedition to Britain as an officer in the 20th Legion, and when they returned was awarded a crown of honour. Appointed high priest at the Temple of Hermes in Alexandria and head of the state university there, he foretold an eclipse which fell on one of the Emperor's birthdays, and remained adviser to Claudius even after the Emperor had passed an edict expelling all astrologers from Rome. He avoided the fatal end of many astrologers under Nero, who in AD56 appointed him Prefect of Egypt, where he stayed until AD59. He returned to Rome under Vespasian, who thought well of him and honoured him by allowing the Balbillean Games, held at Ephesus in the astrologer's honour until well into the 3rd century.

barren signs The *barren* or 'sterile' signs are Gemini, Leo and Virgo; some astrologers add Aries and to a lesser degree Sagittarius and Aquarius. Signs of the water TRIPLICITY – Cancer, Scorpio and Pisces – are regarded as *fruitful* signs, with Taurus, Capricorn, Libra and Aquarius said to be moderately fruitful. The allusion is of course to the probability of conception or nonconception; but these attributions are unsubstantiated by statistical research.

Behari, Bepin (d. 2005) Indian VEDIC astrologer and consultant, an authority on JYOTISH. He wrote prolifically on the mythological and symbolic aspects of Vedic astrology, and was a regular contributor to *The Times of India* as well as to *The Astrological Magazine*. He lectured widely in India and the West. Among his many books, the most important is perhaps *A Study in Astrological Occultism* (1979).

beholding Aries and Libra, Taurus and Virgo, Gemini and Leo, Aquarius and Sagittarius, Pisces and Scorpio, are pairs of signs which are of equal distance from the tropics, and were traditionally known as 'stars of equal power'. They were also said to 'behold' each other because they rise from the same part of the horizon. *See* SOLSTICES.

belief One of the questions most likely to irritate the astrologer is, 'Do you *believe* in astrology?' The answer, of course, is that which would be given if the question was 'Do you *believe* that the world is round?'. The astrologer *knows*. Proof of any degree acceptable to the scientific mind is probably further away than it has ever been in the history of this oldest of sciences, and it cannot be denied that part of the attraction of astrology, especially in the 21st century, is due to its nonscientific nature, and its symbolic truth. In this sense, the word 'believe' has little meaning, and the distance to be travelled by astrology before it comes within reach of convincing those for whom proof is more acceptable than belief remains very considerable.

benefic aspects *see* BENEFICS

benefics/benefic An archaic term meaning *favourable*; ancient astrologers described Jupiter for instance is as the 'greater benefic', having under certain circumstances the most favourable effect, and Venus as 'the lesser benefic'. The Sun and Moon are also said to be *benefics* when well aspected. A benefic ASPECT is one in which planets and their effects are sympathetic – notably the TRINE and SEXTILE.

Benjamine, Elbert (1882–1951) A well-known American astrologer, Benjamine wrote a series of courses on the branches of occult science, and was the founder in 1915 of the Church of Light, in Los Angeles, where (having studied as a naturalist) he also founded a bird sanctuary. As an author on astrology and occult subjects, he used the pseudonym C C Zain.

Berosus (fl. ca.290BC) A Chaldean priest of Bel who wrote an account of the history and culture of Babylonia, claiming that the study of astronomy there dated back for 500,000 years. He settled on the island of Cos, where there was already a well-established school of medicine, and there wrote about astrology and, allegedly under the patronage of the King of Egypt, established a school in which he taught the subject. He is credited with an early account of the waxing and waning of the Moon, and with devising a particular type of sundial. The historian Josephus claimed that Berosus introduced astrology to the Greek world. Pliny notes that he was such a good speaker and lecturer that a statue of him was erected in Athens, with a golden tongue – a tribute to his efficacy in predicting the future. His work exists only in fragments quoted by other writers.

bestial signs *see* FERAL SIGNS

Bible, the Given the violent antipathy that astrology has prompted during the past two or three centuries from most churchmen, it is not surprising that there has been much controversy about the Bible's allusions or supposed allusions to the subject. Much of the discussion has centred on numerology and the alleged coincidences which have resulted in the twelve zodiac signs being aligned to the twelve Tribes of Israel, the twelve Apostles, and the twelve stones in the breastplate of the High Priest. The truth is that there is no specific reference to astrology as such in the Old or New Testament, either in favour or in condemnation. Those that seem to occur have been shown to be the result of indifferent translation. The Apocrypha on the other hand contains a number of allusions: Enoch has passages on the stars and herbs, gems and numbers, and claims that in the sixth heaven angels attend the phases of the Moon and the revolutions of stars and Sun. In the Arabic *Gospel of the Infancy*, attributed to St James, Jesus is an astronomer, lecturing the priests in the Temple on 'the number of the spheres and heavenly bodies, as also their triangular, square and sextile aspect; their progressive and retrograde motion; their twenty-fourths and sixtieths of the twenty-fourths and other things which the reason of man has never discovered...'. Clement of Rome, a friend of St James, called the twelve Apostles the Twelve Months of Christ. *See also* ANGELS, ARCHANGELS and POPES.

bicorporeal The dual Signs: Gemini, Sagittarius and Pisces.

birth-chart *see* HOROSCOPE

birth control *see* JONAS

birth, moment of The moment of birth of an individual, as accurately recorded as possible. Four minutes is claimed as the optimum time which may be allowed before significant differences will appear in a birth chart (the accuracy of the birth place is equally significant). Astrologers variously take the time of the cutting of the umbilical cord, or of the first cry, as the precise time of birth. Precise timing is, however, rare even in the days of accurate time-keeping – and as to any period before, say, the turn of the 19th century, anything approaching real accuracy must be doubted. In modern times in some countries the time of birth is recorded on the birth certificate; this is generally also regarded as likely to be inaccurate – it is all too often rounded up to the nearest half-hour. There are various views of induced birth as interfering with the 'natural' time when birth would otherwise have occurred. *See* RECTIFICATION, CONCEPTION CHART.

birthstones The association between certain gemstones and certain zodiac signs dates from ancient times, but has been amended by speculative astrologers over many centuries, so that different lists exist. A modern, nonastrological jewellers' list has muddied the waters still further. There is really no reliable correspondence between stones and zodiac signs. The list prepared by AGRIPPA in the 15th century reads:

Aries – sardonyx
Taurus – sard
Gemini – topaz
Cancer – chalcedony
Leo – jasper
Virgo – smaragdine*

*emerald

Libra – beryl
Scorpio – amethyst
Sagittarius – hyacinth
Capricorn – chrysoprase**
Aquarius – crystal
Pisces – sapphire

**a golden-green gem, perhaps a beryl

The list perhaps most common at the time of writing is:

Aries – diamond
Taurus – emerald
Gemini – agate
Cancer – pearl
Leo – ruby
Virgo – sardonyx

Libra – sapphire, jade
Scorpio – opal
Sagittarius – topaz
Capricorn – turquoise, amethyst
Aquarius – aquamarine
Pisces – moonstone, bloodstone

birth-time *see* BIRTH, MOMENT OF

black chart A great number of different theories are attached to the practice of astrology, from the traditional planets in their zodiacal and house positions to the use of MIDPOINTS and many less reputable systems such as the movements of HYPOTHETICAL PLANETS. Teachers warn that if every suggested theory was to be used, and its indicators inserted in a HOROSCOPE, the chart would be completely black, or so nearly so that it would be indecipherable. The recommendation is by all means to experiment, but – especially when beginning to study – to adhere only to those theories which are traditional and well-tried.

Blagrave, Joseph (1610–82) Born in the parish of St Giles, Reading, in 1610, Blagrave studied astronomy, astrology, philosophy and medicine: 'Without some knowledge in astronomy one can be no astrologer, and without knowledge in astrology one can be no philosopher, and without knowledge both in astrology and philosophy one can be no good physician, the practice of which must be laid upon the five substantial pillars of time, virtue, number, sympathy, and antipathy.' He published a number of EPHEMERIDES, and in 1671 *Blagrave's Astrological Practice of Physick*. His *Introduction to Astrology* was published posthumously in 1682, dedicated to his friend Elias ASHMOLE.

Boehme, Jacob (1575–1624) Born of a simple peasant family in Altseidenburg, north of Dresden, Boehme worked first on a farm and then as a cobbler. A religious revelation when he was 25 persuaded him to devote his life to the expression of extremely complex and often opaque theological views in a series of over 50 books. Some of his ideas later influenced the English poet William Blake and the psychologist Carl Gustav Jung. Far from being a conventional astrologer, he wrote about the subject in spiritual, occult terms, in relation to alchemy and the theories of Paracelsus.

Bomelius, Dr Eliseus (d.1579) Born in Holland, Bomelius took a degree in medicine at Cambridge and rapidly became well-known in London for his treatment of the sick. At the same time he had studied and practised astrology, and at one time Sir William Cecil consulted him about the possible marriage of Queen Elizabeth I. In 1567 he was arrested for practising medicine without the licence of the College of Physicians and sent to King's Bench Prison, whence he petitioned Cecil for his release, predicting that the country was in great danger and that he could advise how to avoid it. This was unsuccessful, and the College of Physicians fined him £20 and 15s costs, which he was unable to pay. He remained in prison until 1570, when an ambassador from Russia took him to Moscow, where he settled, and in 1572 was said by a British traveller to be living in great luxury at the court of Ivan IV and holding an official position as astrologer at the court of the Tsar's son. Eventually, suspected of being part of a Polish and Swedish conspiracy against Ivan, he was arrested, tortured and died in imprisonment. He was described (by Sir Jerome Horsey) as a skilful mathematician, a wicked man, and a practiser of much mischief, though another contemporary claims that 'hys learned workes published geve due testimony of his erudicion and godlynes'.

Bonati, Guido (fl.13th c.) Adviser to the Holy Roman Emperor Frederick II and others, and to the governments of Florence and Siena. His *Liber Astronomicus* was a famous and popular text of its time, later reprinted in the 17th century. Dante, in his *Divine Comedy* placed Bonati and Michael SCOT in the eighth circle of Hell, with their heads on back to front, a symbol of their religious deviation.

Booker, John (1603–67) First a haberdasher then a clerk and teacher before becoming an astrologer, Booker published his first almanac in 1631; in this he predicted the deaths of Gustavus Adolphus and the elector palatine, both of whom conveniently died, providing him with considerable publicity. He was a vehement supporter of Cromwell during the Civil War, and in 1643 was made official licenser of books on 'Mathematicks, Almanacks, and prognostications'. LILLY at first admired him, but altered his opinion when without leave Booker made several alterations in Lilly's *Merlinus Anglicus Junior* before consenting to licence it. ASHMOLE bought and preserved his papers, which were said to prove him 'a very honest man, who abhorred any deceit in the art he practised'. He had a large practice, dealing with over 1,000 consultations a year – as many as 16,500 enquiries between 1648 and 1665.

Brady, Bernadette (b.1950) Australian astrologer practising in England. With Darrelyn Gunzburg runs Astro Logos, a teaching body which offers courses in medieval astrology and the use of the fixed stars. Her publications include *Predictive Astrology: the eagle and the lark* (1999), *Brady's Book of Fixed Stars* (2006) and *Astrology: a place in chaos* (2006) – the latter based on her research for her master's degree in cultural astronomy and astrology from Bath Spa university.

Brahe, Tycho (1546–1601) Danish astronomer, the greatest pre-telescope observer of the heavens. Born into a noble family, he was destined for a political career, but impressed by the partial eclipse of 1560 became fascinated by astronomy, and in 1572 observed a new star in Cassiopeia, a discovery which made his name. He established an observatory on the island of Hven and for 20 years carried out observations, measuring the positions of 777 stars. He firmly believed that the planets influenced life on Earth, and lectured in Copenhagen defending astrology, speaking especially in favour of its use in medical practice. He published a number of speculative astrological works – on the supernova of 1572 and the comet of 1577, for example. He gave astrological advice to Frederick II and Rudolph II of Denmark, who were his patrons, and suggested that astronomers should have two mottos: *Despiciendo suspicio* ('By looking down I see upward') and *Suspiciendo despicio* ('By looking up I see downward').

Bruno, Giordano (1548–1600) Born in Naples, Bruno became a Dominican friar, but left the order to travel and study beyond its confines. His championship of Copernicus brought him into conflict with the Church, and after a trial which lasted seven years he was burned at the stake in Rome. Influenced by the work of AGRIPPA, he believed that the reformation of mankind must begin with the reformation of the heavens, the characteristics of the 'bestial' constellations to be driven from the skies as a preface to the driving out of the evils of mankind.

business cycles A considerable amount of research has gone into the use of astrology to help to forecast business cycles. Some astrologers claim a success rate over 70 per cent, whereas professional economists average more like 50 per cent. A close correlation has been found between sunspots and the business index. Many different techniques have been used: some astrologers use the time of a company's foundation to erect a birth-time (*see* BIRTH, MOMENT OF), and use this and PROGRESSIONS from it. Others study the birth-charts of the company's chief officers.

Butler, Samuel (1612–80) English satirist and author of *Hudibras*, the most entertaining of all satirical attacks on astrologer and astrologers.

– C –

calculation (of a horoscope) It is not difficult to calculate and set up a
HOROSCOPE; the work required is tricky rather than complex. It involves the
discovery from the subject of his or her birth-date, time and place, and the
latitude and longitude of that place (which can be found from a reasonably
comprehensive book of maps). The birth-time then must be converted to
Greenwich Mean Time – remembering any adjustments that must be made
for local time changes – summer time, double summer time, or whatever.
This can be difficult to find, especially if the birth took place during
wartime; there are now, however, comprehensive books that list world time
changes. An EPHEMERIS must then be consulted to discover the sidereal time
at midnight or noon, and the local sidereal time at birth calculated, from
which can be found the ASCENDANT, MIDHEAVEN and other features of the
chart. The calculations can now be done with the aid of computer
programmes, several of which are available, and most of which result in the
provision of a full horoscope and list of planetary positions, aspects and
other features.

calendar The accurate measurement of time has always been a preoccupation of mankind, and early attempts were made to define rules for dividing a
year into manageable units, and naming these. First attempts at this may
have been made as long ago as 2000BC, using not only ephemeral means
such as notched sticks or bones, but such monuments as Stonehenge, one of
whose purposes was surely to measure the length of the solar year by
observing the movement of the Sun along the horizon. Months marked by
the observation of a 'new Moon' were an obvious and easy means of
dividing time; in climates where frequent cloud obscured the heavens, early
astronomers devised mathematical means of calculating such periods –
measuring a synodic month (the interval from one 'new Moon' to the next)
as 29.53059 days.

The next step was the division of the year into 12 months of 29 or 30
days each, forming a lunar year of just over 364 days. A lunar year,

however, proved impractical for farmers, and an additional month was added whenever it seemed convenient, in order to allow them to keep in step with the Sun. Such calendars, based on the same observations, sprung up all over the world – in Mesopotamia and Greece, in Rome and India and China. Elsewhere the measurement of the years was organized somewhat differently – the Mayans for instance devised a year of 18 months, each of 20 days, adding 5 days at the end of each.

The ancient Roman year began in March, so that December was the tenth month – hence its name. January became the opening month of the year in 153BC, when Roman consuls decided to take office from the first day of that month (the Julian and Gregorian calendars followed that practice). Until 1752, England and its dependant colonies began each year on 25 March – hence the allusions in historical dates to 'Old Style' and 'New Style'.

The notion of a seven-day week apparently began with the Babylonians, later copied by the Jews (with the seventh day given special significance as the Sabbath). The Romans seem independently to have associated a seven-day cycle with the Sun, Moon and the then five observable planets – thus

- Sunday – *Dies Solis* or Sun's day
- Monday – *Dies Lunæ*, Moon's day
- Saturday – *Dies Saturni*

The other names seem to have derived from more ancient gods:

- Tuesday – from Tiw
- Wednesday – from Woden
- Thursday – from Thor
- Friday – from Frigg

In fact, these gods are the German equivalents of Mars, Mercury, Jupiter and Venus.

In ancient times the years were often calculated from the time when a particular reign began; most famously, of course, this applied to Jesus Christ. In about AD525 a monk called Dionysus Exiguus suggested that in future all time should be measured from the birth of his Saviour, and gradually during the next few centuries the idea was universally accepted by western Christian nations. The year before Christ's birth – or rather before the year generally agreed to mark that event – became known as BC, so that the first century of the Christian era began in AD1, the second in AD101 and so on. (The new millennium actually began in 2001, though celebrations were mistakenly held at the beginning of 2000).

Because it was obviously important that the civilized world should share one calendar, the so-called Gregorian calendar was introduced in 1582, with the average length of the year approximating closely to that of the solar or tropical year, containing about 365.2422 mean solar days. The Julian calendar had created three leap years too many in every period of 385 years, which had resulted in inaccuracies which made it difficult for the Church to determine the date of Easter, which depended on the date of the spring equinox. Pope Gregory XIII therefore introduced a new calendar devised by the astronomer Christopher Clavius. This was to be a determinate calendar, derived solely by numerical rules, which could therefore be laid out for any year in advance. To the horror of many lay people, who believed that they were being deprived of eleven days of their lives, Thursday 4 October 1582 was followed by Friday 15 October, after which leap year occurred only during years exactly divisible by four (with the exception that years ending in 00 were to be divisible by 400 – so that 1600, 1984 and 2000 were leap years, but 1800 and 1900 were not.

A modern exception to the Christian rule occurred during the French Revolution, when a secular calendar was proposed and, for the time, adopted. This began on 22 September 1792, the day on which the Republic was proclaimed, and the months were give new names – including *Nivôse* or Snow (for April), *Ventôse* or Wind (for June) and *Messidor* or Harvest (for October). France returned to the Gregorian calendar in 1806.

For astrologers the comings and goings of various calendrical styles pose obvious problems, equalled only by the differing measurements of time introduced by governments as summer time, or in times of war double and even triple summer time. The best computerized calculating programmes deal with these, and various EPHEMERIDES are also available to those who wish to do historical research. *See also* HEBREW CALENDAR, ISLAMIC CALENDAR, JULIAN CALENDAR.

Campanus house system A house system in which the PRIME VERTICAL is divided into twelve sections which are projected onto the ECLIPTIC in circles that embrace the north and south points on the horizon.

Campanus, Johannes (1220–96) Italian astrologer, astronomer and mathematician, chaplain to Pope Urban IV and physician to Pope Boniface VIII. His work on Euclid is celebrated, and he published a famous book on the planets, *Theorica Planetarum*, in which he gave instructions for building a planetarium. He worked on RETROGRADE motion and published in the West planetary data from Arabian sources.

Campion, Nicholas (b.1953) English astrologer, historian, author and lecturer, creator of the MA in Cultural Astronomy and Astrology at Bath Spa University, later administered by the University of Wales. He has been active in astrological organizations such as the Astrological Lodge of London (President 1984–7, 92) and the Astrological Association (1995–9). He has received a number of awards from astrological institutions. He has also written popular astrological columns for a number of newspapers and magazines. Among his books are *Astrology, History and Apocalypse* (2000) and *The Dawn of Astrology: A Cultural History of Western Astrology – The Ancient and Classical Worlds* (2008).

Cancer ♋

The fourth sign of the zodiac. SUN-SIGN period 22 June–22 July.

> *It should be remembered when reading of the characteristics of the Sun-signs that these will always be affected by the effects of the rising-sign, the planets in various other signs and houses, and the relationships the planets make to each other.*

General characteristics
Defensiveness is a major characteristic of those with the Sun in Cancer. They have a strong need to protect themselves, their family, and their privacy. This can lead to a certain air of suspicion which can worry

acquaintances who may wish to become friends. Their emotional level is high, and they have a strong urge to care for others – and not only family members. The caring professions thus often attract them. A usually vivid imagination can be troublesome, for they tend to worry – often over nonexistent situations or problems. Tenacious and hard-working, once they have decided on a course of action they will follow it to its conclusion, whether it is an important career commitment or a minor domestic task. Sun-sign Cancerians do however have a reliable intuitive sense, and making a decision on the reliability of another individual, the viability of a business project or a course of action will do so almost instantaneously and unhesitatingly; the decision usually proves to be the right one for them. They make good, though sometimes clinging, parents, and are sensitive – perhaps oversensitive – lovers.

The growing child

Quick to fly to the defence of a family member if another child is critical or makes a derogatory remark, a young boy or girl with the Sun in Cancer will adopt the role of father or mother of the family from the moment he or she understands what a family is. A young male Cancerian will be enormously protective of a younger brother or sister, while a little girl will love caring for a family of dolls (perhaps rather too obsessively). Cancerian children enjoy taking care of pets, which will feature in their lives if they have anything to do with it. This helps to nurture a feeling of responsibility, which in many ways chimes in with the Cancerian personality. Children will be strong-willed and courageous, and from a very early age may trouble parents by being rather too eager to take part in slightly risky games. If a friend offends them in any way, they will tend to retire into their shells, and be quite difficult to coax out. They can be moody – at one moment cheerfully talkative, at the next for no particular reason quiet and defensive. This may be the product of the Cancerian imagination, inventing some quite imaginary difficulty or problem – but naturally intuitive they will also very easily pick up a disruptive or tense atmosphere in the home.

Education

Remembering facts – such as historical dates – will be no difficulty for a Cancerian child or young scholar; indeed history is often a favourite subject, one in which the imagination can play a part. Indeed there may be some difficulty in confining a young Cancerian to the facts, for while they will be readily recalled they may equally readily be embroidered from the rich Cancerian imagination. Sometimes it may seem that a young Cancerian knows more about the past than about the present. The imagination will demand free rein, and will probably find it through writing or art, and also through creative movement of some sort – whether in gymnastics or dance. If a young Cancerian shows signs of being worried, it will be quite difficult to persuade him or her to divulge the reason; they will tend to hug the problem to themselves. They will be devoted to home, and boarding schools are not a good idea for them – they will suffer more than most children from being separated from the family. Indeed, they can at first be shy and wary when attending a conventional school, though their naturally plucky personalities will soon come to the fore.

Friendship, romance and sex

The Cancerian reputation as a caring, loving friend is well founded – they are genuinely worried by other people's problems, and always ready to offer help if any problem needs solving. They are, however, equally swift to defend a friend should another be critical. True romantics, they know how to woo a prospective lover, and once won will know how to show their affection, using all their potent imagination. Their sexual attitude tends to be maternal (even in males), which may not suit every taste, but there will be no shortage of affection and Cancer is by nature a sensual sign, so the sexual side of the partnership should be happy enough. There will however be mood swings, the reason for which will not always be readily apparent, and a real or perceived insensitive remark can provoke a very sharp and hurtful response. The Cancerian tendency to possessiveness can lead to a determination to cling on to a partner long after it should have been clear that the affair is over; it is difficult for a Cancerian to tolerate rejection, and the end of an affair needs to be very tactfully conveyed if they are to look forward to the future rather than resentfully back on the past.

Permanent partnership and family

What has been said above applies equally in a permanent partnership. Both men and women make caring partners, and setting a permanent seal on a romance is a matter of urgency for them. When problems arise, it will be an equally urgent matter to solve them and repair any damage. Both men and women will care deeply for the home – women perhaps almost too deeply, for it is possible for them to become bogged down in domesticity, even giving up promising careers for that reason. The need for parenthood is strong in Sun-sign Cancerians, and a partnership will be in difficulty if the Cancerian's partner does not feel as strongly about starting a family. When children reach the age to leave home, a Cancerian parent will miss them more than most. Outside interests of any kind can suffer from a determination to put the home environment first. Once settled into that home, it will be difficult to shift a Cancerian, who will be as attached to it as a crab to its shell – they are not like those crustaceans happy to exchange one shell for another, and even the prospect of a much enhanced standard of living will often fail to persuade someone with the Sun in Cancer to contemplate moving house.

Occupation

Everything that has been said about the caring instinct nurtured by the Sun from Cancer comes into play when one considers a suitable career. Obviously, the caring professions are high on the list – and the list embraces not only the medical profession but the running of nursery schools (most Cancerians are devoted to small children). However, there are other possibilities. Cancerians tend to be excellent cooks (the fact that they can from time to time give vivid displays of ill temper suggests that the profession of chef may be worth considering!). Their interest in history can prompt a position involving the study and perhaps sale of antiques – but they are also shrewd with money, so the running of any small business can be successful. Many Cancerians have a natural pull towards the sea, which can prompt interest in the navy as a profession, or working on cruise liners, or perhaps in boat-building. It is worth remembering that certain Cancerian traits – unaccountable occasional moodiness for instance – can make them uneasy colleagues, until they are well understood.

Health

Anxiety is the most obvious problem likely to lead to ill health, and is often accompanied by digestive difficulties, and sometimes an outbreak of allergies of one kind or another. Their intuition can be employed in mitigating the problem, when and if they learn to trust it as a means of problem-solving. They are naturally physically sturdy, and will often battle on through an illness after others would have given up. Their natural tenacity will carry them through periods of strain and tension. They often have pale complexions, and are among those people who should particularly heed warnings about protecting their skin from the sun. There is of course absolutely no connection between the name of the sign and cancer the disease – but Cancer rules the breasts, and women with an emphasis on this sign are well advised to examine themselves regularly, and have regular medical checks. The best form of exercise for them is that which increases stamina – swimming in particular, but also dance and running.

Finance

A tendency to hoard is joined by a deep-rooted disinclination to take risks. If parents start a bank account for a very young child, it will not be long before he or she will be taking a very keen interest in it. They may themselves have a small hoard of cash which they keep in some secret place, just for emergencies. When the time comes for them to take control of their own affairs, they will invest only under the very safest conditions and with as many firm assurances as possible. They will also want to be able to access their money easily. Usually careful how they spend their money, even when extremely prosperous they will usually be under the impression that they are comparatively poor. As business people they will enjoy making careful financial plans. Shrewd, and to a degree they can err on the side of caution, and a more adventurous partner will be an asset – though he or she will have to work hard every time they wish to persuade the Cancerian to make an additional investment.

Growing older

The Cancerian physique is naturally strong and resolute, and provided that it has not been sapped by psychological difficulties – undue worry, for instance, leading to difficulties with the digestion – there is no reason why they should not be extremely active in old age. They will be reluctant to retire, unwilling to make a change to their lifestyle – and the prospect of a cutback in regular income will concern them, however healthy their retirement funds. They should have no problem in using up their time, probably by extending hobbies which they have been pursuing for years. The common idea of marking retirement by moving to a new locality can make for unhappiness; after the initial excitement, they will particularly miss old friends and places. By the time they retire, Cancerians may well have a collection of antiques of some sort which needs cataloguing, and they will certainly want to go on attending sales of whatever they have been collecting. They may enjoy researching such things in greater depth than they have previously had time to do, and their instinctive interest in history will serve them well, and make the task fascinating.

Cancer as rising-sign

Inner strength, determination and tenacity of purpose will be notable, and the attainment of objectives extremely important. Much energy, however, will be directed to the care of the partner and family – though this can take the form of working so hard to make money to ensure a good life for them, that the people themselves may feel somewhat neglected. Cancerian shrewdness will be sharpened when Cancer rises, and can be applied in every way, but most rewardingly perhaps in business. The tendency to worry can also be emphasized, with a reluctance to talk problems through even with close family members. The attitude to the lover or partner may seem somewhat cool and even distant, though sexually there will be the same vivacity and enjoyment as with a Cancer Sun-sign. The effect upon the health is much as with the Sun-sign – care must be taken not to expose the pale skin to the sun, and women in particular should make regular appointments for medical checks (though again it should be emphasized that there is no connection between Cancer the sign, and cancer the disease).

Traditional associations

- Ruling Planet – the Moon
- Triplicity/Element – water
- Quadruplicity/Quality – cardinal
- Colour – silver grey
- Gemstone – pearl
- Metal – silver
- Flowers – acanthus, convolvulus, white flowers in general

- Trees – those rich in sap
- Herbs and Spices – saxifrage, verbena, tarragon
- Foodstuffs – milk, fish, fruits and vegetables with a high water content
- Animals – creatures with a shell covering
- Countries – USA, Scotland, Holland
- Cities – Manchester (UK), Amsterdam, Tokyo
- US States – Idaho, New Hampshire, Virginia, Wyoming

* * *

Capricorn ♑

The tenth sign of the zodiac. SUN-SIGN period 22 December–20 January.

It should be remembered when reading of the characteristics of the Sun-signs that these will always be affected by the effects of the rising-sign, the planets in various other signs and houses, and the relationships the planets make to each other.

General characteristics

A concern always to do 'the right thing' – which too often means rigid conformity – is perhaps the strongest element of the Capricorn nature. Their tendency to grumble and to be at least very 'careful' with their finances is often offset by an unexpected deadpan sense of humour. Patience and insight are two qualities which, if they do not seem present, can certainly be nurtured – as can confidence, for lack of confidence can be a surprising problem for them. A negative reaction can persuade them that their progress is blocked – that 'things are against them'. But then suddenly the position can be reversed and they will be full of aspiration and hope. They may find it hard to show their feelings, which can make partnership difficult; their involvement with their careers can lead to neglect of a partner. Capricorns often feel they should know everything, and relish a position of power, even if it results in a degree of solitude. A major problem with Capricorn health, especially if long hours are spent behind a desk, is with stiffness in the joints, which can lead to arthritic conditions.

The growing child

A Capricorn child may well be more conventional than his or her parents –
something to consider when planning their education. They may also, from
a surprisingly early age, be slightly pompous and over-serious – but they
have a natural sense of humour, to which appeal can be made to lighten
them up. They will be eager to show their mettle and be 'top of the class',
from infants' school right up to university – and this can persuade them that
life should be all work and very little play; encouragement to relax and
enjoy life will be rather suspiciously received. Young people may be slow
to show their emotions, and be perceived as slightly cool. They will enjoy
reading and music, and may neglect sports, especially those which take
place in the open air.

Education

The young Capricorn's ambition to succeed will be seriously but sensibly
cultivated – there will be no rush for top marks, but rather slow, confident,
meticulous study. A gradual increase of knowledge is the way to go, and the
way they will follow. They will be popular with their peers, and will cope
well with the school routine, and with discipline – which they will be
inclined to follow even when they disagree with the reasons for it. They
may not, on the whole, consider that their masters and lecturers are necessarily superior to them in intellectual potential, and may well after a while
strike out for themselves into areas of study they think will be more
profitable than those on offer. They will happily study any subject which
they conceive will be useful to them in furthering their ambitions; they may
be particularly drawn to the study of architecture.

Friendship, romance and sex

People with the Sun in Capricorn will sometimes tend to use their friends as
sponges to soak up their current complaints and grumbles; but once these
are over they can usually be persuaded to lighten up and enjoy themselves.
They are loyal and faithful friends, though if they find someone who is one
step up on the social level they are capable of a little pretension. It will take
some time for a Capricorn to decide that he or she is in love; they fear
rejection, which can make them slow to commit. They will want to impress
the object of their attentions – but may spend less on this than might be

expected. The affair will develop cautiously. With the Sun in Capricorn a man or woman may find it difficult to relax into sex and regard it as fun – while often enthusiastic enough about it, Capricorns often seem to regard it as somehow separate from romance, love and affection, and to regard it as one might regard a healthy but rather uninteresting snack when one is hungry, to be taken because it is good for one and satisfies the appetite – simple lust may take the place of romantic love.

Permanent partnership and family

With the Sun in Capricorn a man or woman may tend to marry for reasons unconnected with love; ambition or money, for instance. In a permanent relationship they will show a strong protective instinct, and perhaps as a result will tend to want to manage the life of the partner completely. They can be dutiful rather than deeply loving husbands or wives. Working hard to keep up their standard of living, they may neglect the personal relationship with partner and children, treating the home as an extension of the office. Women with the Sun in this sign will, if they do not themselves have a career in which they are fully involved, devote themselves to building their husband's, and can frequently be extremely successful in doing so. Capricorns are not vindictive, but can be unforgiving – if the non-Capricorn partner strays, forgiveness will be hard to come by. Having said all that, Capricorn marriages are often long-lasting – they rarely marry in haste, and their caution often pays off.

Occupation

A driving ambition coupled with a desire for security makes for a man or woman who is thrusting but careful in whatever career is chosen. Routine presents no problems for them – they enjoy knowing just what they will be doing at whatever time of the clock (this is part of their blanket of security); they do well therefore in big business – banking, for example, though those who enjoy the outdoors also do well in agriculture, where their tempera- ment makes it easier for them to deal with unexpected crises than some others. If they start their own businesses they usually do well; they enjoy 'going it alone'. The successful self-made man is quintessentially Capricornian; working with a partner is not easy for them, and they must take particular care if they are thinking of doing so. Forced to work as members of a team, their sense of humour often comes to their rescue when they feel tempted to be authoritarian. They work particularly well when they are in positions of authority – professions such as business chief, head teacher and high-ranking officer in the armed services have more than their fair share of Capricorns.

Health

A particular problem for those with the Sun in Capricorn tends to be a stiffening of the joints, with age; since many Capricorns are likely to spend their working lives behind desks, a regular routine which keeps them moving is therefore valuable. The knees and shins (the Capricorn area of the body) are vulnerable, and knee injuries (particularly cartilage problems) are common, especially when the Capricornian man or woman plays sport. The skin is also governed by Capricorn, and may need attention, as may the teeth and bones. (As always, this is true for everyone; but for Capricorn problems with these areas of the body tend to be above average). Capricorns do not worry about temperature, and react well to cold – but this can nevertheless bring problems, for it can bring on rheumatic pains.

Finance

Capricorns are enthusiastic investors, probably from an early age; given pocket money, a Capricorn child is quite likely to set it, or a proportion of it, aside, and watch it grow. Both sexes have a reputation for being 'careful' with money, and the word 'mean' may even be apt. They are more concerned to set money aside, 'just in case', than to spend it on such flippancies as entertaining a girl- or boy-friend. They are among the people who will keep their private account books as carefully as any accountant. As investors they are cautious and usually wise; they dislike risk-taking, and will tend to gravitate to the safest possible financial institutions rather than taking the leap of investing in what may seem 'a good thing', but without the evidence to support the claim. As collectors, they will concentrate on things which have a chance of making a profit – antiques, perhaps, or paintings, or silver. If they remember that they are traditionalists they are unlikely to go wrong.

Growing older

Capricorns usually plan ahead, and the chances are that they will make well-considered plans for retirement long before the situation arises. They will have saved prudently against the moment when they no longer receive a salary, and will probably be as well-off in retirement as when in employment. Similarly, they will have a very good idea of what activities they will take up – or elaborate – to fill the spare time they may have; gardening on a large scale may certainly be one of these, but literature and music are enjoyed by most Capricorns and may play an enhanced role in old age.

Capricorn as rising-sign

Stability and common sense are strongly accented when Capricorn rises, though there may be some difficulty with the positive expression of emotion (the Sun-sign will have much to say about this, however). The talent to plan ahead will be enhanced, and self-expression will be channelled in a considered and therefore effective way. There may be some lack of self-confidence, which can be cramping in the career; shyness, too, which may inhibit courtship – but contrary to the effect of Capricorn as a Sun-sign, this rising-sign (through the influence of its POLAR SIGN, Cancer) will contribute to the development of a really tender, sensitive and caring quality once a commitment has been made to a permanent relationship. Loyalty will be paramount.

Traditional associations

- Ruling Planet – Saturn
- Triplicity/Element – earth
- Quadruplicity/Quality – cardinal
- Colours – dark grey, dark brown, black
- Gemstones – turquoise, amethyst
- Metal – lead
- Flowers – ivy, hemlock, medlar, heartsease
- Trees – pine, elm, yew
- Herbs and Spices – hemp, comfrey, knapweed
- Foodstuffs – potato, barley, beet, spinach, malt
- Animals – goat, all cloven-hoofed animals
- Countries – Afghanistan, Australia, India, Saudi Arabia

- Cities – Atlanta, Charleston, Delhi, Mexico City, Oxford (UK), Salt Lake City, Seattle; the administrative areas of capital cities
- US States – Alaska, Connecticut, Georgia, Iowa, New Mexico, Texas, Utah

* * *

Cardan, Jerome (Gerolamo Cardano) (1501–76) Mathematician, physician and astrologer much in demand at Renaissance Italian courts for his medical skills (he was the first to describe typhoid). His services were highly valued at the courts. In 1554 he published his own calculated horoscope of Christ. For a while he was merely criticized for this, but some years later was arrested and accused of blasphemy. After a short imprisonment he was released and given a pension by Pope Gregory XIII. He died in Rome on the day he had astrologically forecast (sceptics accused him of committing suicide in order to make his prediction true).

cardinal signs The cardinal signs are Aries, Cancer, Libra and Capricorn. They are each related in some way to activity, to expressing oneself through enthusiastic and considered action. Ambition is a motivating force, and there is little delay in seeking to fulfil it. The driving force of cardinal signs is strong, and can result in selfishness and the treading down of rivals. The cardinal HOUSES are the first, fourth, seventh and tenth. Planets in these houses will contribute a cardinal flavour to the HOROSCOPE.

Carter, Charles Ernest Owen (1887–1968) Carter graduated from the University of London in 1913 and practised as a barrister. He became interested in astrology, studied it, and co-founded the Faculty of Astrological Studies. Attending the meeting at which Bessie Leo proposed the founding of an astrological lodge of the Theosophical Society, Carter became its second president. He started *The Astrological Quarterly* in 1922, and edited it until 1959. He correctly forecast his own death based, he said, on the observation of indications of grief expressed in the charts of his friends and relatives. Among his many books the most respected is perhaps *The Astrological Aspects*.

Case, John (fl.1680–1700) Case set up business as astrologer and physician in premises in London first used by William LILLY, whose name could still be seen faintly inscribed over the door where the younger astrologer had set up his board:

Within this place
Lives Doctor Case.

He became extremely popular and well known, which did not protect him from the ridicule of Swift and Addison. In 1697 he published *The Angelical Guide, shewing men and women their lott or chance in this elementary life.* He rose above criticism with some wit. The story is told that when a colleague proposed the toast of 'those fools, your patients', Case replied, 'Good brother, let me have all the fools and you are heartily welcome to the rest of the practice'.

Cassini, Giovanni Domenico (1625–1712) French astrologer and astronomer. He was introduced to astrology as a young man, and in 1644 a Bolognese senator with an interest in the subject offered him a position at his private observatory, where he worked on the production of reliable EPHEMERIDES for astrologers. Subsequently he became professor of astronomy at the University of Bologna and later director of the Paris observatory.

celestial equator A great circle on the CELESTIAL SPHERE midway between the celestial poles – i.e., the projection of Earth's equator onto the celestial sphere.

celestial latitude The measurement of any planet's or star's distance north or south of the ECLIPTIC.

celestial longitude Celestial longitude is measured along the zodiacal circle or ECLIPTIC, eastward from the first point of Aries.

celestial meridian A great circle on the CELESTIAL SPHERE passing through the poles and north and south points of the horizon. The meridian of LONGITUDE of an observer projected onto the celestial sphere.

celestial poles The points of the sky directly overhead from the Earth's poles – the axis of the Earth extended into space.

celestial sphere The apparent great sphere surrounding the Earth, on the surface of which the ancients believed the planets and stars were placed.

cell-salts In homeopathic medicine the signs have been allied to the twelve cell-salts, and this is taken into consideration when diagnosing and prescribing. The links are as follows:

- ARIES – *Kali Phos* (potassium phosphate)
- TAURUS – *Nat Sulph* (sulphate of sodium)
- GEMINI – *Kali Mur* (chloride of potassium)
- CANCER – *Calc Fluor* (fluoride of lime)
- LEO – *Mag Phos* (phosphate of magnesium)
- VIRGO – *Kali Sulph* (sulphate of potassium)
- LIBRA – *Nat Phos* (sodium phosphate)
- SCORPIO – *Calc Sulph* (lime sulphate)
- SAGITTARIUS – silica
- CAPRICORN – *Calc Phos* (lime phosphate)
- AQUARIUS – *Nat Mur* (sodium chloride)
- PISCES – *Ferrum Phos* (iron phosphate)

Celsus, Aulus Cornelius (fl.1st c. AD) One of the greatest of all Roman medical writers also wrote *The True Word*, an anti-Christian tract, which took the view that it was idiotic of Christians to deny the power of the planets.

Ceres The largest and first ASTEROID to be discovered – in 1801, in orbit between Mars and Jupiter. Ceres is believed to speak of necessary nurture – physical (such as the early care received from parents) and psychological (the kind of nurture which makes one feel safe). It also reveals how a subject will care for his or her own children. Some astrologers claim that it affects the design and choice of clothing and food.

Chaldean astrology The Chaldeans were a Semitic people originally from Arabia, who ruled Babylonia between 625BC and 538BC. They were famous astronomers and astrologers – it is likely that the zodiac was devised by them, although it was later adjusted by the Greeks. The prediction of future events was regarded as a 'Chaldean' art, and the term *Chaldean* came to be synonymous with *astrologer*. It was they, predominantly, who carried astrology to other nations and broadened its scope, claiming for instance that not only a man but a city could have its HOROSCOPE, and that an astrologer could advise on its foundation, in order to secure its prosperity (in 312BC Seleucus I founded the city of Selucia on astrological advice, and Antioch was founded on 22 May 300BC for the same reason).

'changeable' signs Taurus and Gemini, Leo and Virgo, Sagittarius and Capricorn (thus paired) were traditionally described as *changeable* signs (the other six were described as *fixed*). They were linked to the astrological QUALITIES, Taurus being described as cold, Gemini as cold and moist, Leo as hot and moist, Virgo as cold and moist, Sagittarius as hot and dry, and Capricorn as cold and moist (this according to Western astrology; in the East, there were different attributions). This archaic theory is now largely discarded.

chart ruler The chart ruler is the planet which rules the ASCENDANT or rising-sign. However, any planet which may be considered as the most powerful in a HOROSCOPE or BIRTH-CHART can be described as the chart ruler, and regarded as of equal importance to the Ascendant. *See* PERSONAL PLANETS.

Chaucer, Geoffrey (ca.1343–1400) English poet, famous for *The Canterbury Tales*, in which the characters of the pilgrims who walk from London to Canterbury represent stars and planets, coming into conjunction and forming other aspects to each other. Modern literary scholarship has revealed, and is still revealing, the many astrological allusions in the poem, in which astrology is presented as an acknowledged fact:

The death of every man is there to see,
Patterned in stars clearer than in a glass,
Could one but read how all will come to pass.

Chaucer also wrote a treatise on the use of the ASTROLABE. His young clerk, Nicholas, was an astrologer, and drew up horoscopes for people.

Cheiro *see* WARNER, WILLIAM JOHN

Chennevière, Daniel *see* RUDHYAR, DANE

Childrey, Joshua (1623–70) A schoolmaster at Faversham, Childrey was in 1660 appointed as chaplain to Henry Somerset, Lord Herbert, and swiftly rose to become Archdeacon, Prebendary of Salisbury Cathedral and Rector of Upwey in Dorsetshire. In 1652 he published *Indago Astrologica, or a brief and modest Enquiry into some principal points of Astrology*, and the following year *Syzygiasticon instauratum; or an ephemeris of the places and aspects of the planets.*

Chinese astrology Chinese astrology is very different from Western astrology, and attempts to equate the two by comparing the symbolic animals linked to the Chinese 'years' with the Western zodiac (i.e., the Rat with Aries, the Monkey with Gemini and so on) are deeply mistaken.

Chiron Discovered in 1977, Chiron – technically Comet 95P, minor planet 2060 – has an orbit of 50.7 years, within the orb of Uranus. Astrologically it is regarded as a 'healer', teaching one how to come to term with one's 'wounds', and encouraging bravery in adversity.

Chiron in ARIES

Chiron in this sign tends to make a person impatient and subject to boredom, so that while Arien enthusiasm and vigour are accentuated, the enthusiasm will tend to be brief. These people want to perform every task themselves, or at least over-see everything – the idea of entrusting an assignment to anyone else is foreign to them. There is natural daring and an ability to seize the moment and make the most of it, and this can be used to cover – and sometimes also to overcome – a sense of insecurity.

Chiron in TAURUS

The physical body is of great importance to those with Chiron in this sign – there will be a preoccupation with bodily health and wellbeing, and much consideration of sexuality and the part the body plays in attracting partners. Just as there will be concern to keep healthy, there will be an interest in staying wealthy – which may lead to an overcareful attitude to money, to materialism and possessiveness, for these folk will never be confident that they are wealthy enough – or as wealthy as they feel they should be.

Chiron in GEMINI

Natural Geminian quickness and liveliness of mind is accented by this placing of Chiron, but there may be need of an effort if the individual is to keep in touch with his or her inner emotions, and find a solution to questions which may have been nagging at them for years. Ideas and opinions are likely to be presented in original and perhaps unsettling ways, which may prove a barrier when these people want to explain themselves. This can lead to frustration and the inhibition of positive thought.

Chiron in CANCER

A need to feel part of society is basic to people with Chiron in Cancer, in the sense that they must feel that they are a necessary part of a family, a partnership, a business, a group of some kind, if they are to feel really secure. This however does not mean that they will want to play a strong social role – on the contrary, they may be regarded as loners because of a disinclination to join in with usual social activities: the other members of their group or even family may feel they know little about them.

Chiron in LEO

A sense of restriction is often shown when Chiron is in Leo: the subject's strongest desires will remain in some way unfulfilled, because of outside influences or the intervention of others (probably of parents, when they are young). There will be a tendency to achieve in order to impress, rather than for the joy of achievement, and this can be negative, especially if there is an ambition to be creative. Their instinct is always strong, even when a lack of talent or ability hampers it.

Chiron in VIRGO

If a workaholic is governed by routine and the desire for perfection there is likely to be pressure, stress and therefore ill health; learning some relaxation technique is therefore mandatory for those with Chiron in this sign. When calm and repose are achieved, that achievement will be more fully enjoyed. Intellectual liveliness and quickness of mind are natural to these folk – but so is a critical sense, which can be too often sharply and sarcastically expressed. This placing of Chiron sometimes bestows a talent for healing.

Chiron in LIBRA

A tendency to feel resentful of others' success when contrasted to what is seen as their own failures can damage these people's understanding of their own worth, and they can find it difficult to grasp the conception of fairness and justice when applied to themselves. They also sometimes find it difficult to be straightforward in discussing anything which affects them strongly. The need to develop sensitive and sympathetic rapport in relationships is vital if they are not to appear selfish.

Chiron in SCORPIO

Everything is seen in primary colours by those with Chiron in Scorpio; there are few pastel shades. Doubts or inadequacies will provoke sullenness rather than the desire to cope with and conquer them. A highly developed competitive spirit can be valuable in, for instance, sport, but when expressed in a career can become ruthlessness. The urge to reach the top and stay there should not be allowed to lead to extreme action or the total disregard of the feelings and attributes of others. The Scorpio's healthy enjoyment of sex often results in considerable expertise – which may be used to conquer rather than woo.

Chiron in SAGITTARIUS

Whatever success is achieved, whatever happiness is attained, those with Chiron in Sagittarius will be certain that there is something better, more rewarding, further along the road. While this is healthy if expressed as hopeful assurance, the desire – the need – to be always taking action, always moving on, can result in disillusion and frustration. Experience should teach a degree of caution, the need for thought before indulging in yet another speculative endeavour without thoroughly thinking it through.

Chiron in CAPRICORN

Reliability is a keynote when Chiron occupies the sign of Capricorn – and
indeed people with this placing of the planetoid are often steadfast and true.
However, it is sometimes the case that the note is sounded in order to
impress, and the reputation for dependability is less reliable than might be
thought. These people place a great deal of value on material success,
sometimes for the sake of self-aggrandizement, and (especially if Chiron is
conjunct the MIDHEAVEN) they can rush in and take responsibility without
the power or capability to impose it.

Chiron in AQUARIUS

This is an extremely helpful placing of Chiron for anyone who suffers from
ill health, mental or physical, for its curative powers are considerable, and
can lead not only to better health but to a stronger realization of the self and
of self-value. There can be a degree of perversity, and a fear of commitment
in personal relationships – the idea of total faithfulness to one person will
be difficult to comprehend, as will any restriction of personal freedom in
any area of the life. 'The right partner', if found, will be an enormous
source of pleasure, but it is entirely possible that the life will be lived,
equally happily, without a permanent partner.

Chiron in PISCES

Intelligence married to firm spiritual values characterizes those with Chiron
in Pisces, though balance will not be achieved without some confusion as
emotional responses intervene in an attempt to make purely intellectual
decisions. Practicality will be at a premium, and the desire to help others
may be so strong as to make undue demands on physical and emotional
energy. A sense of direction is invaluable.

* * *

Choisnard, Paul (*pseudonym* Paul Flambert) (1867–1930) The most influential of the 20th-century French astrologers. Choisnard was in the main a
researcher into the history of astrology and the statistical evidence collected
to support the theory; he pioneered modern attempts to 'prove' astrology by
scientific means (he influenced Michel GAUQUELIN, who followed up much
of his work). He was highly critical of individual predictions and of the use

of astrological charts for personal counselling. The author of over 30 books, he founded the magazine *L'Influence Astral*. Among his theories was the suggestion that a child will be born under planetary influences which were also present at the birth of its parents.

Christian Astrology The earliest textbook of astrology to be published in English, *Christian Astrology* was written by the famous 17th-century astrologer William LILLY and published in 1647. The work is in three books: in Book One he describes the use of an EPHEMERIS, the drawing up of a BIRTH-CHART, and the 'nature' of the twelve zodiac signs and planets. Book Two deals with the questions an astrologer may wish to resolve by the use of astrology, and Book Three shows how to interpret a birth-chart and RECTIFY it by the use of 'annual accidents'. Lilly's style is often informal, amusing and shrewd: qv his remarks on the effect of Venus when 'well dignified': it gives one 'a lovely Mouth and cherry Lips, the Face pretty fleshy, a rolling wandering Eye, a Body very delightfull, lovely and exceeding well shaped, one desirous of Trimming and making himself neat and compleat both in Cloaths and Body, a love Dimple in his Cheeks, a stedfast Eye, and full of amorous enticements.'

For modern astrologers Lilly's book is particularly important as regards HORARY astrology, and many of his precepts are considered still to be accurate and useful.

Christianity and astrology In AD312 the Emperor Constantine became a convert to Christianity, and instigated a campaign against pagan practices. In AD358 astrologers were among those threatened with death. Over the following centuries the most antagonistic of Christian theologians were, however, somewhat confused by the apparent scientific basis of astrology, and what seemed a very obvious relationship between medicine and astrology which it would be foolish to deny. Their attempts to assert that some areas of the subject were theologically dangerous while others were permissible resulted in great confusion. The great example of a precarious balance between the two attitudes to astrology was seen in the work of the Greek philosopher PLOTINUS, who asserted that men and women must be in control of their own destiny, while aspects of their life – including their physical health – were evidently influenced by the planets. There was also the difficulty, for those Christians who abhorred astrology, that God had apparently chosen to signify the birth of his Son by astrological means; the easy way out was to have it both ways, as did Tertullian, who accepted the Star of Bethlehem while asserting that the twelve PLANETS had now been replaced by the twelve Apostles. Others, Origen among them, teetered uneasily on the edge of accepting 'the stars' as having been placed in the sky by God as symbols, while failing to reconcile this with the suspicion that astrology was deeply anti-Christian. ST AUGUSTINE was a fierce critic of astrology as a thing of the Devil, though many of his arguments were based on a fallacious understanding of the history of the subject. Later, mediaeval Christians found it easier to reconcile their faith with their view of astrology as a useful tool which God had given them; many of the popes were sympathetic, accepting the dedications of books on astrology, sometimes employing their own astrologers, and in a few cases being themselves competent astrologers. It was even permissible to speculate about the horoscope of Christ Himself, and from the 13th century onwards the development of natural science seemed to support the view that it was impossible to deny the effect that the planets had on the life of mankind, that (as Robert Grosseteste, the Bishop of Lincoln, put it) 'nature below effects nothing unless celestial power moves it and directs it'.

It seemed possible at one time that astrology would become totally acceptable, taught in every European university as a matter of course. The waves of approval and disapproval that affected the Christian view of astrology rose and fell over the centuries, however – at one extreme astrologers were being persecuted and condemned (though there was no such pogrom against them as against alleged witches; and none was burned by the Inquisition), yet at the other extreme, members of the clergy were openly practising astrology, in some cases positively from the altars of their churches. The pendulum swung decidedly against astrology after the Reformation, and Pope Sixtus V issued a papal bull in 1586 which had the result that Italian universities at least ceased to teach it. Elsewhere the Pope's condemnation had a more limited effect, which resulted in Pope Urban VIII subsequently condemning as heretics everyone who approved of the subject (presumably including his papal forebears). Astrology, however, refused to die, and during the Renaissance there was renewed intellectual discussion of the subject. At a political and social level it was in the ascendant, and the voice of the Church was much diminished. With the coming of the Age of Enlightenment, churchmen – however suspicious they were of science – welcomed increasing criticism of astrology as a pseudo-science, and from then until the present day a steady if generally ineffectual antipathy has been maintained. The Catholic Church, as might be expected, has continued to condemn the study of the subject, and has been joined in general by other Churches, the fiercest condemnation coming from right-wing evangelicals. Since it is probably the case that only a minority of modern astrologers assert that the prediction of events is possible, there seems no more reason why modern Christians should condemn astrology than that they should condemn psychiatry or weather-forecasting, but tradition dies hard. *See* ANGELS, POPES.

circumpolar stars Stars which are always to be seen above the horizon.

cities ruled by signs *see* GEOGRAPHICAL ASTROLOGY

combust A planet is said to be combust when it is placed very near the Sun in the BIRTH-CHART. Traditionally, the planet is then believed to lose some of its force. An ORB of 5° is usually considered.

comets Unsurprisingly, considering the drama of their sudden striking appearance in the sky, comets have always been taken as omens – sometimes of disaster, sometimes as reflections of events on Earth (the death of Julius Caesar, for instance, was said to have been followed by the appearance of a comet). In general, their appearance has been believed to presage ill events – the nature of which astrologers attempted to foretell by considering the signs in which the comets appeared and moved, and their relationship to the planets. If comets were discussed during Greek and Roman times, it seems to have been informally; PTOLEMY does not deal with them in the *TETRABIBLOS*, though he does say elsewhere that comets forecast an attack by an invader. In medieval times, however, astrologers began to publish their opinions on them; some believed that God sent them to warn humanity of war, drought, flood, disease and the death of kings:

> *When beggars die there are no comets seen;*
> *The heavens themselves blaze forth the death of princes.*

Other astrologers claimed that comets simply underlined what the planets already had to say. The most notable of such interpretations in English history is the connection made between the appearances of a spectacular comet in 1066 and the death of King Harold at the battle of Hastings (the comet is famously depicted in the Bayeux tapestry). The victor, King William, is said to have exclaimed before the battle that such a comet was only seen 'when a Kingdom lacks a king'. Four centuries later Halley's comet was believed by the Turks to presage the destruction of the Christian nations; later still the appearance of various comets was said to signal the destruction of the monarchy at the start of the English Civil War. Astrological ALMANACS did much to demystify comets by explaining their astronomical nature; but their astrological character continued to be discussed. Modern astrologers generally think of comets as signalling, in a personal HOROSCOPE, disorder followed by new associations and opportunities – but the other indications in the chart show whether the result will be good or bad. *See also* METEORS.

conception chart Some astrologers claim to have made valuable use of a chart drawn for the moment of conception of a child. Such a chart must, however, be entirely speculative, for unless there is scientific examination of the journey of the sperm and its entry into the egg, the time of conception is impossible to determine. This fact has not prevented astrologers from attempting it – *see* for instance the adventures of MORIN in the bedchamber of the King of France.

conjunction A conjunction between two or more planets takes place when they occupy the same degree of LONGITUDE. A conjunction is a crucial feature of a HOROSCOPE, and will be interpreted according to its relationship to the other planets and the houses of the chart. An ORB of 8° is allowed – up to 12° in the case of the Sun or Moon. A conjunction can be positive or negative.

constellations The two hemispheres of the sky are divided into 88 areas; every star, galaxy or other celestial body lies within, or sometimes overlaps, one of these constellations, the boundaries of which were established in 1930 by the International Astronomical Union. Ancient civilizations marked certain constellations by imagining that the stars that composed them could be joined to picture mythical figures. PTOLEMY in his *Almagest* listed 48 of these, visible from the Middle East. The main ones were believed to have specific influences on humans and affairs on Earth, but there are no constellations in the zodiac.

contra-parallel aspect *see* PARALLEL ASPECT

co-ordinates The mathematical factors that describe the position of a point in a HOROSCOPE or BIRTH-CHART. *See* LONGITUDE, LATITUDE.

Cooke, Roger (b.1552–ca.1612) At the age of 14 Cooke became assistant to John DEE, and remained with him for 14 years. Though they continually quarrelled, Dee not only tolerated this ill-tempered young man, but carefully instructed him. Eventually, they parted company and presumably Cooke set up in business on his own account; but despite Dee's teaching, he vanished from sight, and all that remains is an almanac for 1585 published under his name.

Copernican system The heliocentric version of the solar system developed in the 16th century by the Polish astronomer Nicolas COPERNICUS (influenced by earlier Indian and Greek astronomers and mathematicians). His system replaced the GEOCENTRIC system which had been used since the time of PTOLEMY – at least as far as astronomers are concerned; astrologers continue to use the geocentric system. *See* HELIOCENTRIC ASTROLOGY.

Copernicus, Nicolas (1473–1543) Polish astronomer, priest, and founder of modern astronomy, Copernicus studied mathematics at Krakow university His *De Revolutionibus*, proving that the Sun was the centre of the solar system, was completed in 1530 and published just before his death.

co-ruler The RULERSHIP of signs by planets was determined before the invention of the telescope, and when additional planets – Uranus, Neptune and Pluto – were observed some centuries later, astrologers assigned them to certain signs as co-rulers. So in modern astrology Uranus shares the rulership of Aquarius with Saturn, Neptune rules Pisces with Jupiter and

Pluto rules Scorpio with Mars. Uranus is considered the dominant ruler of Aquarius, and Neptune of Pisces. Pluto has a stronger influence on Scorpio than Mars; but in all three cases the traditional influences are also considered. A minority of astrologers still claim that the so-called 'modern' planets should not be allowed rulership at all, and that the original list should remain the only reliable one.

cosmobiology *see* MIDPOINTS

countries ruled by signs *see* GEOGRAPHICAL ASTROLOGY

critical days In traditional MEDICAL ASTROLOGY astrologer-doctors would carefully calculate the critical days on which an illness could be expected to take a turn either for the better or for the worse. An unpromising development could be expected on a day when the Moon made a SEMI-SQUARE ASPECT to its original position in the HORARY chart of the illness (drawn for the moment when it was first observed, or sometimes the moment when the doctor was called in). A day when the Moon made a SEXTILE ASPECT was one on which a positive change in the patient's fortunes should make itself felt.

critical degrees Particular degrees in an HORARY chart were regarded by medical astrologers as *critical* or important in devising treatment for a patient or watching the progress of an illness. There were various lists of these, and there remains some confusion about them. Gettings (*Arkana Dictionary of Astrology*) lists as characteristic the 1st 13th and 26th degrees of Aries, Cancer, Libra and Capricorn, the 9th and 21st degrees of Taurus, Leo, Scorpio and Aquarius, and the 4th and 17th degrees of Gemini, Virgo, Sagittarius and Pisces.

Crophill, John (fl. ca.1420) Practised as an astrologer in Suffolk, where he specialized in giving matrimonial advice to young men and women; a notebook MS in the British Museum lists the couples he has advised, together with money due to him for his advice.

culmination When a planet crosses the MERIDIAN – i.e., the point of the MIDHEAVEN, or the CUSP of the tenth house – it is said to culminate.

Culpeper, Nicholas (1616–54) The author of a number of books on astrological and herbal medicine, whose herbal became wildly popular, and is still consulted today. At first a physician, accused of witchcraft in the early months of the English Civil War, he joined the army on the Parliamentary side (he was anti-Church as well as anti-Royalist) and assisted the injured until himself badly wounded. He wrote several medical works, including a book on childbirth which circulated widely in England and America. Originally entitled *The English Physician, or an Astro-Physical Description of the Vulgar Herbs of this Nation . . . whereby a man may preserve his body in health, or cure himself, being sick, for three pence charge, with such things only as grow in England*, his book on medicinal herbs and some following books were attacked by the College of Physicians for demystifying medicine by being published in English.

Cuningham, William (fl. ca.1586) A physician and astrologer, he studied at the university of Heidelberg and settled in Norwich, where he practised until 1559, when he moved to London to become extremely well known and popular, and a lecturer at Surgeons' Hall. He published several astrological works, the most popular of which was *A Newe Almanacke and Prognostication collected for ye yere of our Lord mdlviii., wherein is expressed the change and ful of the Mone, with their Quarters. The variety of the ayre, and also of the windes throughout the whole yeare, with infortunate times to bie, and sell, take medicine, sowe, plant, and journey, etc.*

cusp The imaginary boundary between one zodiac sign and the next: for instance, where Aries ends and Taurus begins. Those unfamiliar with the practice of astrology will say they are born 'on the cusp' when the Sun is within a few degrees of the imaginary line that separates one sign from the next – and if, for instance, at the time of their birth the Sun was a few degrees – or even days – from the division between (for example) Gemini and Cancer, will claim that they possess some of the characteristics of each sign. While this may be true, it will have nothing to do with being born 'on the cusp', but will be due to other planets – especially Mercury and Venus – placed in the two signs in question. Astrologers agree that the influence of the Sun is never divided between two signs.

cycles *see* RETURNS

– D –

Davison, Ronald C (1914–85) English astrologer, President of the
London Astrological Lodge of the Theosophical Society and editor of its
astrology magazine. Credited with inventing KEYWORDS, a valuable aid for
interpreting HOROSCOPES. The author of *A Classic Guide to Synastry*.

day for a year *see* SECONDARY PROGRESSIONS

daylight saving time In wartime – since 1916 – clocks have often been
advanced in order to give extra light to farmers and other workers. During
the Second World War for instance, the clocks were advanced for one or
two hours between spring and autumn. Alas, this was not done on a regular
basis, and the dates vary from year to year and often from place to place. In
North America daylight-saving time, otherwise known as War Time, was
observed from 2 February to 30 September every year between 1942 and
1945. The USA still uses daylight-saving time. In the UK double summer
time was used, the clock being advanced by two hours. The experiment
continued after the war: in 1968 all clocks were advanced one hour ahead of
GMT from 28 February; since 1972, clocks in the UK have been advanced
by one hour from March to October every year. In Europe, various
countries have various habits. Reference books are available which detail
the changes. To calculate the STANDARD TIME of the country for which a
HOROSCOPE is calculated, astrologers must *deduct* the amount of time by
which clocks are advanced from the given clock time in that country.

debility *see* DIGNITY

decan Each zodiac sign occupies 30° of the circle of the HOROSCOPE, and is
itself divided into three decans of 10° each. These were considered of great
importance in ancient (particularly Egyptian) and medieval European and
Arabian astrology. In modern astrology there are various theories as to how
the decans can most profitably be used. In the most common, each

decanate, or 10° arc, is ruled by the sign of its own triplicity so that all the decanates of the fire signs relate to each other, as do those of the earth, air and water signs. The first decanate of a sign is ruled by its own sign, the second by the next sign of the same triplicity, and the third by the third sign of the same triplicity. *See* ELEMENTS.

declination The declination of a planet, or any celestial body, is its angular distance (from 0° to 90°) north (positive) or south (negative) of the CELESTIAL EQUATOR. The Sun has maximum declination when it reaches the TROPIC OF CANCER in the north and the TROPIC OF CAPRICORN in the south.

decumbiture A chart drawn up for the moment when an illness begins, with the intention of foretelling its duration. In MEDICAL ASTROLOGY it was also used to forecast the CRITICAL DAY or hour of an illness.

Dee, Dr John (1527–1608) Astrologer, geographer and general magus, Dee was born in London and studied at St John's College, Cambridge, of which he became Fellow in 1545. He studied also in Paris, and his lectures there on Euclid were wildly popular with students. King Edward VI granted him a pension. It must be presumed that his astrological studies predisposed him to favour Princess Elizabeth, during whose imprisonment he himself was arrested in connection with an alleged plot to poison Queen Mary. Narrowly escaping being burned at the stake, he was freed, and when Elizabeth succeeded to the throne the Earl of Leicester invited him to propose a date and time for her coronation. He successfully proposed 15 January 1559 (his astrological argument for this date has not survived), the date on which the coronation indeed took place. The Queen continued to patronize him, commanding him to comment on the comet of 1577, and even calling on him at his own house.

His belief was that everything in the universe was governed or at least informed by 'rays' from the planets, which he believed could be scientifically studied. His *Propaedeumata Aphoristica* argued that these 'rays' could affect the human body and soul, and that they emanated from all physical objects, as well as the planets. They were so mysterious that they would be forever beyond scientific explanation. It might however, by the use of lenses and mirrors, be possible to discover some of the properties of the rays.

Understanding of the scope of his astrological work is hampered by lack of evidence: he does not seem to have kept files of charts – not surprising, considering the dangerous times in which he lived (there is a parallel to the difficulties of astrologers in imperial Rome – *see* THRASYLLUS). He certainly advised a number of prominent men of his time, however – a 62-page astrological profile of Sir Philip Sidney has survived, foretelling an adventurous life between the ages of 15 and 31, at which age he would suffer mortal injury from a sword or pistol. Sidney was killed in battle in 1586, at the age of 31. Dee believed that the appearance of a new star in 1572 indicated the discovery of 'some great Treasure' (a new gold mine was discovered two years later), and made the usual connection between astrology and ALCHEMY.

Increasingly distracted by his interest in magic, especially communication with angels and spirits – and no less by his interests in world exploration, the mapping of unexplored regions, the setting up of a British national library and other matters – Dee neglected his astrological studies, and is thus not as important to astrology as some other figures. One of the most remarkable men of his age, he died in miserable poverty, Queen Elizabeth having (not unusually) reneged on her promises to support him.

degree The ZODIAC circle is divided into 360 degrees (usually written 360°), each degree divided into 60 minutes (60'), and each minute into 60 seconds (60''). Each degree has significance in the interpretation of a HOROSCOPE, depending on the SIGN and DECAN in which it is placed.

degree rulers Traditionally, each degree of the zodiac circle is associated with a particular planet. Vettius VALENS recorded one of the earliest lists of degree rulers, in the 1st century AD.

degree symbols A number of astrologers have produced lists of symbols attached to each degree of the zodiac. Some are ancient – viz the Volasfera symbols clairvoyantly produced by Anytonio Borelli in the 16th century and popularized by SEPHARIAL in the 19th. Though they are much ridiculed in some quarters, the SABIAN SYMBOLS and others such as the Sepharial and Charubel symbols, are said by some astrologers to be extremely helpful in interpretation, presumably by assisting occult meditation.

delineation The term used for the interpretation of a HOROSCOPE.

Denderah Zodiac In the Louvre in Paris, torn from its place with the use of gunpowder and removed to France by Napoleon, is a bas-relief representation of the zodiac dating from the late Ptolemaic period, between about 30BC and AD17. The oldest known representation of the zodiac – claimed by some authorities to be based on depictions dating from as early as 2900BC – it once formed part of the ceiling of a room in a chapel to Osiris on the roof of the Hathor temple at Denderah in Egypt, where a plaster cast now hangs. The Denderah Zodiac shows ancient Egyptian constellations or groups of stars together with Babylonian and Greek groupings. Figures – men, snakes and other animals – around the circumference of the Zodiac mark out the DECANS, and within the Zodiac signs themselves are the planets, shown as gods holding staffs. The circle of the Zodiac is supported by four feminine figures standing at the four corners of the ceiling – the goddesses of the four points of the compass. There are two similar zodiacs at Esna which have been dated to 137BC.

Descendant The CUSP of the SEVENTH HOUSE.

detriment *see* DIGNITY

dignity A planet placed in its own sign is said to be in its *essential dignity*, and is also dignified when it is in the sign of its EXALTATION.

- The Sun is *exalted* in Aries;
- the Moon in Taurus;
- Mercury in Virgo (its own sign);
- Venus in Pisces;
- Mars in Capricorn;
- Jupiter in Cancer;
- Saturn in Libra.

Modern astrologers have placed

- Uranus in exaltation when in Scorpio;
- Neptune in Leo;
- Pluto in Aries.

When exalted, a planet's influence is strengthened. The opposite of dignity is *debility*, when a planet's influence is somewhat weakened. A planet is debilitated when it is in *detriment* – in a sign or house opposite its own. Some astrologers have suggested other circumstances in which this may be the case. A planet's position in a HOUSE or on a particular degree of a HOROSCOPE is sometimes described as having an *accidental dignity*, according to complex and variable rules. *See also* RULER.

directions To interpret 'directions' is to make a study of a PROGRESSED CHART in order to estimate possible future trends in the life of a subject.

direct motion The normal apparent motion of a planet through the zodiac (as opposed to RETROGRADE motion).

disjunct signs *see* DISSOCIATE SIGNS

dissociate aspects Aspects which are outside the bounds of the aspecting sign, although they may be within ORB, are described as *dissociate*, or sometimes *out-of-sign*. The connection is with the theory of the ELEMENTS and the sympathy between planets which are of the same element.

dissociate signs According to PTOLEMY signs which are adjacent or five signs apart.

diurnal A planet which is above the horizon in a HOROSCOPE is described as *diurnal*. One below the horizon is *nocturnal*.

diurnal arc The measurement, in degrees, of a planet's movement from rising to setting.

diurnal chart The HOROSCOPE of someone born during the day. Someone born during the night will have a *nocturnal chart*.

Dixon, Jeane (1904–97) American astrologer and psychic who claimed to have accurately predicted the assassination of President John F Kennedy (writing in a magazine article in 1956 that the 1960 election would be won by a Democrat who would be assassinated in office). President Nixon is said to have taken her advice, as did Nancy Reagan during her husband's presidency.

Dorotheus of Sidon (fl.1st c.) A Hellenistic astrologer probably working in Alexandria, who wrote a textbook, *Carmen Astrologicum,* which has survived only in fragments but was evidently important in its time, influencing Middle Eastern medieval astrologers. It offered an explanation of how to set up a HOROSCOPE, and dealt among other things with KATARCHIC ASTROLOGY, for instance laying down rules for recovering stolen goods and catching the thief.

Draco Draco is a large straggling constellation in the northern hemisphere, containing Thuban, which was the pole star in ancient times, when the constellation was known as the Dragon. Astrologers who use it contend that it can indicate a sharp and methodical mind, and promise extensive travel.

Dragon's Head and Tail The Moon's NODES – i.e., the points at which the ORBIT of the Moon intersects the ECLIPTIC to north and south – are sensitive points in a HOROSCOPE, and are known as the Dragon's Head (the north node) and Tail (the south node). The Dragon's Head marks the north node, because it is the point at which the Moon crosses the ecliptic from southern to northern LATITUDES; the Tail marks the south node. In general the Head is considered on the whole to be beneficial, and the sign in which it is placed indicates an area in life which one needs to develop and encourage. The Tail, on the other hand, marks an area of life which, consciously or unconsciously, one longs to develop but perhaps fails to do so. Some astrologers regard the Tail as almost the equivalent of Saturn in its negative effects. *See also* NODES.

dual signs Gemini, Sagittarius, Pisces.

– E –

earth *see* ELEMENTS

earth signs Three of the zodiac signs, Taurus, Virgo and Capricorn, have traditionally always been associated with the earth ELEMENT. This grouping contributes certain basic qualities common to all three signs, and while the characteristics are manifested in subtly different ways in each sign (*see* the respective entries) individuals in whose horoscopes the signs are prominent will tend to be extremely practical, cautious and with ready common sense – they may be described as 'down to earth'. They have considerable financial flair and many are very ambitious and determined, though often stubborn and reluctant to change their opinions.

Earth signs often indicate those who are successful in finance and banking, agriculture and horticulture, land management, real estate, food production, the building trades and architecture. Enjoying creature comforts, they need to make a lot of money to support the comfortable lifestyle which gives them an all-important sense of security – and not only financially, for there is also a considerable need for emotional security, without which a full expression of feeling does not always come easily, and as a result shyness and inhibition can be present.

Those in whom the element is strongly expressed are usually very much in tune with nature. Most love their gardens, or if deprived of them will carefully nurture potted plants on the smallest windowsill. There is also a love of natural materials; wood, wool, linen, cotton and leather will feature in their interior decoration schemes. Many are good at various forms of craft-work and here we find carvers, weavers, knitters, potters and embroiderers in plenty since most are not lacking in patience.

The earth element often adds strength and a certain toughness to a character, so that difficult and sometimes dangerous conditions can be endured (this vividly contrasts with their need for creature comforts). There is often a love of rock climbing, caving and mountaineering more than.

Many individuals are commonly concerned about the Earth's resources and will become involved in conservation and climate changes. Those who are in a position to do so will make their opinions known publicly.

Ebertin, Elspeth (1880–1944) German astrologer and professional graphologist. She taught herself astrology and began publishing during the 1914–18 war – becoming the first popular German writer on astrology. Her 1918 almanac, *Ein Blick in die Zukunft (A Glance into the Future)* was immediately popular, and she went on publishing popular books and magazines for many years. In her 1924 almanac she published an analysis of HITLER's chart, anonymously, warning that he could 'trigger off an uncontrollable crisis', should 'be taken very seriously indeed' and was 'destined to play a "Führer-like" role in future battles'. She was subsequently introduced to Hitler, but there is no evidence that he took any interest in her or her work. Her almanacs ceased publication in 1937, due to the Nazi opposition to astrology. She was killed in an air raid in 1944.

Ebertin, Reinhold (1901–88) The son of the German astrologer Elspeth Ebertin, Ebertin is best known for his research into possible empirical evidence of the truth of the astrological theory, including its use in medicine. This began secretly during the 1939–45 war, when astrology in all its facets was banned in Germany by the Nazi government. After the war he founded a School of COSMOBIOLOGY, using the term *cosmogram* to describe his own version of the horoscope, and employing 'planetary pictures' involving MIDPOINTS. His best-known book is *The Combination of Stellar Influences* (1940, later revised).

eclipses An eclipse occurs when a celestial body passes through the shadow of another body. Because they are very clearly seen from Earth, solar and lunar eclipses have always been popularly regarded as important astrological events – but they have been given much more importance by lay people than by astrologers, no doubt because they appeared in ancient times to be magical interferences with the natural order of things and the great lights in the heaven. In time, and especially after the invention of printing and the publication of ALMANACS, astrologers were able to explain how eclipses occurred, and thus divest them of their 'magical' reputation.

A lunar eclipse – an eclipse of the Moon – always occurs when the Moon is full. It is generally recognized, even by nonastrologers, that at the time of a full Moon mankind seems to be under special psychological pressure, and this will be exacerbated when there is a lunar eclipse. The drama of a total solar eclipse is an unforgettable experience, and the ancient view of it as signalling significant disaster is not at all surprising. Astrologers continue to regard eclipses in general as malevolent, in particular if they occur on a degree of the HOROSCOPE conjunct the Sun, Moon, ASCENDANT or MC. *See also* SAROS CYCLE.

ecliptic The great circle in which the plane of the Earth's orbit intersects the CELESTIAL SPHERE. It coincides with the Sun's apparent path across the sky. The orbits of the Moon and planets, apart from PLUTO, lie very close to the ecliptic when projected onto the celestial sphere. The EQUINOXES lie at the two points of intersection of the ecliptic and the equator.

Egypt The idea of Egypt as the home of astrology and the civilization under which it reached its apogee, is mistaken. It might have been so, were it not that compared to Babylon, Egypt had a relatively weak command of mathematics.

The Egyptians did, however, make contributions to the early development of astrology, notably in devising a simple calendar (probably based on the date of the Nile flood at the beginning of the third millennium BC) which presented a year consisting of 12 months of 30 days each, with 5 'extra' days (later the 'leap year' was proposed, adding a day every 4 years). The other major gift of the Egyptians to early astrology was the system of time measurement according to the rising of the constellations over the eastern horizon (the first illustration of this is in a coffin of the period of the Tenth Dynasty, ca.2100BC). This resulted in the devising of the DECANS.

In the 7th century BC, during the reigns of Esarhaddon (681–669) and his successor Assurbanipal, astrologers were attached to the temple of Ea, the god of oracles, and employed among other things to calculate the best time for the building of sanctuaries. Treaties were signed 'in the presence of the planets'. At first, predictions were made for the king and interpreted as applying to the whole kingdom; the earliest individual HOROSCOPE to have survived is from 410BC.

Predictions were, however, fairly primitive, based on eclipse-omens. A number of HERMETIC texts, often astrological in origin, have survived under the authorship of Nechepso and Petosiris – Petosiris was allegedly the priest-astrologer who wrote an astrological book for King Nechepso, who reigned sometime between 663 and 522BC. The text, as it has survived, seems in fact to be an anthology of omens, including eclipses and meteorological phenomena, plus work on astrological predictions for individuals – good and bad periods in a life, and advice on travel, injury, children, illness and death. Petosiris claimed to possess the birth-chart of the world, which he obtained directly from Hermes.

Other Hermetic texts dealt with the brightness of the stars, planetary CONJUNCTIONS and the positions of planets in the zodiac signs, and examined how to predict the length of one's life, the value and effects of marriage, and the nature of one's children. It was probably the spreading of these texts which resulted in Egypt having, by the 1st century BC, the reputation of being the natural home of astrology.

eighth house The eighth house of the zodiac is the house of Scorpio and Pluto. Traditionally known as the house of death, it must not be regarded as a fatalistic indicator of the end of life. As in dreams, 'death' represents, in this instance, regeneration, change, and is the harbinger of new beginnings. These may follow either a simple desire for change, or the deepest examination of what the subject wants and needs from life. It is also the house of the 'life force', and so of the deepest and most imperative sexual instincts and needs (cf. the link with Scorpio). It represents the income a subject has from his or her own efforts, though it is also linked to inheritance, and to crime and the investigation of crime. It rules the genitals. In MUNDANE ASTROLOGY it is concerned with a country's national income and balance of trade; also with public sexual mores.

election chart A chart cast to discover the most auspicious time for such a special event as a marriage, the setting up of a business, an important journey, buying a house, or whatever.

elements The four elements from which the Earth and everything we know of it are composed (according to traditional astrology and alchemy) are fire, earth, air and water, held together by a fifth element, quintessence – a spiritual element not used in astrology. Traditionally, FIRE SIGNS are said to be enthusiastic by nature, EARTH SIGNS practical, AIR SIGNS intellectual with a need to communicate, WATER SIGNS emotional. The elements are also called triplicities.

elevation The planet nearest the MIDHEAVEN is said to be *elevated*; astronomically, the elevation marks the distance in altitude of a planet above the horizon.

eleventh house The eleventh HOUSE of the HOROSCOPE is the house of Aquarius and Uranus and represents the social life, social conscience, political awareness, and friends. One's objectives in life – though not those connected with a career – are also the concerns of this house, as is the attitude to such matters as world poverty and ecology. Study of this house will reveal how far a person is likely to interest him- or herself in good causes, and whether the impetus to do this is self-centred or altruistic. It will show how well a person is likely to integrate with others in, say, committee work, or as a leader of a group. In MUNDANE ASTROLOGY it has to do with the stock exchange, world financial centres and political affairs. This is not regarded as a very powerful house, but should be studied carefully when examining a person's capacity to relate to other people.

Elliot, Roger (1937–93) British astrologer and SUN-SIGN columnist (notably for *The News of the World* in the UK), Elliot was a gregarious man and a popular lecturer on the astrological circuit. He published annual Sun-sign books which sold worldwide.

elongation The angle between the Sun and a planet when observed from Earth. The maximum elongation that Mercury and Venus can attain is 28° for the former and 48° for the latter. Therefore, Mercury can only be placed either in the SUN-SIGN of a HOROSCOPE, or in the sign before or after it; Venus can only be placed in the Sun-sign or in one of the two signs before or after it. All the other planets can reach an elongation of 180°. When a planet is east of the Sun, it is at *eastern elongation*; when west, at *western elongation*. In the first case the planet will set after the Sun, and is known as an *evening star*; when in the west it rises before the Sun and is called a *morning star*.

ephemeris/ephemerides A compilation of astronomical/astrological data giving the information essential for the setting up of a BIRTH-CHART or HOROSCOPE.

Epigenes of Byzantium (d. ca.200bc) A Greek astrologer who, according to the historian Seneca, claimed to have been taught astrology by the CHALDEANS, and may therefore have been one of the first to bring Egyptian and Babylonian knowledge of the subject into Greece.

equal house A system of HOUSE DIVISION in which the zodiac is divided into twelve equal houses, beginning at the FIRST HOUSE cusp, the degree of the ASCENDANT. The MC can appear in any house (not only the cusp of the TENTH HOUSE as in most other systems) and is a particularly sensitive point.

equal power *see* BEHOLDING

equator The imaginary line drawn around the Earth at its maximum circumference: 0° LATITUDE. *See also* CELESTIAL EQUATOR.

equatorial chart An equatorial chart is erected in the plane of the Earth's EQUATOR. Planetary positions are measured in RIGHT ASCENSION, and form the basis of PRIMARY DIRECTIONS.

equinoctial points The first degrees of Aries and Libra.

equinoctial signs Aries and Libra.

equinox The point in the ECLIPTIC at which day and night are of equal DURATION. *See* AGES, ARIES (FIRST POINT OF), PRECESSION, TROPICAL ZODIAC, ZODIAC.

esoteric astrology The study of the 'secret', spiritual aspects of astrology, the symbolic meanings of the planets and signs, as derived (it is believed) from ancient Egyptian and Greek texts, often Hermetic, and frequently informed by a belief in reincarnation.

essential dignity *see* DIGNITY

Evangelists The Christian symbolism attached to the four Evangelists has been related to four of the astrological signs:

- the bull of St Luke to the symbol of TAURUS;
- the lion of St Mark to the symbol of LEO;
- the angel of St Matthew to the urn carried by the Aquarian maiden (see AQUARIUS);
- the eagle of St John to the image of SCORPIO (in very ancient times the earthly symbol of the scorpion was counterweighted by the soaring symbol of an eagle).

exaltation *see* DIGNITY

– F –

face each sign is divided six positive and negative faces of 5°, each with its own planetary RULER.

Fagan, Cyril (1896–1970) Born in Dublin but settling in the US, Fagan was a SIDEREAL astrologer whose books include *A Primer of the Sidereal Zodiac*. His studies stimulated John ADDEY's work on HARMONICS, and his own theories included the possibility of several varied zodiacs in the sky, based on different points of departure.

fall A planet is described as being 'in fall' when it is in the sign opposite that of its EXALTATION. *But see* DIGNITY.

familiarity A term traditionally used to describe any relationship between planets, though particularly ASPECTS.

Favorinus (fl.2nd c.) A Gaulish philosopher and friend of Plutarch who held high office under the Emperor HADRIAN. He was fiercely antagonistic to fatalistic astrology as making a mock of morality, and sneered at those who consulted astrologers about law cases and such matters.

feminine planets *see* MASCULINE PLANETS

feminine signs The so-called feminine signs, originally selected by PTOLEMY, are Taurus, Cancer, Virgo, Scorpio, Capricorn and Pisces; they are also referred to as 'negative'.

feral signs The feral or *bestial* signs are said in some traditions to be those named after animals – i.e., Aries, Taurus, Leo, Scorpio, Capricorn and the last half (the non-human part) of Sagittarius. The Moon is said to be feral when VOID OF COURSE. Interpretation of feral signs is tentative, and for the most part the term is ignored.

fiducial degree Any degree, such as a fixed star, which can be used as a flagpost at which to start the zodiac. The SIDEREAL fiducial consists of two fixed stars, Aldebaran and Antares, which stand at the centre of the signs Taurus and Scorpio. The fiducial in Aries can be found by subtracting 45° from the position of Aldebaran along the ECLIPTIC. Then from this point, called 0° Aries, the signs of the zodiac can be set out.

fiery triplicity Aries, Leo and Sagittarius, the FIRE SIGNS. *See* ELEMENTS.

fifth house The fifth HOUSE of a HOROSCOPE is the house of Leo and the Sun, and is the house of creativity – expressed not only in artistic endeavours but perhaps in cooking, gardening or accountancy. Sometimes called the house of children, it is also concerned with a parent's relationship with his or her children (rather than the other way around; a child's relationship with parents is a matter for the FOURTH HOUSE). It is worth remembering that artists often regard their creations – a book, a picture, a piece of music – as their 'children'. This is also the house of lovers: a new affair will almost certainly be reflected by some fifth house event (but look to the SEVENTH HOUSE to discover whether it will last). The house will also show a subject's thoughts about procreation – whether or not to have children. It rules the heart, loins and back. In MUNDANE ASTROLOGY it rules a country's children and education system, public recreation and arts.

figure The traditional name for a chart or HOROSCOPE. Astrologers were sometimes referred to as 'figure-flingers'.

Firebrace, Roy (1889–1974) Born in Halifax, Nova Scotia, Firebrace was a professional soldier, attaining the rank of brigadier. He was an enthusiast for SIDEREAL astrology, and a close colleague of Cyril FAGAN. One of the founders of the British Astrological Association (1958) he was its first president. In 1961 he resigned, having failed to persuade members of the Association to devote themselves exclusively to sidereal astrology. The founder of the sidereal journal *Spica*, he published it until his death.

fire signs Aries, Leo and Sagittarius. *See* ELEMENTS.

Firmanus, Lucius Taruntius (fl.86BC) A Roman astrologer and philosopher, friend of Varro and Cicero, commissioned by the former to speculate the astrological chart for the foundation of Rome and that of its founder, Romulus. He concluded that Romulus was born on 23 September 771BC.

Firmicus Maternus (fl. AD330) A Sicilian Christian Latin writer of noble birth, published in 354 the *Matheseos*, in which he attempted to demolish Christian objections to astrology. He also attacked 'magicians', and demanded that magic should play no part in astrology; astrologers must place themselves under the protection of God, praying that He give them 'grace to attempt the explanation of the courses of the stars'.

first house The first house of a HOROSCOPE is the house of Aries and Mars, and is considered the most important, covering as it does the ASCENDANT. It has been called the House of Fulfilment. It 'describes' the personality of the horoscope's subject, attitude, temperament, health and wellbeing. Physical characteristics are also reflected here. Any planet placed in this house, especially if it is within 8° and 10° of the Ascendant, will be extremely powerful and will underline the characteristics of the Ascendant itself. Such a planet can also be expected to have a strong effect on a subject's personality, behaviour and appearance. The first house represents the head and face, and is linked to a subject's grandparents (the grandmother of a male subject, the grandfather of a female). In MUNDANE ASTROLOGY it rules a country's whole 'personality'.

fixed signs The fixed signs of the zodiac are Taurus, Leo, Scorpio and Aquarius, and as their quadruplicity or QUALITY suggests, they make for calm individuals, single-minded, determined, composed and self-contained. Recognizing their goals, those with an emphasis on fixed signs in their HOROSCOPES advance steadily, sometimes stubbornly, towards them. They are, in their own eyes, always right. The fixed HOUSES are the second, fifth, eighth and eleventh. Planets in these houses will contribute a 'fixed' flavour to the horoscope.

fixed stars Fixed stars have been part of astrology from time immemorial, but there has been continual argument and discussion as to how they should be used. Most of the astrological tendencies attributed to them have been negative – disaster, blindness, scandal, chaos. Modern interpretations have taken on a powerful mythical/psychological dimension.

Flambert, Paul *see* CHOISNARD

Flamsteed, John (1646–1719) The first Astronomer Royal, Flamsteed publicly attacked 'ye Vanity of Astrology and the practices of astrologers', but nevertheless drew up a horoscope for the foundation of the Royal Greenwich Observatory. This may have been a joke; but John Evelyn in his diary records that that when he attended the laying of the foundation stone he noted Mr Flamsteed 'observing the punctual time by instruments' to ensure that the stone was laid at precisely 5 o'clock.

Fludd, Robert (1574–1637) Sometimes Robertus de Fluctibus. English astrologer and physician who studied widely on the continent and was a correspondent of KEPLER. He put forward a theory that the blood travelled around the veins of the body because the Sun took the part of the heart, and the blood circulated around it, just as the planets circle the Sun.

Fomalhaut One of the four ROYAL STARS of the Persian astrologers. Set at 2° 27′ Pisces, it is the 17th brightest star in the sky. It is said to confer honour on a subject except in conjunction, when it is 'unfortunate' and may provoke 'secret affairs'.

forecast When speaking of the possibility of using astrology to look into the future, many astrologers use the word 'forecast' rather than 'predict', by which they suggest that the prediction of events is either impossible or extremely difficult, and that a better way of regarding attempts to estimate future possibilities is to look at them as similar to weather or stock market forecasting.

Forman, Simon (1552–1611) The best-known Elizabethan astrologer, next to Dr DEE, Forman was virtually self-taught, became a schoolmaster, then entered Magdalen College, Oxford, as a poor student. He became again a schoolmaster, was arrested (the charge is unknown), then worked as a carpenter, travelled to the Low Countries, spent some time as a seaman, and became increasingly interested in and adept at astrology and medicine. His practice as an astrologer and physician in London became wildly successful: in 1597 he held 1,819 consultations with all manner of men and women on all manner of subjects. Extremely highly sexed, he drew up horary charts to discover whether a client might be susceptible to seduction; many proved to be so. One, Emilia Lanier, was (dubiously) claimed by the historian A L Rowse to be the Dark Lady of Shakespeare's sonnets. Certainly another was Mrs Mountjoy, the playwright's landlady in Silver Street. Forman's work as an astrologer was basic – he wrote no books, published no texts and left no notes. He is admirable at least in that when plague broke out he declined to flee, like so many physicians, but remained in London to do what he could for the sick and dying.

foundation chart A horoscope drawn up to determine the most advantageous moment at which to lay the foundation stone of a building (*see*, for instance, BONATI). Astrologers were much consulted on this matter in medieval times by both secular princes and princes of the Church planning the building of palaces, temples or churches. Astrologers were consulted about the founding of cities – there was much discussion by historians of the possible date of the foundation of Rome. Astrologers have also speculated about the foundation charts of nations – taking, for instance, the moment of the crowning of William the Conqueror as that for which the 'birth-chart' of England should be drawn. *See also* CHALDEAN ASTROLOGY, GAURICO, SAN MINIATO ZODIAC.

fourth house The house of Cancer and the Moon, the fourth house of the HOROSCOPE is strongly focused on a subject's family background, and particularly on parents. Traditionally called the House of the Mother, it relates to a subject's attitude to both parents, and will have something to say about a child's earliest years of life in the home environment. An astrologer must be cautious however, for of course the horoscopes of each parent will show much more than a subject's fourth house can say about them. However, it will show how a subject (especially perhaps a child) will relate to his or her parents. Home life in general will also be reflected by whatever is going on in the fourth house, which has also to do with land and is linked to the breasts and the ribs. In MUNDANE ASTROLOGY it is related to opposition to the established government; also to agriculture, architecture and a country's laws.

free will A chief weapon in the modern Christian Church's objection to astrology is the assertion that if it can be used by human beings to predict events it insults the doctrine of free will. Many of the popes failed to subscribe to that supposition, and the ancient Church had no truck with it. Astrologers themselves have always gone out of their way to assert that astrological prediction only offers estimates of the shape the future may take – that, in the words of William LILLY, 'the stars incline, they do not compel'. Very few have ever suggested that the planets force decisions upon man. Prospero, in Shakespeare's *The Tempest*, considering his future, says:

I find my zenith doth depend upon
A most auspicious star, whose influence
If now I court not but omit, my fortunes
Will ever after droop.

Thus expressing the general view that astrology offers opportunities; that mankind is free to make choices, including the freedom to take advantage of astrological opportunities or to ignore them.

fruitful signs *see* BARREN SIGNS

frustration When a planet ASPECTING another is deflected by a third before the aspect is complete, it is described as having been *frustrated*. This situation is observed mainly in HORARY ASTROLOGY, when the matter affected by the frustrated aspect is likely to come to naught.

full Moon A full Moon occurs when the Moon opposes the Sun. The Moon's phases are the crescent, half-moon, gibbous and full. Publicly, the time of the full Moon is generally accepted to be one of some frustration and too often of violence. From the earliest times it has been observed that both humans and animals bleed more freely at this time; this has been observed in blood donation centres and by surgeons during operations. The time of the new Moon is one at which it is good to start new projects: personal energy is often high, and accompanied by a mood of optimism and a desire to move ahead. *See also* GARDENING.

– G –

Gabriel The ANGEL of the Moon.

Gadbury, John (16271628–1704) Born in Wheatley, Oxfordshire,
Gadbury met LILLY in London and began a serious study of astrology in
Oxford. He published a great number of books on astrology and other
subjects including navigation. Settling in London, he became an extreme
monarchist, and in 1659 published *The Nativity of the late King Charles,
Astrologically and Faithfully Performed. with Reasons in Art of the various
success and mis-fortune of His whole Life. Being (Occasionally) a brief
History of our late unhappy Wars.* His extreme right-wing views made him
enemies, and PARTRIDGE in particular attacked him, accusing him of
debauchery and murder. Becoming a Catholic, he was arrested and
imprisoned on suspicion of complicity in 'Popish plots' against William III.

Gaffarel, Jacques (1601–81) First trained as a physician, and then
as a priest, Gaffarel became interested in oriental astrology, and published in 1629 an important text, *Curiosité inouyes sur la sculpture talis-
manique des Persans, horoscope des Patriarches et lecture des étoiles,*
which was translated into English in 1650 as *Remarkable Curiosities
of Talismanic Persian Sculpture, with the Horoscope of the Patriarchs
and a lecture on the Stars.* In this he claimed that the patterns of the stars
could be read like the text of a book. His work was extremely popular, and
much read by scholars and philosophers throughout Europe. Gaffarel
became librarian to Cardinal Richelieu, and collected books for his
library from Greece and Asia.

galactic centre The centre of gravity of our GALAXY, around which the
Sun revolves.

galaxy Galaxies are giant assemblies of stars, gas and dust containing the
visible matter of which the universe consists. Our own galaxy, the Milky

Way, is estimated to contain about a hundred billion stars, of which the Sun is one.

Galen (AD129–ca.216) A Greek physician and philosopher, Galen was a major influence on medical theory and practice in Europe and the Middle East from the Middle Ages until the mid-17th century. He attacked those physicians who relied too much on astrology, but did use it himself, for instance noting the constellation prevailing at the time his patients fell ill, and accepting the influence of certain fixed stars (the Dog Star in particular) on the course of an illness. Herbs, he asserted, should be picked and administered at the proper astrological moments.

Ganymede One of the satellites of Jupiter. Ganymede is particularly associated with Aquarius.

gardening The connection between astrology and husbandry is almost as long as the history of astrology. In America particularly, early ALMANACS were packed with information and advice as to how astrology could forecast the weather, and how the positions of the planets could be used to good effect in the planting and gathering of crops and the breeding of cattle. This could be as simple as advising the picking of apples when the Moon was full, thus drawing the juices into the fruit, or more complex, but it was always practical and forthright, viz Jerome CARDAN:

> *Graft not Trees, the Moon waning, or not to be seen, and if you shear sheep in her increase their wool will grow again the better.*

or,

> *Sow or plant when the Moon is in Taurus, Virgo or Scorpio in good Aspect of Saturn, but when she is in Cancer set or sow all kinds of pulses, and in Libra or Capricorn dress your Gardens and trim your small Trees and Shrubs.*

Planting by the Moon is traditional in the East, and there have been somewhat inconclusive studies by Western astrologers.

Garnett, Richard (1835–1906) Linguist, philologist, author and assistant keeper of printed books at the British Museum, Garnett eventually became the superintendent of the Library. He published several collections of poetry and a number of biographies and translations. He began to study astrology when he was in his twenties, but took the precaution of using an alias ('A G Trent') when he published on the subject. He insisted that the subject was 'strictly empirical' and in no sense occult; its principles had been drawn from thousands of books which were open to examination, and based on arithmetical calculations. He was perhaps the most serious writer on astrology of his time. He agreed to write the entry on astrology for the 11th edition of *Encyclopaedia Britannica*, but died before doing so.

Gauquelin, Michel (1928–91) A French psychologist and statistician, Gauquelin in collaboration with his wife Françoise was the first modern researcher to collect a major body of statistical data rigorously observed and collated. He had been interested in astrology from his youth (his father had been an enthusiast) and was calculating horoscopes at the age of ten. He published much of his work, in particular recording the planetary positions at birth for many thousands of men and women, divided into professional groups such as actors, artists, business executives, doctors, journalists, politicians, scientists, soldiers, sports champions and writers as well as criminals and schizophrenics. He claimed to observe specific patterns of planetary positions common to the charts of those with similar occupations – in particular, the rising and culminating of Mars in the birth-charts of notable athletes. His research was taken seriously not only by astrologers but by some professional psychologists, and remains, if not conclusive, highly interesting and to a degree significant.

Gaurico, Luca (1476–1558) Sometimes known as Lucas Gauricus, he was born in Naples in poverty, but somehow contrived to reach the position of astrologer at the court of Catherine de Medici, who he impressed by forecasting in 1489 that her great-uncle Giovanni, then aged 14, would become pope – which he did in 1513, as Leo X. He was less successful when Giovanni II of Bologna consulted him; finding Gaurico's prediction unpalatable, Giovanni had him tortured and exiled. Pope Julius II favoured him however, and when he successfully predicted the accession to the papacy of Alessandro Farnese (who became pontiff in 1534 as Paul III) his fame spread throughout Italy and further abroad. Pope Paul III knighted him and in 1539 appointed him Bishop of Giffoni in Salerno, and six years later Bishop of Civitate, in southern Italy. He accurately forecast to the day the death of Pope Paul III, who died on 20 November 1549, after which Gaurico moved to Rome.

There he worked on his *Tractatus Astrologicus*, an archive containing hundreds of astrological birth-charts of notable people, comparing chart with chart and attempting to rationalize a theory of prediction. Among other successes, he accurately predicted the death in a duel in1559 of Henry II of France, and the type of wound that would kill him. He is said to have warned the King, in a letter, to avoid single combat during his 41st year, but his advice was ignored.

Gaurico's skill as an astrologer extended to the planning of a favourable time for the laying of the foundation stones of important buildings. There is a reliable account of Pope Paul III instructing him to calculate the most fortunate time at which to lay the cornerstone of a new building near St Peter's in Rome. Gaurico and an assistant processed to the site with an astrolabe, calculations were made, and the astrologer struck a gong when the proper moment arrived.

Gell, Robert (1595–1665) Astrologer and chaplain to the Archbishop of Canterbury, and at his death rector of St Mary, Aldermanbury, London, he preached before Charles I, the lord mayor and aldermen of London and (twice) before the Society of Astrologers.

Gemini ♊

The third sign of the zodiac. SUN-SIGN period 22 May–21 June.

It should be remembered when reading of the characteristics of the Sun-signs that these will always be affected by the effects of the rising-sign, the planets in various other signs and houses, and the relationships the planets make to each other.

General characteristics

'Versatility' is the word that springs most readily to mind when one thinks of Gemini as a Sun-sign. It seems virtually impossible for someone with the Sun in this sign to do, or even think of, one thing at a time; and if they are forced into that position, boredom will swiftly ensue – and boredom is the second word which comes instantly to mind – this time as the one thing to be avoided at all costs. The sign contributes a need to communicate, and usually makes communication easy and natural – both with a partner and with anyone else who will listen. There is a natural rationality and logicality about the sign, and emotions are often mistrusted – and sometimes slow to be expressed. This can give the impression of superficiality – and sadly this can often be the case; in their constant desire to find out more about any subject which comes to mind, Geminians often skim the surface, and end up knowing relatively little about an enormous number of subjects. One result is that they are natural journalists, able and eager to explore the current 'story', but finding it very easy to drop it and move on to the next. Flirtatious by nature, they find it equally easy to pick up and drop acquaintances, sometimes not allowing time for a relationship to develop. In a permanent relationship they can be entertaining, fun, sexually lively – but naturally reluctant to confine themselves to one partner.

The growing child

From the moment when he or she starts to talk – which may be phenomenally early – the Geminian child will be bright, communicative, entertaining, a bit of a show-off, and so naturally friendly and approachable that there may be a danger in the readiness to approach or receive the attentions of strangers. These will be challenging children – always asking questions and requiring intelligent answers, refusing to be put off by flippancy or an 'I don't know.' If an adult doesn't know a fact, they should find it out, otherwise how is the Geminian to learn? – the idea that they should do the hard work of finding out for themselves is not so attractive. They will often be argumentative and again demand a rational response, only accepting discipline if the reason for it can be rationally explained, and seems to them to be logical. Their energy will be continual and stimulating, not to say tiring, to the adults caring for them.

Education

At school – from infants' school to university – teachers will notice a certain superficiality in Geminian students, and often a disinclination to hard work and real study. For instance they will tend to parrot the opinions of others rather than take the trouble to think things out for themselves, quoting from a book, a lecture or an internet site without attribution, often presenting the opinion or fact as their own. Reading a serious subject, they will quickly get bored with the necessary groundwork of facts, and in history (for example) will tend to remember anecdotes rather than dates, the characters of politicians rather than their political views. Committed, in further education, to one subject they will find it extremely difficult to confine themselves to it, always ready to scamper away down a sidetrack. They are likely too to spend too much time in extramural activities: the university debating society, students' union, drama club will be infinitely more appealing than the lecture room, while the idea of settling down alone to study one subject in isolation will be anathema, to be avoided at all costs.

Friendship, romance and sex

Lively, entertaining, full of surprises, eager for new experiences, a Geminian makes a stimulating friend – but one easily bored, and likely suddenly to disappear if the company or the conversation begins to pall. Anyone unable to meet quip with quip, to share the enjoyment of a book, a play, a concert, or to be unwilling to join in a vigorous argument about everything and anything from politics to global warming to contemporary fashion will very quickly be dropped. Naturally flirtatious, a Geminian often looks on it as a challenge to gain the attention of someone he or she finds attractive; but once again, if the mind and personality aren't as interesting as the face or figure, the flirtation will rapidly cease. The Geminian's enjoyment of sex can be equally flippant, and is often described as cool. This does not mean that Geminians are not capable of ensuring that they and their partner don't have an extremely good time in bed, but that the partner should not make more of this than is on offer – which is often just a good time, not necessarily anything to do with love, 'whatever that is', as a Geminian might say.

Permanent partnership and family

Once a commitment has been made, the Geminian may intend to be
faithful, but the partner should be under no illusion that this will be easy. To
a typical Geminian, it may seem entirely natural to want to spend a lifetime
with one other person – but the idea that this should mean total sexual
monogamy will not commend itself. The partner will have to deal with this
as best he or she may; with luck, the problem will have been thought – and
talked – through before the commitment is fully realized. This – undoubtedly major – problem out of the way, partnership with a Geminian will
never be less than entertaining, like a fairground ride, full of ups and downs
and violent changes of direction. The Geminian will take it for granted that
the partner enjoys all this, and enjoys the partnership – so there are unlikely
to be regular deep expressions of loving emotion; these will be taken as
read. It will also be taken for granted that the family is important – that the
children enjoy life as much as the Geminian and partner, and the family
means friendship as well as love – this is likely to be a case where a child
and parent are indeed 'best friends'.

Occupation

Everything about Gemini suggests journalism as the ideal career, and an
above-average number of people with this Sun-sign will be found working
in print journalism, in radio and television, as journalists, newsreaders,
interviewers, commentators, and disc jockeys. Any work that involves communication may well be suitable, and one in which travel is involved would
commend itself – Geminians like to move around. Work in telecommunications would suit – though not on the technical side – and part-time work
interviewing for public opinion polls will also be of interest. A job with a
regular routine and no variety would not attract anyone with this Sun-sign,
and should they get trapped in such a job, release will be sought in spare-
time activities. However, many Geminians make excellent lecturers in
advanced education centres, though not necessarily in conventional schools,
where boredom can too easily set in. On the other hand this is often
combated by their finding ways of making repetitive lessons or examina-
tions interesting for themselves and their pupils.

Health

Geminian energy levels and metabolism are high, and need expression; nervous energy too burns brightly. They can get caught up in a frenzy of activity, and can become tense and sometimes nervously apprehensive. This can result in burn-out unless time is found for relaxation, preferably involving steady exercise such as walking, jogging or running. Exercise machines do not usually interest Geminians; what is the point of expending all that effort to stay in the same place? It is also important to find a spare-time activity which can take the mind off pressing problems. Yoga can be helpful. Gemini rules the shoulders, arms and hands, which can be vulnerable – the hands, especially, which are of above-average importance, not only because Geminians tend to gesture freely, but because they use them for writing and often for playing a musical instrument. Gemini also rules the lungs, and it is too often the case that these are susceptible – a cold can often turn into bronchitis. This is a Sun-sign whose members would be particularly rash to take up smoking.

Finance

Those with the Sun in Gemini are rarely particularly interested in money. They enjoy having it, but the idea that they should spend time nurturing investments and carefully planning for the financial future does not appeal, and is sometimes found confusing. Impetuosity can dangerously involve them in financial schemes which sound appealing and undemanding; they may be shrewd but their tendency to make sudden off-hand decisions can result in disaster. Finding reliable advisers is vital. Those who insist on managing their affairs alone, should spread their investments widely, and resist any idea of loading their eggs into one or two baskets. Their tendency to spend freely and often thoughtlessly – usually on the latest books, videos, sound systems – can result in difficulties with the bank; all too often they ignore bank statements, assuming them to be more satisfactory than they are. In business they make excellent, persuasive salespeople, but if setting up on their own account they need a more financially savvy partner.

Growing older

Geminians often retain their looks longer than those with any other Sun-sign, and their sprightly movements together with their youthful attitudes and continuing liveliness of mind keep them young longer than may be reasonably expected. Provided that their bodies and minds are free of ailments, they retain their interest in every aspect of life to its very end, and their addiction to newspapers, TV and radio news and discussion programmes also keeps them right up to date with the latest developments not only in their own but in the wider world. Regular exercise, in the form of daily walks, is valuable – and since they like being in company, a dog is often an excellent means of persuading them to keep these up, even when they are confined to the same walk every day. They are usually good at ignoring the gradual slowing down which age brings, and will happily pretend that such ailments as arthritis simply do not exist.

Gemini as rising-sign

When this sign is rising over the horizon it has an interesting effect on the Sun-sign, for Geminian characteristics (wide interests, the desire to communicate, a tendency to be easily bored) will somehow make themselves felt even when the Sun-sign character is very different. Someone with Gemini rising may express the more outgoing side of his or her nature more vigorously when out and about than at home or with really close friends. Unlike those with Gemini as Sun-sign, those with the sign rising will tend to pay attention to a number of projects in turn, rather than dealing with two or three at once, giving each rather more attention than the Sun-sign Geminian may. There will be need for challenge and perhaps risk-taking in every area of life, and a partner must be prepared to deal with a strong need for personal freedom.

Traditional associations
- Ruling Planet – Mercury
- Triplicity/Element – air
- Quadruplicity/Quality – mutable
- Colour – yellow, but a love of all colour
- Gemstone – agate
- Metal – mercury
- Flower – lily-of-the-valley
- Trees – nut-bearing

- Herbs and Spices – aniseed, marjoram, caraway
- Foodstuffs – nuts, vegetables grown above ground, carrots
- Animals – small birds, parrots, butterflies, monkeys
- Countries – Azerbaijan, Wales, Italy, Belgium, Vatican City
- Cities – London, Plymouth (UK), Cardiff, San Francisco, Melbourne
- US States – Arkansas, Kentucky, Rhode Island, S. Carolina, Tennessee, W. Virginia, Wisconsin

* * *

generation influence   Those planets that take many years to circle the Sun, and thus spend seven or more years in one sign are said to have a generation influence, because they affect everyone born during the time they spend in that sign. *See* URANUS, NEPTUNE, PLUTO.

genethliacal astrology   The Greek term for the interpretation of the personal BIRTH-CHART.

geniture   The nativity of the person for whom a HOROSCOPE is being calculated. PTOLEMY described the RULING PLANET of a horoscope as the Lord of the Geniture.

geoarc   The HOUSE DIVISIONS relating to a HOROSCOPE drawn up for a particular moment, considering the effect on a subject of his movement around the centre of the Earth, as he stands on its surface. A *heliarc* refers to the same house divisions when considering the actual movements of the planets, including Earth, around the Sun. Heliarcs are measured in 30° segments from the Sun's position on the day for which the horoscope is set up.

geocentric   A geocentric view of the solar system is one in which the Earth is visualized as its centre. This has traditionally always been used in astrology for the purpose of drawing charts showing planetary relationships. However, *see* HELIOCENTRIC ASTROLOGY.

geographical astrology From ancient times there have been reputed links between countries and cities, even the different areas of some cities, and the zodiac signs which are said to 'rule' them. The reason why the associations were first made is now obscure, and geographical changes have made them even more so. But the tradition dies hard, and it continues to be argued that the associations often work – that a person can be particularly happy in an area or place associated with a sign which is emphasized in his or her HOROSCOPE. A few of the places linked to specific zodiac signs will be found listed under those signs. *See also* ASTRO*CARTO*GRAPHY.

George II, King *see* HEMMINGS, SAMUEL

Gerard (d.1108) Archbishop of York, Gerard was an enthusiast for astrology. When he died, a book by Julius FIRMICUS was found under his pillow. His enemies asserted that his death was a divine judgment for his addiction to 'magical and forbidden arts', and he was refused burial within his cathedral (though his body was later brought in by a later, sympathetic archbishop).

Glastonbury Zodiac There is a tradition, which existed as long ago as the 17th century but crystallized in the 1920s, that a zodiac, its circle some nine miles across, exists near Glastonbury, in Somerset, the figures outlined by natural features including pools, rivers, ancient earthworks and the contours of the landscape. It must be said that the outlining of the lion, the ram, the bull and the other images of the zodiac as postulated by K Maltwood, who elaborated her theory in a book published in 1929, has a relationship to the natural features which is certainly no more graphic than the relationship between the images and the stars in the constellation patterns, but the romanticism of the theory has attracted many followers, and a great number of highly fanciful legends has been attached to the Zodiac, including the allegation that it originated after the visit to England of Chaldean astrologers in ancient times. It has also been sentimentally associated with the legend of King Arthur, the knights of the round table, and the search for the Holy Grail.

glyphs The 'short-hand' graphic symbols used to represent the signs and planets – viz, ? representing Venus, ? Mars, and so on. It has been pointed out (*see* Gettings, *The Arkana Dictionary of Astrology*) that the term is in fact a misnomer, and that the proper word should rather be *sigils*; but the usage is so common that it is unlikely ever to change.

Goodman, Linda (1925–95) American astrologer. The author of arguably the best-selling SUN-SIGN book of the 20th century, *Linda Goodman's Sun Signs* (1968), followed in 1978 by *Linda Goodman's Love Signs*.

grand cross An astrological ASPECT made when four planets are in such a position that when two pairs are connected by lines, a perfect right-angled cross is formed. This is said to be an aspect which, while it may result in considerable tensions in a character or a life pattern, contributes a strong emphasis on creativity and originality. It is said to be a 'make or break' pattern, often instilling remarkable determination.

grand trine A grand trine is formed when two planets form a TRINE aspect (i.e. are separated by 120°) and each is trine a third planet. This is a highly favourable and helpful aspect to have in a birth-chart, but inclines the 'fortunate' individual to a laid-back attitude.

Grasshoff, Carl Louis von (1865–1919) Born in Denmark, von Grasshoff worked briefly in England as an engineer (he was employed by Cunard for some years) then moved first to New York City and then to Los Angeles where, failing to make a living in his profession, he became interested in theosophy, studied astrology and began lecturing on occult subjects. Having (he reported) being visited and given spiritual counsel and instruction by a spiritual being, an Elder Brother of the Rosicrucian Order, he wrote and lectured widely on Rosicrucianism. He wrote on astrology under the pseudonym Max Heindel.

Greece, astrology in Astrology came to the fore in Greece in the 2nd century BC, after the death of ALEXANDER THE GREAT. The theory was probably transmitted via the school set up on the island of Cos in about 280BC by BEROSUS of Babylon, though no manuscripts have survived to show the precise nature of his teachings. Within a century, various textbooks of astrology had begun to circulate, and the intelligentsia began to take sides on the subject. Intellectual discussions were never, however, as heated as they were in Rome.

Greene, Liz (b.1946) American astrologer, author and lecturer whose astrological books are informed by Jungian psychology; a co-founder with Howard Sasportas of the London Centre for Psychological Astrology, in which she was later associated with Charles Harvey. Her books include *The Astrology of Fate* (1986), *The Outer Planets and their Cycles* (1996) and *The Dark of the Soul* (2003).

Greenwich Mean Time The local MEAN TIME at Greenwich, in England. The difference between Greenwich Mean Time and local mean time at any one moment is the LONGITUDE turned into time. Many EPHEMERIDES are set for Greenwich at noon or midnight GMT – which means that astrologers must convert the LOCAL TIME of birth into the equivalent Greenwich time *and date*.

Gresham, Edward (1565–1613) Born in Yorkshire, Gresham studied at Trinity College, Cambridge (MA in 1606). He was a diligent and serious astronomer, and wrote an erudite Copernican-based book about the planets, *Astrostereon*, defending astrology against the accusation that it was contrary to religion. He published a number of EPHEMERIDES, and his ALMANACS were popular until (it is reported) he foretold the Gunpowder Plot so accurately that he was suspected of having a part in it. This was not the end of his troubles. The Countess of Essex had employed Simon FORMAN to advise her on ridding herself of her husband and securing the love of the Earl of Somerset. When Forman died, she consulted Gresham, who promised by a magic spell to make Essex impotent – and indeed three years later a royal commission granted a divorce on the grounds of Essex's impotence. Gresham then went on to use his magical arts on the Countess's behalf against her enemy Sir Thomas Overbury. A plot against Overbury was discovered, but perhaps fortunately for him Gresham died before his complicity was revealed.

– H –

Hadrian, Publius Aelius Hadrianus Roman Emperor AD117–38. Said himself to be able to practise astrology, which he may have learned while studying Greek and Roman culture in Rome before entering the army. He is the earliest Roman emperor whose complete horoscope has survived, in several MS copies discovered in the 4th century. He was born with the Sun, Moon and Jupiter in Aquarius, Saturn and Mercury in Capricorn, Venus and Mars in Pisces. He is said to have written down at the beginning of each year the major events in his life for the following twelve months, and to have predicted his own death to the hour.

Hali (sometimes Haly Abenragel) (10th/11th c.) Court astrologer to a Tunisian prince, Hali wrote an authoritative astrological textbook only part of which survives in its original form, but which was translated into Latin in the 15th century as *Praeclarissimus completes in judiciis astrorum*, commonly known as *De iudiciis astrorum*.

Hand, Robert (b.1942) American astrologer, historian, author and lecturer involved for many years in the translation and publication of ancient and medieval astrological manuscripts, forwarding the study of ancient, classical and medieval astrology. Among his publications are *Planets in Transit: life cycles for living* (2002), *Planets in Youth: patterns of early development* (1997) and *Astrolabe World Ephemeris 2001–50* (1998).

Hanussen, Eric Jan (1889–1933) A Czech Jew who became famous in Germany as a mind-reader, hypnotist and astrologer, and despite his Jewish origin was friendly with many Nazi Party members. He is rumoured to have advised Hitler, and in 1933 predicted the Reichstag fire, the event that assisted Hitler to seize power. His almost immediate mysterious assassination led to the supposition that he was murdered by the Nazis as being too intimately connected with that event.

harmonics The English astrologer John ADDEY researched a new way of examining a HOROSCOPE based on the examination of all numerical relationships between the planets and other characteristics of the chart – some thousands of possible relationships, which he called 'harmonics'. The basic theory is that in for instance the seventh harmonic chart, the zodiac circle will be divided into seven sections each of 360°÷7. The idea was not a completely new one: Karl Ernst KRAFFT had applied roughly the same sort of statistic analysis to charts in the 1920s, and the basic notion can be seen to be related both to numerology and to ancient Hindu techniques; but Addey, publishing in the 1970s, elaborated and perfected the theory, and claimed to show that when intervals between (for instance) planets were divided by certain numbers, certain results could be predicted. His earliest work was based on the examination of the birth-charts of a large number of subjects (among others over 7,000 doctors, about 3,000 artists, 4,500 clergymen and 1,000 victims of poliomyelitis) and seemed to show patterns which had nothing to do with traditional astrology but much to do with harmonic analysis (carried out by computer). These were most reliable when associated with traits of personality rather than with, say, occupations. Addey's theory has no relationship to traditional astrology – indeed, one of his own books is entitled *Astrology Reborn* – and while interest in harmonics persists it is a long way from being accepted as a mainstream theory. *See* FAGAN, KEPLER.

Hartmann, Franz (1838–1912) German astrologer, doctor and theosophist, who worked with Helena Blavatsky, and founded the German Theosophical Society in 1896.

Hebrew calendar The Hebrew calendar is claimed to have begun at the Creation, which occurred 3,760 years before the Christian era. The week consists of 7 days, ending with the Sabbath. There are 12 lunar months in the year:

Tishri	Nisan
Cheshvan	Iyar
Kislev	Sivan
Tebet	Tammuz
Shebat	Ab
Adar	Elul

These consist alternately of 29 and 30 days. A 13th month, Veadar, is added several times during each 19-year cycle, to remedy the inconvenience that a year is 11 days longer than 12 lunar months.

Heindel, Max *see* GRASSHOFF, CARL LOUIS VON

heliacal rising and falling The first rising and first setting of a star during a period of visibility (previously having been invisible due to a conjunction with the Sun).

heliarc *see* GEOARC

heliocentric astrology A heliocentric astrological chart has the Sun rather than the Earth at its centre, and the angles between the planets are shown as they would be as 'seen' from the viewpoint of the Sun. Astrologers who work on such charts use specially calculated EPHEMERIDES; the placing of the zodiac signs present special problems which have not been solved by any common consent – and since the Sun and Moon have no place in a heliocentric chart, there is no such conception as a 'SUN-SIGN' – nor is there an ASCENDANT. There is no system of HOUSES. The planetary NODES are seen as important, and new ASPECTS to Venus and Mercury must be interpreted, often in different ways by different astrologers. In fact there is little resemblance between heliocentric and traditional geocentric astrology. Such research as has been done on heliocentric astrology has been skimpy and uncorrelated; it may be that there is room for work on the theory, but it seems unlikely that it will ever be regarded as anything but a sideline.

Hemmings, Samuel There has always been much discussion of 'ASTRO-LOGICAL TWINS' – people born at the same place on the same date at the same time. 'Raphael' (*see* SMITH, ROBERT CROSS) in his *A Manual of Astrology* (1828) reports the case of Samuel Hemmings, born at the same time and date and in the same London parish as the baby who became George III. Hemmings went into business as a baker in October 1760, the month the king acceded to the throne; they were both married on 8 September 1761, and died on the same day, 29 January 1820. The story continues to be quoted, but is unauthenticated except by reports in the popular press of the time.

Henry VIII (1491–1547) King of England. He prevented his bishops from preaching against astrology, and received advice from two astrologers, the German Nicholas Kratzer and the English William Parron.

Hephaistion of Thebes (ca. AD380) An Egyptian astrologer who published (as *Apotelesmatics*) a summary of Ptolemy's *TETRABIBLOS* towards the end of the great period of Byzantine astrology, after the Emperor Constantine was converted to Christianity in AD312, and before the closure of the 'pagan' Athens schools by the Emperor Justinian in 549.

Hercules An HYPOTHETICAL PLANET said to rule Leo.

Herman of Carinthia (ca.1100–60) A scholar, mathematician and astrologer whose first known book was a translation of one of the books of a text, *Liber sextus astronomie,* by the Jewish writer Saul ben ibn Bishr, which dealt with the influences of the planets and comets on Earth, and means of predicting by observing them. He subsequently translated books of astronomy as well as astrology, many of which were used by later scholars.

Hermes A HYPOTHETICAL PLANET said to rule Gemini. In mythology Hermes is identical to the god Mercury.

Hermes Trismegistus The Greek name for the alleged author of an amalgam of religious themes and beliefs expressed by the Greek god Hermes and the Egyptian god Thoth. Both were gods of writing and magic, and Thoth in particular, the god of intellect, was related to astrology. It was he who was named Hermes Trismegistus, or thrice-great – as king, priest and philosopher. He collected together an enormous number of texts relating to astrology, alchemy, magic, medicine, philosophy and religion. Many of these were supposed to date back to extreme, not to say incredible, antiquity – in some cases over 9,000 years before the birth of Christ. The Egyptians were said to preserve in one temple sacred writings by Hermes himself, which contained the rites to be performed by all Egyptian priests. These documents which have been preserved date from the 2nd century AD.

In about 1460 Cosimo de Medici acquired a collection of documents which were supposed to be copies of the original Hermetic writings. He commissioned Marsilio Ficino to translate them, and they were published ten years later. Ficino believed that Hermes was an historical figure (and at one point speculates that the name might be the pseudonym of Moses). In many ways the documents prefigure Christian beliefs and attitudes, though the Church condemned them because of their association with astrology – and magical astrology at that, or so they believed. In fact, the astrology put forward in the Hermetic texts is highly traditional: the creator made the seven planets to govern the Earth, and their movements caused all earthly events. The DECANS fashioned the affairs of men; zodiac demons, the products of the signs, influenced humankind.

Herschel The planet URANUS was for a short time named after its discoverer, Sir William Herschel.

Hesiod (fl. ca.700BC) One of the earliest known Greek poets, who in his poem *Works and Days* notes the effect on farming of the rising of certain constellations. This is the earliest known reference to astrology in Greek literature.

Heydon, John (1629–67). Born in London, Heydon joined the army of Charles I before completing his education, and later travelled extensively in Europe before studying law and practising as an attorney in Clifford's Inn. Interested in astrology, he foretold Cromwell's death by hanging, was arrested and imprisoned for two years, and his library burned. Released, he was re-arrested on a charge of treason, and yet again for debt; but his friend the Duke of Buckingham intervened. In 1667 he was again in prison, once more accused of treason, but managed to talk himself out of trouble. Heydon 'loved a lady in Devonshire, but when I seriously perused my nativity, I found the seventh house afflicted, and therefore resolve never to marry'. However, in fact he married the widow of Nicholas CULPEPER. Among his publications is the ambitious *The Holy Guide: leading the Way* *to the Wonder of the World: (A Compleat Phisitian), teaching the Knowledge of all things, past, present, and to come* (1662) and books on the Rosicrucians and Cabballa.

Hindu zodiac Hindu astrologers have different names for the astrological signs according to whether they appear in their TROPICAL or SIDEREAL zodiacs. They are as follows – the tropical name being given first:

- Aries – Maish/Acvini
- Taurus – Vrishab/Krittika
- Gemini – Mithun/Mrigasitas
- Cancer – Karka/Punarvasu
- Leo – Simha/Magha
- Virgo – Kanya/Phalguni
- Libra – Tulam/Citra
- Scorpio – Vrishchik/Vicakha
- Sagittarius – Dhanu/Mula
- Capricorn – Makar/Ashadha
- Aquarius – Kumbh/Cravishta
- Pisces – Meena/Bhadrapada

Hipparchus (190BC– ca.120BC) The greatest pre-Ptolemaic Greek astronomer, Hipparchus's work towers over that of his contemporaries. He discovered PRECESSION and compiled the first *star catalogue* to be set down in the West. He is believed to have invented the ASTROLABE. He wrote at least 14 books, though none has survived. His work was of great value to astrologers, and he may at least have theorized about the subject: Pliny states that he 'can never be sufficiently praised, no one having done more to prove that man is related to the stars and that our souls are a part of heaven'.

Hippocrates of Cos (460BC– ca.370BC) One of the great figures in the history of medicine, Hippocrates argued that all illness was the result of imbalance between the four HUMOURS, and also postulated a crisis occurring in all illnesses at which the patient would either begin to recover, or continue to slip downwards to death. Naturally, astrology was important in deciding when such a crisis was to occur, or had occurred. *See* MEDICAL ASTROLOGY, CRITICAL DAYS.

Hitler, Adolf (1889–1945) German dictator. Gossip has always asserted that Hitler had an interest in astrology, and even employed astrologers. There is no evidence to support this, and his table-talk shows no interest in the subject. However it is clear that a number of Nazi ministers and officials of the Third Reich were closely associated with astrologers, and it is certainly the case that many German astrologers cast Hitler's horoscope and wrote about his birth-chart (*see*, for instance, EBERTIN, Elspeth). The one apparently substantiated anecdote about Hitler and astrology comes from the diaries of Count Schwerin von Krosigk, Hitler's Minister of Finance. Josef Goebbels, the Reich's chief publicist, was with Hitler in the bunker in Berlin in the last days of the war, and showed the Führer copies of the horoscope of Germany and Hitler's own horoscope, pointing out that these predicted the outbreak of war in 1939, the victories until 1941, and then a series of defeats. But it was clear that they also showed an over-whelming victory for Germany in the second half of April 1945, and an arranged peace in August. Later, when Goebbels heard of the death of President Roosevelt, he went to Hitler with a bottle of champagne, and proclaimed 'My Führer, I congratulate you! It is written in the stars that the second half of April will be the turning point for us. This is Friday, April the 13th – it is the turning point.' Within a fortnight both men had killed themselves.

Hitschler method The Swiss astrologer Kurt Hitschler has allocated a particular degree of the zodiac to every known chemical element or compound, the theory being that this can be usefully adapted to therapeutic practice.

Holst, Gustav (1874–1934) English composer best known for his orchestral suite *The Planets*. Holst was introduced to astrology by his writer friend Clifford Bax, and conceived the idea of a suite of orchestral movements each of which attempted to describe the astrological disposition of one of the planets. He used a book by ALAN LEO as an astrological text.

Hone, Margaret (1892–1969) English astrologer and author of the *Modern Textbook of Astrology*, published in 1951 and one of the most important astrological textbooks of its time, setting a new standard for the teaching of the subject. It was used for many years by the English Faculty of Astrological Studies, which she founded with Charles CARTER, Jeff Mayo and others, and of which she was principal for some years. In 1958 she was one of the founders of the UK Astrological Association.

horary astrology This term is sometimes loosely applied to the astrological consideration of an event rather than of a person. Its real application however, is the answering of a particular question put by a client. The question is answered after consulting a HOROSCOPE drawn up for the moment when it is asked. The approach is different from that employed when a birth-chart is considered. William LILLY, the 17th-century astrologer who was particularly expert in this field, clearly to some extent used his charts as an aid to intuition or clairvoyance; but the rules for drawing up and considering the chart were and are very particular. There is a significant timescale which must be applied, and the planets do not have the same significance as in a BIRTH-CHART, but represent symbols which apply to the question asked by the QUERANT. Lilly's notebooks record a great number of horary queries from as many as 2,000 clients a year; they asked him all manner of questions, from whether a man would be hanged for stealing a cow to the whereabouts of lost pets or stolen property, the safety or otherwise of men going to war, and the sexual availability (or not) of particular men and women.

horoscope *or* BIRTH-CHART. Astrologers use both terms somewhat indiscriminately; it is perhaps sensible to use 'birth-chart' when the natal horoscope is discussed, and 'horoscope' when the chart is drawn for some other purpose. In any event, both terms relate to a diagram drawn for a particular date, time and place, showing the precise positions of the Sun, Moon and planets on that date, at that time and for that place. This may refer to the birth of an individual, or in HORARY ASTROLOGY, the moment when a particular event takes place or a particular question is asked.

An EPHEMERIS is consulted which provides a note of the daily movement of the elements of the solar system (these details may now also be easily found on-line on the World Wide Web); with the aid of the figures provided and CALCULATION, a round map of the sky is produced on which the relative positions of the Sun, Moon and planets are shown, within the circle of the zodiac and relative to the twelve zodiac signs and the astrological HOUSES. It is by examining the positions of these bodies within the signs and houses, and the angles made by each to each, with other factors, that the astrologer is able to interpret the chart.

horoscope, earliest The earliest horoscope to have been discovered, in Babylon, dates from 409BC, probably for the end of April 409. It is damaged, but partly reads:

> *Month Nisan night of 14th ... son of Shuma-usur, son of Shuma-iddina, descendant of Deke, was born. At that time the Moon was below the Horn of the Scorpion, Jupiter in the Fish, Venus in the Bull, Saturn in the Crab, Mars in the Twins, Mercury, which had set [for the last time] was [still] invisible ... the 27th was the day when the Moon appeared for the last time. Things will be good for you.*

The next earliest horoscope, dated 4 April 263BC tells the subject that

> *he will be lacking in wealth ... his food will not suffice for his hunger. The wealth he had in his youth will not stay. His days will be long. His wife, whom people will seduce in his presence, will bring it about. He will have women. He will see profit.*

horoskopos An ancient name for the ASCENDANT.

hours, planetary The hours of the day are traditionally ruled by the planets, in order from Saturn to the Moon – but this system was devised before clocks, when the 'hours' were simply arbitrary divisions of the hours of daylight, from sunrise to sunset, and so could differ wildly in length.

house division The HOROSCOPE or BIRTH-CHART is divided not only into twelve sections attributed to the zodiac signs, but also to twelve sections known as HOUSES, the lines which divide them known as CUSPS. Each of these houses represents an aspect of life (*see* FIRST HOUSE, SECOND HOUSE, etc.) and planets placed within them or related to them, have something to say about these areas of the character of the person to whom the horoscope belongs. Over the centuries, a great number of different means of house division have been devised. The Equal House system, one of the earliest, is still very common, having the advantage that it enables horoscopes to be drawn for every part of the world, whereas with others, such as the PLACIDUS or KOCHIAN systems, this is impossible – though both of these systems remain popular as to some extent do the REGIOMONTANUS and CAMPANEAN systems. Information to assist the astrologer to calculate house positions and place the house cusps is published in Tables of Houses. *See* ALCHABITUS, CAMPANUS, EQUAL HOUSE, KOCH, KRUSINSKY, MERIDIAN, NEO-PORPHYRY, PORPHYRY, PLACIDUS, REGIOMONTANUS, TOPOCENTRIC, whole sign.

house ruler In traditional astrology a house was ruled by the planet that ruled the sign on its CUSP. In modern times the planet associated with a particular house is said to 'rule' it – the first house is ruled by Mars because Aries is the first sign and is ruled by Mars, the second by Venus because Taurus is the second sign, and is ruled by Venus, and so on. This system seems to have been devised by ALAN LEO in the last century.

houses The HOROSCOPE is divided into twelve sections, separate from those that show the zodiac signs. These are the houses. The first house begins at the horizon line – the horizontal line across the circle – and lies below it and left of centre; the rest follow, anticlockwise, until the twelfth ends above the horizon line, ending at the line. The houses are not always regular in size, but may vary according to different means of HOUSE DIVISION, of which there are many. Each house governs particular areas of the life of the owner of a horoscope: for these *see* under FIRST HOUSE, SECOND HOUSE, etc. For the effect of the placing of Sun, Moon and planets in different houses, *see* under the relevant planet.

Huber, Bruno (1930–99) A Swiss astrologer, a follower of Alice Bailey, who with his wife Louise founded the Huber School of Astrology in 1962, later bringing it to England.

humours In early Greek medicine it was believed that four 'humours', kept in balance, governed the health of the human body. The degree of phlegm, black bile, yellow bile and blood in a patient must be carefully estimated before treatment could be begun. Phlegma was associated with water, black bile with earth, yellow bile with fire and blood with air. The lack or diminution of one or the other inevitably resulted in illness – not only physical but psychological, hence the association between the humours and the TEMPERAMENTS, themselves associated with specific astrological types.

Hyades A group of stars in Taurus which both Pliny and PTOLEMY believed to be 'evil', and to suggest violence.

hyleg A planet which is regarded as 'the giver of life'. The Sun or Moon can be hyleg if either is in the 1st, 7th, 9th or 11th house, though PTOLEMY laid down that the *hylegiacal place* was between 5° above and 25° below the Ascendant.

Hypatia of Alexandria (ca.360BC–AD415) A mathematician who taught astrology and astronomy, Hypatia was murdered by Christians, perhaps because of her steadfast defence of astrology, which the Christian world was beginning to condemn.

hypothetical planets Nonexistent planets, usually 'discovered' by mediums, and said to have an effect within a horoscope in the same way as real planets. There are probably currently over a hundred of these, and EPHEMERIDES have in some cases been prepared for the more 'important' ones, showing their alleged movements. None of them has been observed by even the most sophisticated of telescopes. The theory by which they are used is obscure to many astrologers, but those who do use them take them seriously. *See* ISIS, JANUS, LILITH, TRANSPLUTO, VULCAN, HERCULES, HERMES, URANIAN ASTROLOGY, WITTE, BLACK CHART.

– I –

Ibn Yunus (ca.950–1009), born in Egypt, worked as an astronomer for the Fatimid dynasty. His best-known work, a collection of astronomical tables, is remarkable for its accuracy, and was used in Europe as late as the 19th century. This accuracy must have relied on very large instruments, and it is said that he possessed an armillary sphere with 9 rings, each weighing 2,000lbs, and large enough for a horse and rider to pass through. He is said to have predicted his own death to the day, though immediately before it he appeared perfectly well.

IC *see* IMUM COELI

Imum Coeli (*sometimes wrongly spelled Immum Coeli*) In a HOROSCOPE or BIRTH-CHART, the lowest point of the ECLIPTIC, opposite the MIDHEAVEN; it is sometimes called the anti-Midheaven. The Latin original translates as 'the lowest point of the heavens'. Usually abbreviated, in a chart, as IC.

immersion The beginning of an ECLIPSE or an OCCULTATION.

impeded A planet is impeded when it is AFFLICTED, especially by MALEFICS (Mars, Saturn or Uranus). The Moon is impeded when it is in a CONJUNCTION, SQUARE or OPPOSITION to the malefics, and also when it is afflicted by the Sun.

inclination The inclination of an ORBIT is the angle between the orbit's plane and the plane of the ECLIPTIC.

inferior planets The term should really be in inverted commas: Venus and Mercury are in no way 'inferior' in astrological terms; the reference to them as such is because they lie closer to the Sun than the Earth.

infertility *see* JONAS

ingress When a planet enters a zodiac sign it is said to have made its ingress.

intercepted When, in a chart, a SIGN is placed entirely within a HOUSE, without being on either CUSP, it is described as being intercepted. Some astrologers assert that planets placed in such a house are strengthened, others that they are weakened.

International Date Line On the opposite side of the globe from the Greenwich line of LATITUDE is the International Date Line, 180° west or east. It was agreed at an international conference in 1884 that each day should begin immediately west of the line, and end immediately east of it – which means that time zones on each side are 24 hours apart, with the still somewhat surprising result that travellers crossing from west to east repeat a day, while those crossing from east to west lose one. The line avoids crossing land, so as not to cause disorder within a country or state.

interpreting a horoscope As in medicine a doctor will balance a number of symptoms and relate them to the character and personality of the patient, an astrologer will similarly weigh the effects of all the elements of a HOROSCOPE or BIRTH-CHART, weighing this one against that one, estimating how the strength of one will affect the influence of another. Certain elements are of greater importance than others: the RISING-SIGN and SUN-SIGN are of course two of the most important, but their effect can be seriously influenced by the positions of the planets within them, or possibly within one or two particular other signs, and by the influence of the Moon. While no serious astrologer will allow any kind of occult influence to affect the judgement, again as with the practice of medicine, there will necessarily be the development of an instinct which will assist the interpreter in reaching conclusions. There is, of course, no substitute for experience in interpretation if results are to be reliable.

Iris An asteroid, discovered in 1847.

Isis There are three HYPOTHETICAL PLANETS named Isis, 'discovered' by three different astrologers.

Islamic calendar The Islamic calendar is dated from the day when Moahmmad fled from Mecca to Medina – i.e. 16 July 622. There are twelve lunar months of alternate 30 and 29 days:

Muharram	Rajab
Safar	Shaban
Rabi I	Ramadan
Rabi II	Shawwal
Jumada I	Zulkadah
Jumada II	Zulhijjah

This makes the year 354 days long, so the months move backward through the seasons, completing a cycle every 321–2 years.

– J –

Janus A HYPOTHETICAL PLANET.

Jillson, Joyce (1945–2004) A popular American astrologer who wrote widely syndicated SUN-SIGN columns. One of several astrologers who claimed to have advised President Reagan and his wife. She is said to have been employed by Hollywood film studios to advise them on the best dates for the release of films.

Jonas, Eugen (b.1928) A Czech psychiatrist and astrologer, Jonas claimed to have discovered, after studying 30,000 cases, an association between the ovulation cycle and certain transits of Sun and Moon in the BIRTH-CHARTS of his women patients, and that he could, by using his theory, aid infertile women to conceive. The publication of this theory in the early 1970s, and the suggestion that it could also be used as a reliable instrument of birth control (he claimed a success rate of 98 per cent) naturally received a great deal of publicity. Jonas also asserted that the tropical sign position of the Moon at conception indicated the sex of a child (male for alternate signs beginning with Aries, female for the other signs). His work was banned by the then Communist government of Czechoslovakia, and does not appear to have been published more recently, though certain Internet sites suggest that it is still being pursued. What is known and has been published in the West about the basis of his theory has not proved promising, and neither testing nor experience has substantiated it.

Jones, Mark Edmund (1888–1980) American astrologer, Christian Scientist and theosophist. On the one hand Jones was ambitious to help place astrology on a scientific basis, yet on the other hand he published the SABIAN SYMBOLS, widely derided by many astrologers who shared that ambition. He developed a system of recognition of certain patterns made by planets placed within a HOROSCOPE – the 'bundle', 'bowl', 'bucket' and others – asserting that these show how an individual may cope with certain problems.

judicial astrology Astrological forecasts which concentrate on public, often political affairs.

Julian calendar Julius Caesar ordered a reform of the existing Roman CALENDAR system, and the so-called Julian calendar, largely devised by the astronomer Sosigenes, was the result. The year 46BC was given 445 days, to compensate for accumulated errors of several months, and thereafter, starting in 45BC, there were to be 365 days in each year, with an additional 'leap year' every fourth year during which February had 29 rather than 28 days. The year 46BC, during which two months were inserted into the year, was known as the Year of Confusion – but thereafter the new system settled down surprisingly quickly. A second correction was made to the calendar by Augustus Caesar in AD8, after which the month of August was named after him, just as July had been named after his great predecessor. Nevertheless, three leap years too many were found to occur every 385 years, and consequently the actual equinoxes and solstices drifted away from their assigned calendar dates.

Juno Discovered in 1804, the ASTEROID Juno was the third to be discovered. Juno, the Roman equivalent of Greek Hera, was the queen of the gods, wife of Zeus and goddess of marriage – so the asteroid, according to its sign and house position, is said to present a picture of the person with whom one is most likely to form a lifelong partnership.

Jupiter ♃

The largest planet of the solar system – its mass twice that of all the other planets combined – Jupiter orbits the Sun in 11.9 years. Astrologically, it affects the individual's outlook on life, and the intellectual capacity and potential. Expansion is the planet's KEYWORD, and the sign in which it falls at birth will strongly affect the way in which one reaches towards new possibilities and an enhanced future. The planet is concerned with higher education and the expansion of the mind through travel and study. Jupiter takes twelve years to complete a journey through the zodiac, and every twelve years RETURNS to the precise position it was in when one was born.

This is known as the Jupiter Return, and at such times individuals usually take important steps forward, increasing prestige and income; it is a time at which to watch for opportunities and grasp them.

Jupiter and the zodiac signs

Jupiter in ARIES

People with Jupiter in Aries tend to be straightforward and uncomplicated – the influence of Aries as a SUN-SIGN. Loving a challenge, they are quick to grasp opportunities, often without troubling to analyse the situation in any depth. Coping with detail is not a strong point with them; it is their grasp of an overall plan or situation which is dependable and valuable. They will have a broad vision and the determination to carry plans through with a fiery enthusiasm, taking adventurous risks when this seems necessary, and often finding that their positive and optimistic nature is rewarded with success.

Jupiter in TAURUS

Slow to study, those with this placing of Jupiter will assimilate and retain information. They will be content to work steadily and cautiously within the boundaries they set for themselves, and will concentrate with enthusiasm on making financial progress – and if other planets suggest a good business sense, Jupiter will strengthen this, and they will watch with pleasure as the value of the business increases. They will not be eager to travel, which may slightly hinder the expansion of a business which relies on international contacts. They will enjoy a life of material comfort, delight in good food and wine; and reflecting Jupiter's KEYWORD, *expansion*, may consequently have above-average difficulty in keeping their weight down.

Jupiter in GEMINI

In Gemini, Jupiter scarcely knows which way to look: the pressure of various opportunities will make it difficult for individuals to decide their priorities, and even their direction in life. Versatile, witty, and with an intellectual flair, they will need variety in their personal and professional lives, in whatever career they eventually decide upon. Work in the travel industry will satisfy them – ameliorating their natural restlessness; work in the media will also be satisfying – their magpie-like love of collecting bits and pieces of (often half-digested) information will serve them well. They should make good salespeople. Though restlessness may be a problem, they will have a basically happy and optimistic temperament, and the ability to get a lot of fun out of the trickiest situations.

Jupiter in CANCER

'Caring' is a word that comes strongly to mind when considering this placing of Jupiter, which contributes a gently compassionate preoccupation with the wellbeing of others. 'Caring' is strongly linked with 'challenge', and practicality married to an excellent memory and good imagination is joined by a canny business sense. All this means that faced with the most difficult situation, these people will fight for those for whom they are caring – whether family members, or professional patients. While those with Jupiter in Cancer (where the planet is EXALTED) are sensitive, emotional and imaginative, they are also shrewd, often making excellent businessmen and women with a natural ability to make money and invest it profitably. The planet is traditionally well placed in this sign, so its influence is insistent.

Jupiter in LEO

Exuberance, a zest for living, powers of leadership, love of challenge and very probably creative ability – all these Leonine traits are encouraged when Jupiter is in this sign; but so are the less advantageous qualities of self-satisfaction, the conviction that one is always right, and a tendency to flamboyant self-advertisement and 'showing off.' These people will have a high-spirited zest for life, and their determination to enjoy whatever position they occupy may contribute to their tendency to be overexuberant. They will have big ideas and get through an enormous amount of work, which they will thoroughly enjoy. Though they may make a good deal of money, they are free-spending and extremely generous. Their abilities are great, but they should watch a tendency to become too conservative and overdogmatic as they grow older.

Jupiter in VIRGO

Discrimination, an acute critical sense, the ability for careful, attentive study and excellent judgement are encouraged by this placing, and challenges are unlikely to present a problem. However, every test will be met with careful consideration; there will be no desire to rush thoughtlessly into adventurous risk-taking. There will be a highly practical, commonsense attitude to life, and this placing of Jupiter will be especially helpful to anyone working in the teaching profession. Medically, there could be problems with the bowels and digestive system, and there should be some attention to diet, especially when rich food is on offer.

Jupiter in LIBRA

The desire for a pleasant, enjoyable, relatively untaxing life will make it unlikely that someone with Jupiter in Libra will be over-eager to take up challenges – and when these are accepted, it will be with a degree of blind optimism that may not be justified. These people love a life of pleasure and enjoy having fun – what they want is an untaxing routine, with the finer things of life – good food and wine, comfortable surround-ings, an elegant existence. The usual tendency will probably be to take life sitting or even lying down, appreciating comfort and the good things which are offered. The influence of other planets will be needed to instil energy and determination.

Jupiter in SCORPIO

'Moderation' is not a word that will commend itself to those with this placing of Jupiter; they will jump into any challenge with both feet – indeed, challenges may be determinedly sought out. An enquiring mind will focus on opportunities, and breadth of vision will ally itself to Scorpio intensity. But in all this, despite seriousness of purpose and a shrewd assessment of problems, there will also be a capacity to enjoy and appreciate life with enthusiasm. Jupiter will encourage this, and these people will work as hard when they are enjoying themselves as when they are facing problems and defeating them. They will actually relish 'facing fearful odds', and it is when they feel that they are making the most of their potential that they are at their happiest.

Jupiter in SAGITTARIUS

Jupiter rules Sagittarius, and works well and strongly from the sign. Development of the more serious side of the nature may take time to show

itself, but gradually experience will sharpen the intelligence and
bring balance to a youthful, carefree spirit which may last rather longer
than adolescence and is likely to be expressed through sport. This is
by no means a bad thing, and the youthful quality will be enormously
attractive on a personal level. In time however, the more serious side of
the nature will emerge, possibly demonstrated through an interest in
theology, philosophy or the law. Many writers and publishers share
this placing of Jupiter, which may indicate a possible career or at least a
strong interest. There will be a facility for learning languages, usefully
allied to a love of travel.

Jupiter in CAPRICORN

Rather soberly placed in Capricorn, Jupiter will assist with the achievement
of their objectives, and often denotes considerable ambition. It will also
contribute an off-beat sense of humour and fun to a generally rather serious
outlook on life. Methodical minds will be brought to bear on carefully
devised plans for career-building and/or money-making; the ability and
desire to look at every aspect of a situation and carefully calculate any
move in advance will be an enormous asset. No decision will be made
without its consequences being thoroughly estimated and considered.
Jupiter is an optimist; Capricorn somewhat pessimistic – these opposing
characteristics will have to be balanced, but both these qualities have their
positive and helpful side, and can be used to advantage.

Jupiter in AQUARIUS

Onlookers may attribute a degree of eccentricity to those with this
placing of Jupiter, which will certainly encourage the individual to go his
or her own way, expressing an independent spirit in an individual way
and showing the world evidence of a thoroughly inventive and
original mind. Originality will be positively expressed, and if ideas seem
extreme, they will turn out to have been thoroughly thought through, and
will be followed up with determination and completed to general applause.
These people have not just a desire but a positive need to break new
ground in whatever area of work they choose, and are thoroughly determined to stick to the course they have chosen, however doubtful colleagues and friends may be of the result.

Jupiter in PISCES

An idealistic turn of mind will express itself via a compelling interest of some sort – an idea, a faith, a philosophy, a way of life, perhaps an art form. There may be a strong religious faith, and since Pisces is a sign much related to charity and sacrifice, inhabiting it Jupiter may well turn to work for the alleviation of local or world poverty and starvation. This does not mean, however, that the individual will lack the capacity to enjoy life – so much so that the Jupiter KEYWORD, expansion, is expressed all too literally. It should be kept in mind that these individuals can be artful and occasionally deceptive. They will, incidentally, be excellent mimics.

Jupiter and the houses

Jupiter in the FIRST HOUSE

Jupiter's influence from this house is stronger the nearer it is to the ASCENDANT, and will strengthen the characteristics of the ascending sign. It will at best add a splendidly optimistic, enthusiastic, positive and infectious attitude to life, and a warm-hearted gusto which will prompt those with this placing of Jupiter to live it to the full. There will be considerable breadth of vision and a philosophical outlook which will be enriched with age. The pleasures of life will include a love of good food and wine, which may (because of the possibility of a vulnerable liver) lead to medical difficulties as well as trouble with weight gain.

Jupiter in the SECOND HOUSE

An enjoyment of the comforts of life will be joined to a distinct appreciation of the advantages of a sound financial base, and there will be an interest in making and investing money – often with considerable success; financial risks may well be taken, and are likely to pay off with greater than average success. Depending on influences from elsewhere in the BIRTH-CHART, there can however be blind optimism, leading to overinvestment and loss. Money will be freely spent on creating a comfortable, even luxurious home, on entertaining friends – and on the partner (sometimes under the sad impression that love can be bought).

Jupiter in the THIRD HOUSE

As the planet of the mind, Jupiter in the Geminian house will strengthen the need to exercise and use the intellect, and challenges in this area will be enthusiastically met. There will be an equally strong urge to share opinions and to shape those of others, and excellent communication techniques will be freely used to this end. Happily, this is joined to a strong sense of justice and the need to see that it is available to all. Restlessness may be a problem, especially if indicated in other areas of the birth-chart. The need to ingest knowledge will probably lead to the person with Jupiter in this house to continue to study long after formal education has ended. There will be a need for freedom of movement, for both physical and mental mobility.

Jupiter in the FOURTH HOUSE

There will be an admirable warm, affectionate and realistic attitude to the upbringing of children, and the home should be one in which any child will be happy. This may well stem from the happy childhood experiences of the person with Jupiter in the fourth house, who may have had a positive and comfortable relationship with his or her own parents. There may be a somewhat sentimental attitude towards the family, though not a damagingly maudlin one. Money will not be of prime importance, and where security is concerned it may turn out that the home itself, possibly with a house improved by enlargement and care, will be the best of possible investments.

Jupiter in the FIFTH HOUSE

Overenthusiasm may affect and possibly be a disadvantage in almost every area of the life of a person with Jupiter in the fifth house. At best, if kept under control, it will be an advantage – at worst it will mean that the individual may take undue risks and run into trouble through seizing opportunities and putting plans into action before they are ripe. A liking for gambling – even an obsession with it – is an equal possibility. But there will be an enormous zest for and enjoyment of life, and as far as the love life is concerned the individual is likely to have an above-average number of partners (not necessarily, however, at the same time). There will be great pleasure in children, and an excellent relationship with them.

Jupiter in the SIXTH HOUSE

There is likely to be a concern with the physical health of the body, with this placing of Jupiter. The metabolism is likely to be low, and overindulgence in food and wine may lead to problems with weight (and subsequently problems with losing weight). There could also be problems with the liver. Needless to say, smoking is specially to be avoided. Too much work may have an equally deleterious physical effect, and regular exercise is highly desirable, together with a disciplined lifestyle, which should make it possible to avoid all these difficulties. Psychologically, there will be generosity of spirit, a genuine desire to help others, and a contagious optimism.

Jupiter in the SEVENTH HOUSE

The attitude to the love life and to personal relationships will be important, but may be rather offhand. Enthusiasm for the idea of partnership and the challenge of finding and capturing a partner will tempt someone with Jupiter in the seventh house to premature affairs; there will be high expectations of success and pleasure. These may be disappointed, and then the partner will be quickly dropped, on the grounds that there is a better chance of pleasure and success with someone else. If a partnership is to last there must be consideration for the feelings of the other, and the subject's potential for enthusiasm must be shared, on the intellectual as well as the physical plane. A partner who leads rather than following will have the best chance of imposing success.

Jupiter in the EIGHTH HOUSE

There is the prospect of an extremely active and happy sex life, provided that the partner of the person with this placing of Jupiter shares an enthusiasm for that pastime and is happy to indulge it. Considerable demands are likely to be made in this area of life, and if for some reason they are not met there will be an equally high degree of frustration and dissatisfaction, and in that case it is highly probable that a solution to the problem will be found outside the partnership. There is, in any event, a strong love of freedom, and attempts to restrict this are likely to be unsuccessful and negative. The financial effect of Jupiter working from the eighth house should not be underestimated, especially if the planet is well ASPECTED.

Jupiter in the NINTH HOUSE

A positive outlook on life is joined by breadth of vision and a healthily positive imagination; there will be a love of travel, both intellectual and physical. This will be joined by an interest in languages, and probably a talent for learning them. Promising intellectual potential should be developed, for the need to study and acquire knowledge will be important. Versatility may be accompanied by a tendency to restlessness (especially if Jupiter is in a FIRE SIGN).

Jupiter in the TENTH HOUSE

The person with Jupiter in the tenth house will seize every opportunity and make the most of it; he or she will also create opportunities, and dramatic flair will give them a distinct advantage in presenting ideas to colleagues, though they must be careful not to act in such a way that they appear over-dramatic and self-important. There will be an ability to grasp an overall view of things, and to estimate the future effect of present decisions with a high degree of practicality. Ambition will be strong, and as success comes wisdom will grow with it. This is a house position much associated with acting – whether professional or amateur!

Jupiter in the ELEVENTH HOUSE

A natural enthusiasm and ability to turn it to effect in work and at play will result in the person with this house placing of Jupiter enjoying both activities – and inspiring others to do so. A strongly social animal, he or she will have a large circle of friends and acquaintances and contribute a great deal to any groups to which they belong. They will be strongly attracted to social work, for the needy of every variety, and make excellent friends, always ready with help and advice – sometimes very challenging advice. The attitude to love is in general rather cool, and it is sometimes the case that friendship is more important.

Jupiter in the TWELFTH HOUSE

A philosophical approach to life, together with a sense of vocation, may make those with this house placing of Jupiter seem rather cool – and indeed there can be a tendency to keep themselves very much to themselves. They usually need to work alone under solitary conditions. Attention should be paid to staying in touch with reality. A sense of religious vocation is not unlikely, though a sense of dedication can apply to any set of circumstances – for instance in the medical profession; work which produces some concrete effect – a painting, a book, a piece of sculpture – is also possible.

* * *

Juste, David French historian and scholar. Engaged in research into medieval (Latin) astrology and all aspects of medieval and early modern culture, science and magic, including studies of MSS. At present working on *The Uses of Astrology, AD 1200–1700*. Has completed two books cataloguing the astrological MSS in the Bayerische Staatsbibliotek in Munich and the Bibliothèque nationale de France in Paris. Publication: *Les Alchandreana primitifs: Etude sur les plus anciens traités astrologiques latins d'origine arabe*.

Jyotish *see* VEDIC ASTROLOGY

– K –

karma The effect of past actions, including those from previous incarnations, on our present lives. As we live through a number of earthly lives, our actions shape future incarnations. The term is much used in ESOTERIC ASTROLOGY, when astrologers consider the BIRTH-CHART as an indication of the problems or circumstances with which the subject has to deal in the life which is just beginning. *See* VEDIC ASTROLOGY.

Katarchic astrology The setting up of an astrological chart for the start of a project in order to estimate its chances of success and/or discuss how to develop it.

Kepler, Johann (1571–1630) German astronomer and astrologer, professor of mathematics at Graz, then (1600) assistant to Tycho BRAHE at Prague, succeeding him as court astronomer to the emperor Rudolf II. Much of what is known about his early years comes from the astrological diary that he kept. At Graz he published four annual almanacs, for which he was paid 20 florins each (his salary was only 150 florins a year). In his first almanac (1594) he predicted very cold weather and an invasion by the Turks; both events occurred – it was so cold (he told a correspondent) that people died of it, and when they blew their noses, those noses fell off. Meanwhile promptly on 1 January the Turks marched in, destroying much of the country between Vienna and Neustadt.

　　He was not a conventional astrologer of his time. He took a great interest in planetary HARMONICS, based on the ASPECTS, which formed a basis of his *Harmonice Mundi*, or *Harmony of the World*. His general theory is to be found in *On the More Certain Fundamentals of Astrology* (1601), in which he writes of the effects of the planets not only on human life but on terrestrial weather. He was eager that statistical evidence should be produced to establish a definite connection between terrestrial events and the movements of the planets. He himself kept careful records – over 800 horoscopes calculated and drawn by his own hand have survived, including those of the Emperor Augustus and the Prophet Muhammad. He was the first astrologer to propose the importance of the now familiar astrological aspects, and proposed a number of new ones, including the QUINDECILE and the QUINTILE. These emerged from his interest in numerology, and he used them in his astrological work as adjuncts to the traditional ones.

keywords Astrologers, especially when teaching, use 'keywords' to describe the principal functions or characteristics of signs, planets and houses – a useful shorthand. There are different keywords for the SIDEREAL and tropical systems of astrology, but many are similar. The following are those devised by Julia Parker, using the TROPICAL ZODIAC:

The signs

- Aries – assertively, urgently, forthrightly, selfishly
- Taurus – possessively, permanently
- Gemini – communicatively, adaptably, restlessly, versatilely
- Cancer – protectively, sensitively, moodily
- Leo – impressively, creatively, powerfully
- Virgo – critically, analytically, carpingly
- Libra – harmoniously, sympathetically, resentfully
- Scorpio – intensely, passionately, jealously
- Sagittarius – philosophically, freely, exploratively, high-handedly
- Capricorn – prudently, aspiringly, calculatedly, grumblingly
- Aquarius – independently, humanely, distantly
- Pisces – nebulously, impressionably, deceitfully

The planets

- Sun – self-expression, vitality
- Moon – response, instinct, intuition, fluctuation, emotion
- Mercury – mind, communication
- Venus – harmony, unison, love
- Mars – physical energy, initiative
- Jupiter – expansion
- Saturn – stability, restriction, limitation, control

- Uranus – change, disruption, shock
- Neptune – cloudiness, unreality
- Pluto – elimination, eruptive change

The houses

- First – psychological motivation, wellbeing
- Second – possessions, feelings
- Third – brothers, sisters, transport, environment, early education
- Fourth – home, domesticity, parents (especially mother)
- Fifth – creativity, pleasure, children, romance, risk-taking, the father
- Sixth – health, diet, exercise, hobbies, routine work
- Seventh – partnerships, relationships
- Eighth – sex, inheritance, investment
- Ninth – higher education, travel, ideals, challenge, dreams
- Tenth – aspirations and ambitions
- Eleventh – social life, objectives, social conscience, friends
- Twelfth – seclusion, escapism, faith, institutions

Koch house system A system of HOUSE DIVISON advocated by Walter Koch, who derived it from Fiedrich Zanzinger and Heinz Specht. It was first published in 1971, and is a complicated version of PLACIDUS. Like most other systems, other than EQUAL HOUSE, it is inapplicable in northern latitudes, only working indeed between 66° north and 66° south.

Krafft, Karl Ernst (1900–45) Born in Switzerland, Krafft took a degree in mathematics and, fascinated with astrology from his childhood, worked in Germany for ten years on a book which was to establish a way of predicting an individual's future based on an astrological study of his or her personality. He had made himself well known by the time the National Socialists came to power, and in the autumn of 1939 wrote to an acquaintance, Dr Heinrich Fesel, who was on the staff of Reichsführer-SS Heinrich Himmler, warning him that there would be an attempt on HITLER'S life between 7 and 10 November – 'possibility of an attempt of assassination by the use of explosive material'. When a bomb exploded in a Munich beer-cellar on 8

November, just after Hitler had addressed a meeting there, Krafft was arrested by the Gestapo on suspicion of planting the bomb. He was able to prove that he had nothing to do with the assassination attempt, and was released. In 1940 he was engaged by Dr Josef Goebbels (the propaganda minister) to work on a new translation of the prophesies of NOSTRADAMUS, with a view to showing that that ancient prognosticator prophesied success for the Axis. Krafft had no difficulty in doing this, and leaflets bearing Nostradamus' positive view of the Reich were dropped all over Europe.

There has been much discussion of a possible connection between Krafft and Hitler himself. It appears that they never met, and what evidence there is from the Führer's table talk suggests that he discounted astrology. However, there is a record that in spring, 1940, Krafft prepared a copy of Hitler's BIRTH-CHART and an interpretation, which was given to an aide, and Krafft used to claim that he had advised the leader to postpone his attack on the USSR for some months, with, initially, some success.

Nemesis caught up with Krafft when in 1941 Rudolf Hess suddenly flew to Britain, apparently with an offer of a peace settlement. Some excuse had to be found for the Deputy Führer's action, and it was put about that he – who indeed had been a devotee of Krafft's – had been 'crazed by astrology'. There was a huge purge of astrologers and occultists and Krafft was imprisoned for a year before being released to work on the horoscopes of members of the Allied High Command. One of his statements was that the chart of General Montgomery was 'certainly stronger' than that of Rommel. The psychological pressure on Krafft appears to have affected the balance of his mind; he was rash enough to prophesy that bombs would soon destroy Geobbels' propaganda ministry in Berlin. The Gestapo arrested him for treason, and the almost instantaneous destruction of the ministry was of no assistance to the astrologer, who died (of typhus fever) in the train which was carrying him to Buchanwald concentration camp. *See also* WOHL, Louis de.

Krusinsky house system A system of HOUSE DIVISION published in Poland in 1995, based on a circle passing through the ASCENDANT and the ZENITH, divided into twelve sections, and projected to the ECLIPTIC through MERIDIAN circles.

– L –

Lambe, John (d.1628) At first a private tutor in Worcestershire, Lambe briefly studied medicine, and then decided there was money to be made by setting up as a general magician and astrologer. In 1607 he was tried for practising against Lord Windsor of Bromsgrove and attempting to kill him by magical means. He was found guilty, but his alleged victim's continued good health (he lived another 40 years) secured his release. His astrology was somewhat outweighed by his supposed magical powers, and a year later he was rearrested, accused of raising impious spirits and successfully predicting the death of several people. He was again imprisoned and sent do the dungeons of Worcester Castle, but when a number of men concerned with his trial died, the terrified authorities arranged for his transfer to King's Bench prison in London, where he lived comfortably for 15 years, receiving clients in his cell – including the Duke of Buckingham. In June 1623, he was found guilty of seducing an 11-year-old girl – but freed, presumably as a result of Buckingham's patronage. He shared the Duke's unpopularity, and, accused of magically procuring virgins for Buckingham's pleasure, was attacked by a crowd as he left a theatre, and so severely beaten that he died.

latitude The latitude of any place on Earth is its distance north or south of the equator. The equator marks 0° latitude, and the latitude lines drawn around the Earth are measured from it by degrees, minutes and seconds. Used with the lines of LONGITUDE, lines of latitude can give a precise location to any point on Earth. CELESTIAL LATITUDE is the distance of any planet north or south of the ECLIPTIC.

latitude celestial *see* CELESTIAL LATITUDE

laxative According to *The Secret of Secrets*, a lost text by Aristotle, laxatives should never be taken unless the Moon is in Scorpio, Libra or Pisces; if one is taken when it is in Capricorn, the result will be severe constipation. *See* ALEXANDER THE GREAT.

legal action against astrology *see* ALAN, WILLIAM FREDERICK

Lehman, J Lee (b.1953) American astrologer and historian, especially interested in classical HORARY technique and in attempting to recover the obscured methods of PTOLEMY and other ancient astrologers. She has been research director of the National Council for Geocosmic Research, and has written especially on the asteroids, producing the first EPHEMERIDES of a number of them. Among her books are *The Ultimate Asteroid Book* (1988), *Essential Dignities* (1989) and *The Book of Rulerships* (1992).

Leo ♌

The fifth sign of the zodiac, Sun-sign period 23 July–23 August.

It should be remembered when reading of the characteristics of the Sun-signs that these will always be affected by the effects of the rising-sign, the planets in various other signs and houses, and the relationships the planets make to each other.

General characteristics

The ability to lead, to command, to organize other people's lives as well as their own, are primary characteristics of those with the Sun in Leo. These people will make the most of their lives, and do their best to encourage others to do the same – thereby running the risk of being considered inter-fering if not domineering (and these are indeed possibilities, though they will be willing slaves to those they admire). Kings and queens of their own particular area of life, they will make the most of their resources, psycho-logical, intellectual and material. Naturally creative, they must express their creativity in some form or another if they are to be psychologically healthy. Ambitious, they need to do things in a big way, and will be eager for material success in order that they may do so – though a happy lifestyle need not be an extravagant one, as long as it is comfortable. The Leo sense of drama can result in exaggerated self-promotion and the suggestion that they know best about everything, which can occasionally prove not to be the case. Their fiery enthusiasm is contagious, however, and is freely expressed in every area of life, not least romantically.

The growing child

Energetic exuberance can make a Leo child an extremely tough proposition for any parent who cannot match it – and also control it, for if it is not to a degree controlled, the child will eventually become exhausted and tetchy. From the earliest age he or she will marshal friends and tell them which are the best games to play, and how to play them – a diminutive five-year-old may be seen informing an eight-year-old where to stand and what to do. This does not always make him or her popular. Later, however, it will be so obvious that Leo is good at organization, and gets good results, that others will fall into line and happily obey. The tendency to show off, present in all Leo children, must be tactfully curtailed. They are willing to accept that other children must be given a chance to shine – but a suggestion that they might shine more brightly than Leo will *not* be welcome. Praise is important to a Leo child, and parents who do not reward them in this way will not get good results, especially when discipline becomes necessary. Criticism is never welcome, for the Leo self-confidence can be surprisingly susceptible, and can crash under the pressure of harsh criticism or ridicule.

Education

Teachers who do not recognize that, beneath the sometimes brashly self-confident manner of a Sun-sign Leo child there is not only promise but a rather under-developed sense of self-confidence, will miss out on the opportunity to help the child and young student to develop. Sometimes overassertive, the student will be utterly deflated by too sharply or unkindly administered criticism. Basically honest and straightforward, they will react positively if criticism is rational and kindly rather than destructive, and their reaction to encouragement and firm direction is second to none – they profit enormously from being exposed to the creativity of others, which will stimulate their own strongly creative instincts. A Leo child who becomes interested in a particular subject when young will be extremely unlikely to turn away from it, and it will be likely to remain important to him and her for a lifetime. It is important to distinguish between determination and stubbornness, which the Leo child itself can sometimes confuse.

Friendship, romance and sex

Leos are eager to make friends, but are by no means quick to do so. They accept people on face value, in whatever strata of life, but an acquaintance will be tried and tested before being called a friend. When admitted to that rôle, however, Leo's enthusiastic attitude to friends translates into a desire to encourage enjoyment of life in every possible way. This involves generosity on a scale which can sometimes be embarrassing – and a new friend will often be somewhat discomfited by the way in which a Leo can sweep one off one's feet, making decisions without much consultation, and taking command of an outing or a proposed meeting in a way which can be overpowering. Romantically, the same can be true: the romance will be of Hollywood proportions, prompting the question whether so much enthusiasm can really be sincere. It almost always is. Sexually, as in everything else, Leo likes to be admired; criticism of a perhaps too smothering technique will not be welcome. Leo tends to put the loved one on a pedestal; few can permanently keep their balance, but if they fall the effect on the Leo will be far more damaging than to themselves.

Permanent partnership and family

Intensely loyal, generous and magnanimous, with an almost too charitable and trusting nature, Leo has qualities which should make for great success in partnership. The fact that this is not always the case may be due to several factors: the trusting nature may lead to a partnership with someone who does not merit that trust. The tendency to admire and look up to a partner can lead to disillusion and disappointment when the partner proves to be all too human. It is also the case that the Leo propensity to take charge, to take the lead in every area of a partnership, is not always helpful, and unless the Leo is prepared to be tactful and reject any idea of domination, and unless care is taken to give way from time to time in arguments, there is likely to be trouble. This may be especially true where the partner is noticeably weaker in asserting him- or herself, for that partner's confidence can then be completely destroyed. The managerial talents of Leos can be of enormous value in a partnership however, from arranging the family's finances to organizing a good party or holiday – though the tendency to extravagance can tend to be a problem in both cases.

Occupation

A dull, routine job which does not allow Leo to show flair and enthusiasm and display a talent for organizational ability and showmanship is the last thing to be considered. A young Leo just starting work will want and need to be able to show what he or she is capable of, and will be ambitious to start climbing the ladder to success, and without delay. Sun-sign Leos are not afraid of work, and do not expect others to lag behind, so they are usually employees who can be depended upon, and are employers who insist on a dependable and hard-working workforce. They need to be emotionally involved with their work, and if this is difficult they will contrive some way of becoming involved; the most menial task will be interesting to them as long as they can see their way to perform it better than someone else, or to make it in some way significant.

High standards and quality are important to them, and they will polish every surface – whether of a speech, an article, a car or a performance of some kind – until it dazzles. Their powerful creative urge serves them well if they are employed in the arts; if they are in the public eye they will ensure that they are impressive both in appearance and in the execution of whatever task is expected of them.

Health

The spine and the heart are both associated with Leo, and attention should be paid to both. A somewhat sluggish circulation can have difficulty in coping with cold weather, while bad posture can have a weakening effect on the spine. It is particularly important for Leos to take regular exercise to encourage the circulation and maintain the heart in good condition – perhaps dancing is the best option, and can also be good for the posture and therefore for the spine, though Leos in general tend in any event to have naturally good posture. When they settle on a regime of exercise that suits them, they will follow it for many years, getting to know their body well, and understanding how best to treat it in order to retain mobility. They will need to take care that they do not over-exercise, for they are highly competitive and will want to be among the leaders of the pack in, for instance, running or even jogging. Leo rules the thymus, which is connected with immunization and the repelling of bacteria; Sun-sign Leos should take advantage of every possible inoculation, especially before travelling. Preventative medicine is on the whole of particular value to them.

Finance

Naturally cautious where investment is concerned, Sun-sign Leos will look askance at vigorously-touted investment schemes promising high financial returns, and will much prefer something well-tried and safe. Having often worked particularly hard to get some capital together, they will be extremely reluctant to risk it, and will be likely to take a lower return on their money rather than invest in anything remotely redolent of a get-rich-quick scheme. They like the best of everything, and from time to time will splash out on something too beautiful and impressive to resist; but at the same time will carefully weigh the effect of the expense on their savings scheme. They are unlikely to spend a lot of money on a second-rate purchase, however useful it might be; they will prefer to save until they can buy the best model on the market. (Even when young, they will prefer a good coffee and cake in an up-market café to a complete meal from some take-away joint.) They will start investing in property as soon as possible, though when affordable, they also particularly enjoy investing in jewellery or *objets d'art* – and the only gamble which might conceivably appeal would be to put money in a theatrical show.

Growing older

The main problem facing Leos as they grow older is knowing when to stop. This is true in almost every area of life – most dangerously perhaps in exercise, for they will want to keep mobile and fit for as long as possible, and may well overdo exercise by insisting on maintaining when they are 75 the régime of exercise they worked out for themselves 50 years previously. A good instructor who can advise a slow amelioration of exercise will be well worth consulting. No Leo will enjoy the idea of retirement – particularly of relinquishing a position for which he or she has worked hard, and in which much has been achieved. In fact, retirement from a job will not mean retirement in any sense understood by those with other Sun-signs, for Leos will have plenty to occupy their time – they will certainly over the years have become skilful in what others would call hobbies, but which for Leos are mini-careers. They will also certainly not want to relinquish their positions on the several committees or organizations with which they have become involved; it will take a unanimous vote to expel them – and it is highly likely that they will not only find a way around that, but will end up by taking over the committee.

Leo as rising-sign

Here is, all too often, an indication of the Leo autocrat, the biggest fish in the pond, who will be all too ready to demonstrate just how admirable and valuable he or she is to society in general. It is likely, in fact, that this brilliant and showy exterior is all camouflage, disguising secret feelings of inferiority, or certainly lack of confidence. Leos who do not come to terms with this problem are all too likely to become depressed and even more lacking in confidence, especially if by their manner they alienate the very people with whom they would like to be on good terms. All these things may be true of someone with a Leo Sun – but with Leo rising the problems are exacerbated and the solution more difficult to achieve. In emotional relationships the Leo needs a partner to admire and who will continually surprise them, someone who is an achiever in their own way. The Leo may expect too much of them, and any disappointment will rankle and may damage the partnership.

Traditional associations

- Ruling Planet – the Sun
- Triplicity/Element – fire
- Quadruplicity/Quality – fixed
- Colours – the colours of the Sun from dawn to dusk
- Gemstone – ruby
- Metal – gold
- Flowers – sunflowers, marigolds
- Trees – palm, orange, lemon, laurel
- Herbs and Spices – saffron, peppermint, rosemary
- Foodstuffs – rice, honey, crops and vines in general
- Animals – big game, especially the cat family
- Countries – South of France, Italy, Greece, Jamaica, Pakistan, Switzerland, Romania, Sicily, S. Korea
- Cities – Rome, Prague, Bombay, Madrid, Miami, Philadelphia, Chicago, Los Angeles, Boston, Bath, Bristol
- US States – Colorado, Hawaii, Missouri, New York.

* * *

Leo, Alan *see* ALAN, WILLIAM FREDERICK

Libra ♎

The seventh sign of the zodiac. SUN-SIGN period 23 September–23 October.

It should be remembered when reading of the characteristics of the Sun-signs that these will always be affected by the effects of the rising-sign, the planets in various other signs and houses, and the relationships the planets make to each other.

General characteristics

The symbol of the sign – the balance – describes very well the major attributes of those with the Sun in the sign of Libra when they are born. Balance and harmony are very important to them, and indeed are vital to their psychological and physical wellbeing. It is important in their relationship to those around them. They need to react comfortably to other people, and particularly to be comfortable within a personal relationship. It is only when they are settled in a relationship that they will feel whole – and their need for one is so strong that they sometimes commit themselves prematurely. Keeping the peace is so important that they will be all things to all people, fearing that any disagreement will disturb the equilibrium of their lives. Sitting on the fence is safer than coming down on one side or the other, and thus perhaps upsetting someone. For the same reason they can endlessly equivocate, waiting to see 'how things turn out' rather than making a decision, however obvious the solution to a question or a problem may be. Their often extraordinary personal charm permits them to get away with this. They make good parents, but again will try to shift the necessity for every decision onto the other partner. Health-wise, the kidneys may be slightly susceptible – at the sign of recurrent headaches, these should be checked. Normally their well-balanced lives keep them healthy.

The growing child

Libran children will show great charm from a very early age, and realize how they can use it. With a tendency to laziness, they will persuade others – including their peers – to do things for them, and whenever possible devote their own time to taking life easily. They will make procrastination into a fine art, and if there is the possibility of passing time away by sitting in front of the television, indiscriminately watching everything that appears on the screen, they will seize it. They are generous and kind, and will delight in pleasing everyone with whom they come into contact, but they may be slow to fix on any one favourite activity or pastime – unless it is daydreaming, which they will enjoy at any and every age. Decisiveness is not a quality natural to them; asked to choose between two, or a number of alternatives they will whenever possible shuffle the decision off onto someone else, lacking the confidence to make a decision.

Education

The children in whose horoscope the Sun is in Libra will not necessarily be unhappy at school, but the minor injustices which are bound to occur from time to time will upset them unduly. 'But it's not *fair*!' will be an all too common phrase, and the lesson that life is *not* always fair will be hardly learned. There should be creative potential, but it will have to be coaxed from the Libran child, for left to itself it will only develop slowly. In further education the major problem will be with laziness, or if not precisely that, with procrastination – 'always put off to tomorrow what you could do today' is all too frequently the motto. There may also be problems when it comes to choosing the course to follow, the subject to read at university, the area in which to specialize. In all these matters Librans will look for advice, and will not always wisely choose those to whom they turn for it.

Friendship, romance and sex

Librans enjoy relaxing and enjoying themselves, and are good at persuading others to do the same. What they are not good at is deciding just *how* to enjoy themselves; they rely often on joining in what others are enjoying – which is no problem as long as the friends are ready to organize every evening out, and make every decision. Shared interests will be very much enjoyed, and there is much to be said for a friend with whom the Libran has a hobby in common. A friend who lets a Libran down, however, even in the most innocent way, will not soon be allowed to forget it. Librans tend to fall in love easily and often; they believe every compliment an attractive wooer pays them, and in love with love accept every declaration at face value. Ironically, hesitant in making every other decision in life, they will rush into a love affair with impetuous speed. Not usually highly sexed, they easily succumb to admiration, and a determined wooer who treats them with the right degree of romantic fervour will not find the bedroom door too firmly locked.

Permanent partnership and family

Normally hesitant to make up their mind, Librans are psychologically so in need of a permanent partner that their hesitancy deserts them once they have convinced themselves they have met the right person. In a lasting relationship, Libra needs to be continually reminded that he or she is loved – and will still demand more admiration. So deep is this need to know they are truly loved that they will sometimes engineer a quarrel in order to be absolutely sure that the partner loves them sufficiently to bear any criticism or nagging, and be ready to kiss and make up. This can be dangerous ground. Generous, even overgenerous, to a partner, they can give the impression that they are trying to buy his or her affection. Librans make easy-going parents, encouraging their children to exercise good manners and charm, but often incapable of making a decision when asked to do so, inviting the child to ask the other partner, or sending them to the partner for punishment. A child is likely to learn very early on that twisting a Libran parent around the little finger is exceptionally easy.

Occupation

Librans will be perhaps most successful in small businesses, where they can get to know the people around them. They hate loneliness, and need the comfort of a circle of familiar friends or colleagues. They work well with these, encouraging and complimenting them, and getting the best out of them. Any occupation which requires them to spend a lot of time alone will not be good for them. This means that sometimes promotion actually damages their psychological attitude to their work, for it can mean a degree of loneliness if the position is one in which they have authority over others. They work well with a single partner – preferably one who is good at the financial aspect of business, leaving the Libran to exercise charm and diplomacy on the patrons or customers. Emotionally involved in their work, they can be somewhat uncharacteristically ambitious, and there will be no sign of the laid-back laziness which otherwise marks them out. They are often at home in glamour industries such as fashion or hairdressing and beauty.

Health

Librans generally have excellent control over their energy, and expend it evenly and steadily. They sometimes neglect their need for exercise, which is considerable – if it is neglected, they can put on weight very easily. An excess of good food and wines (especially sweet food), to which they are somewhat addicted, can have the same result. The Libran metabolism is generally speaking low, and if there is to be any pleasure in exercising (and it will by no means be popular) it must appeal – so membership of a really good health club, where there is a social life attached to working out, and where there is a suite of saunas or steam-baths and the availability of masseurs and masseuses, will be an excellent idea. Otherwise, exercising with friends is an equally good idea – and this will appeal to the Libran competitive spirit, which is quite strong and is well expressed in competitive sports. The Libran body area is the kidneys, which should be checked if any symptoms suggest an upset – an unusual number of headaches, for instance.

Finance

Librans enjoy a comfortable lifestyle, and take pleasure both in making and spending money – the second exercise depending, of course, on the success of the first. They are not much interested in money as such, and the idea of spending hours calculating which shares to sell and which to buy would bore them to distraction; good, reliable financial advisers are therefore both necessary and desirable. From time to time they may get excited by the idea of some money-making scheme; they should consult their adviser before indulging – and if they have none, they should at least weigh up all the aspects of the enterprise in which they are interested, and invest only on the understanding that they put in the amount of money they can afford to lose, if things go wrong. They are all too easily persuaded to put their trust in agreeable friends, and where money is concerned should be extremely careful about this. Balance is as important in this area of their lives as any other, and they should refrain from putting all their financial eggs in one basket.

Growing older

Librans may well look forward to retirement with more pleasurable antici-pation than anyone with another Sun-sign. In theory, the idea of long days without the petty problems of everyday work and with nothing whatsoever to do will appeal enormously. The reality, of course, will be very different, and unless Libra contrives some occupation or other he or she will very soon be driven mad with boredom. It is quite possible that the spare-time occupations which they have built over the years may, as time goes by, be difficult to maintain – those which require a high mobility, for instance – though both Libran men and women enjoy judo, and there are forms of this which can be happily maintained in old age. New, enjoyable hobbies will release fresh areas of potential to be employed and enjoyed. It is *not* a good idea for Librans to plan to move locality, or even house, when they retire – this will be extremely disorientating and stressful, and should be avoided unless the benefits are really overwhelming.

Libra as rising-sign

The need for a really firm and happy permanent relationship becomes paramount when Libra is the rising-sign, and the Libran male and female will be strongly drawn towards achieving this. The need openly to express affection is less vital, however, which may have a negative effect on courtship. The Libran polar sign, Aries, will make these people more interested in sex and more energetic and enthusiastic in pursuing sexual satisfaction than those with a Libran Sun; this can have a positive effect on a permanent partnership in which he or she requires the admiration of a partner – but there may be an element of selfishness in this as in other areas of a Libra-rising personality. The fire of Aries will nevertheless be a delightful surprise to a partner who has got used, during courtship, to the idea of the partner as a slightly hesitant person, poor at making decisions of any kind. When Libra rises it tends to inject an element of self-satisfaction into the character.

Traditional associations
- Ruling Planet – Venus
- Triplicity/Element – air
- Quadruplicity/Quality – cardinal
- Colours – shades of blue – from pale to ultramarine, pinks, pale greens
- Gemstones – sapphire, jade

- Metal – copper, sometimes bronze
- Flowers – blue flowers, hydrangea, large roses
- Trees – ash, poplar
- Herbs and Spices – mint, arrack, cayenne
- Foodstuffs – tomato, pear, asparagus, beans
- Animals – lizards and small reptiles
- Countries – Austria, Burma, Japan, Argentina, Upper Egypt, China, Nigeria
- Cities – Copenhagen, Johannesburg, Vienna, Venice, Lisbon, Frankfurt, Nottingham
- US States – No traditionally associated signs

* * *

lights The term sometimes used to describe the Sun or Moon.

Lilith A HYPOTHETICAL PLANET sometimes described as the Black Moon, supposed to be invisible except when it passes between the Earth and the Sun (and even then never yet observed by astronomers). An EPHEMERIS has nevertheless been produced showing its supposed positions. It has been referred to as the Dark Moon, and said to be an evil planet bringing temptation and ruling abortion and stillbirth.

Lilly, William (1602–81) One of the best known of all English astrologers, the author of *CHRISTIAN ASTROLOGY* (1647), the first comprehensive astro-logical textbook to be published in English. Many of its precepts are still followed by 21st-century astrologers, especially in the field of HORARY ASTROLOGY, in which he specialized. Born in Diseworth, Leicestershire, he began to study astrology in London in 1627, as the result of the chance reading of an almanac. He became the most famous astrologer of his time, credited with predicting the great plague of 1665, during which he remained in London to succour the sick, and the following year with predicting the Great Fire of London (1666) – so accurately that he was later arrested and accused of starting the fire in order to fulfil his prediction (*see* KRAFFT). He published best-selling annual almanacs which made him rich, and became a confidant to many influential men, including Elias ASHMOLE and Bulstrode Whitelocke. He took an interest in the politics of his time, and addressed such questions as 'If Presbytery shall stand'. During the Civil War he adhered to the Commonwealth side, and successfully predicted the defeat of the Royalist army at Naseby and Colchester in 1645 and 1648. At the same time however, he privately advised King Charles I, and was instrumental in procuring a hacksaw with which the King attempted to escape from imprisonment on the Isle of Wight. Though he had always been a Parliamentarian, he was revolted by the execution of the King (he is the only man to claim to know the identity of the axeman who executed Charles). He was twice called before Parliamentary committees and twice imprisoned as a result of the complaints of Presbyterians: his strong opinions were often voiced against Fifth Monarchists and Levellers.

After the Restoration he settled in Hersham, in Surrey, and practised there and in London as a consultant astrologer, charging between half a crown and 40 or 50 pounds according to the depth of his clients' pockets, who included MPs and members of the aristocracy, as well as ordinary people. He also taught astrology, which he insisted was not fatalistic (his motto was *Non cogunt* – 'the stars incline but do not foretell.' His horary work was considered especially reliable, though he was bitterly attacked by some churchmen on the grounds that this form of astrology was irreligious. He was, however, deeply religious himself; in his famous Preface to *Christian Astrology,* entitled 'An Epistle to the Student in Astrology', he advises his readers to 'consider and admire thy Creator, be thankfull unto him, and be humble, and let no naturall knowledge, how profound and transcendant soever it be, elate thy mind to neglect that Divine Privodence by whose al-seeing order and appointment all things heavenly and earthly have their constant motion … the more holy thou art, and more neer to God, the purer judgement thou shalt give.' His advice is such that graduates of one astrological teaching body (the Faculty of Astrological Studies in the UK) are presented with a copy, which among things instructs them to 'be faithfull, tenacious, betray no ones secrets. Instruct all men to live well: be a good example thyself … be not dismayed if evil spoken of …' (he himself was caricatured as Sidrophel by Samuel BUTLER in *Hudibras*).

Towards the end of his life he studied medicine, which had always fascinated him, secured a licence to practise, and worked as a general practitioner – though he continued to do occasional astrological work, and in 1673 was consulted by Charles II about his future relationship with Parliament. He died on 23 March 1681, and was buried at Walton-upon-Thames.

local time Local time is that for a particular MERIDIAN, and differs by four minutes for every one degree of LONGITUDE. *See* STANDARD TIME.

long ascension The planets of long ascension are those that take longer to ascend than others: in northern latitudes Cancer, Leo, Virgo, Libra, Scorpio and Sagittarius. The other six are of long ascension in the southern hemisphere.

longitude A point of longitude marks the distance of a place east or west of Greenwich, England, expressed in degrees, minutes and seconds and measured along a line of LATITUDE. Opposite to the Greenwich line of latitude, on the other side of the Earth, is the INTERNATIONAL DATE LINE. *See also* CELESTIAL LONGITUDE.

Lord of the Horoscope *see* CHART RULER

Lord of the Nativity *see* CHART RULER

lots *see* PARTS

luminaries The Sun and Moon.

lunar calendar *see* LUNAR YEAR

lunar day The rotation period of the Moon – 27.322 Earth days.

lunar eclipse *see* ECLIPSES

lunar mansions A traditional division of the ECLIPTIC into sections, each of 12° 51′ results in a lunar HOROSCOPE consisting of 28 lunar mansions or 'houses', each of which is differently interpreted according to the planets – though chiefly the Moon – placed in them during the Moon's monthly cycle. The best-known such system is used by Hindu astrologers, the sections known as Nakshatras, and in use for at least 2,000 years. Many Hindus still name their children according to the Nakshatra in which the Moon stood at the time of the child's birth. Arabian astrologers use a system of lunar mansions called Manzils, the Chinese a system known as Sieu or Xiu. Most modern astrologers using this system only consider the position of the Moon.

lunar month A period of 29.53059 days between successive new Moons.

lunar year A year of twelve lunar months – i.e., of 354.3672 days. A lunar calendar is based on the motion of the Moon, and has a year of 354 days with a 'leap year' of 355 days, and is made up of 12 months of 29 or 30 days.

lunar zodiac It seems extremely likely that a lunar zodiac, similar to the one we know, once existed and was used by ancient astrologers, though very little material has survived to suggest how it was used. *See*, however, LUNAR MANSIONS.

lunation The time from new Moon to full Moon.

– M –

Magi, the The Magi, the three 'wise men from the East' who advised Herod of the birth of the King of the Jews because they had 'seen his star in the East', were clearly astrologer/astronomers. Herod seems to have been interested in the subject, for he 'enquired of them diligently what time the star appeared'. There has been much speculation about the star – general opinion suggests it may have been a conjunction of Jupiter and Saturn, possibly with Uranus, which would have appeared as a single very bright star moving quickly enough to fulfil the conditions of the Bible story.

Magini, Giovanni Antonio (1555–1617) Italian astrologer, astronomer and mathematician. From 1588 Professor of Mathematics at the University of Bologna, he proposed a theory of planetary movements (the planets placed in eleven rotating spheres) based on the GEOCENTRIC view of the solar system. His chief work on astrology was *De astrologica ratione* (1607). *See* PLACIDUS HOUSE SYSTEM.

malefic An archaic term meaning 'unfavourable'. It was applied to a planet considered to be up to no good in a particular HOROSCOPE. Malefic ASPECTS are the SQUARE and SEMI-SQUARE. (In the past, the OPPOSITION was considered highly malefic, but is now believed to confer strength.)

malevolents *see* MALEFIC

Manilius Antiochus (nd) A slave named by Pliny as 'the founder of Roman astrology'.

Manilius, Marcus (fl. ca. AD1–50) The author of *Astronomica*, an unfinished poem of over 4,000 lines on astronomy and astrology probably written between AD14 and AD27, during the reign of Tiberius. Manilius was the first astrological author of the Graeco-Roman world, and this is one of the two earliest substantial textbooks on astrology *(see also* VETTIUS

VALENS). The tradition of writing informative and educational books in verse now seems surprising, but Manilius shows amazing skill in versifying even the instructions for calculating a birth-chart. The text has often been translated into English (first by Thomas Creech, in the 17th century, and most recently by G P Goold, in 1977). The poet A E Housman spent many years editing it. Manilius opens by describing the zodiac signs and their characteristics and qualities. He emphasizes the effect of the signs much more emphatically than we might now expect, and at the expense of those of the planets. Rather than associating particular planets with particular signs, in the now familiar way, he brings unfamiliar gods and goddesses into the pattern, associating Aries with Minerva, Taurus with Venus, Gemini with Apollo, Cancer with Mercury, Leo with Jupiter, Virgo with Ceres, Libra with Volcanus, Scorpio with Mars, Sagittarius with Diana, Capricorn with Vesta, Aquarius with Juno and Pisces with Neptune He explains ASPECTS very clearly, and HOUSE DIVISION (he calls the houses *loci*), describes DECANS, and places heavy emphasis on the ASCENDANT or rising-sign. He is also one of the earliest astrologers to connect the signs with particular areas of the body (*see* ZODIAC MAN). He takes the view that humankind is ruled by fate: 'no one can escape from this – each must bear the burden imposed on him', although it is possible to understand it more fully with the help of astrology.

mansions *see* LUNAR MANSIONS

Mantreswara A 16th-century Hindu astrologer and author of *Phaladeepika*, an important work on JYOTISH.

Mars ♂

Mars is the fourth planet from the Sun and the nearest SUPERIOR PLANET to the Earth, orbiting the Sun every 687 days. No doubt originally because of its striking reddish colour in the night sky it has always in astrology been associated to some extent with violence and warfare. It RULES Aries and is in DETRIMENT in Libra; it is EXALTED in Capricorn and in FALL in Cancer. In modern astrology it represents human energy and the way it is used, including the sex drive. It has an influence on the red blood corpuscles and the adrenal glands, represents the masculine element in the personality of both sexes, and is related to aggression and heat – the heat of sudden anger as well as physical heat. In the right relationship to other elements of the HOROSCOPE it can represent assertive leadership and a pioneering spirit. Mars can fall in any of the twelve signs of the horoscope, irrespective of Sun-sign.

Mars and the zodiac signs

Mars in ARIES

Placed in Aries – the sign it rules – Mars is at its most powerful, and a high level of physical energy must be positively employed – perhaps in sport, but certainly in some physically demanding exercise. There is usually no shortage of enthusiasm which can be a positive aid to those with an unassertive Sun- or Moon-sign – but there is a tendency to be so enthusiastic about an idea or a concept that, in their eagerness to push ahead, these people will fail to take in all the details about it, or the instructions they are given. Patience will not be a notable quality unless contributed by some other area of the HOROSCOPE. A tendency to avoid the views, opinions and susceptibilities of others is often marked. Especially in young men and women, a tendency to be accident-prone may lead to a greater than average number of minor accidents – cuts, burns and blows to the head. The selfishness hinted at by Mars in Aries will be all too likely to show up in the love-life; the 'wham-bam-thank-you-ma'am' attitude is all too likely to be crystallized here. The tendency to be overeager may lead, embarrassingly, to premature ejaculation in the males, while women with this placing of Aries may find it all too easy to put off a partner less immediately interested in sex than themselves.

Mars in TAURUS

A temper which is usually kept under control can occasionally, given reason, erupt in considerable violence. If this does not happen all that often, when it does happen the explosion is notable. Physical and mental effort will be steadily employed in an effort to achieve a set goal, and in general there will be awareness that 'slow and steady' is the best way forward.

People with Mars in Taurus are usually fully aware that rushing at a problem or a task, or working at it in fits and starts, is not the best way for them. A set routine will be established, maintained and positively treasured, and there can even be an obsession with custom and habit. Powers of physical endurance will be high, and it will be necessary to expend physical energy in a controlled and regular way. Speed, either physical or mental, is not a marked characteristic, and the metabolism may be sluggish. Lovemaking will be leisurely, relaxed and unhurried, with an accent on foreplay. Male lovers should be notably capable of self-control, and the only real problem may be that lovers of either sex with Mars in Taurus may become the slaves of custom, and be unwilling to experiment. They should remember that variety is the spice of love.

Mars in GEMINI

Given a certain amount of ambition and a strong sense of purpose, the degree of restlessness associated with this placing should give relatively little trouble. A lively, assertive – sometimes overassertive – mind and con-siderable versatility is characteristic, and while a tendency to flit over the surface rather than examine in depth can never be discounted, the advantage of the ability to deal with a number of subjects or situations at the same time is a positive advantage. Patience is not characteristic, unless con-tributed by some other area of the HOROSCOPE, and boredom will be all too prevalent if not countered by continual changes of scene and occupation. There is a tendency to use energy unevenly, but if the individual is ambitious and purposeful this should not be too much of a problem. These people will have a ready tongue, and will never be slow to contribute to debate – often starting out asserting one opinion, and ending by arguing for the opposite one. Geminian duality must be accepted – which brings us to the love life, for with the best will in the world people with Mars in Gemini find the idea of restricting themselves for life to one partner difficult to contemplate. In bed, however, an eager appetite for variety will make for exciting, varied and highly enjoyable sex. Oral sex may be a particular pleasure.

Mars in CANCER

There is always a tremendous effort to achieve, and a combination of the energy of Mars and Cancer encourages this – though it can also result in unevenness of effort, and a strong tendency to meet pressure by working overtime and with excess energy can result in a threat to health. Under pressure, the individual may find it difficult to relax, and tension may build. Mars can instigate accidents, and this should always be remembered when even slightly dangerous work is undertaken; with the planet in Cancer, accident proneness is most likely because of overconcern for other people, and a lack of proper concern for one's own safety. People with this placing of Mars usually have a strong, intuitive sexual instinct and understanding of a partner's needs. Their vigorous but extremely loving expression of sex can be second to none as long as they are met by a partner's equal enthusiasm for its enjoyment. Lack of interest or a failure to match a partner's enthusiasm may be fatal to an otherwise positive partnership.

Mars in LEO

A natural leader with abundant enthusiasm and energy can show a worrying love of personal power and of being the centre of attention. Much energy will be spent on the career, and even more on persuading other people of the individual's success and achievements. The energetic pursuit of success should result in the achievement of personal ambitions – however high these are set – but it will be well if individuals reject the temptation to tread on others in their strong desire to reach the top, and remember that displays of bombastic dogmatism are unattractive and counterproductive. The happy knack these people have of persuading others to assist them can be wasted if the tendency to show off is not governed. What time can be spared from the relentless pursuit of success will be turned to the kind of spare-time interests by which others can be impressed – sport, or amateur theatricals, for instance. Everything said above can apply to the sex life: lovers will enjoy using mirrors to impress themselves with their own performances – but certainly the sex will be wonderfully exuberant for both lovers if not spoiled by selfishness.

Mars in VIRGO

The necessity to relax, but an accompanying difficulty in doing so, are characteristic of this placing. The high degree of nervous tension which accompanies this dichotomy can result in headaches and even migraine, which can in turn obstruct a natural love of intellectual pursuits – for which, however, time should always be made, for the individual will really enjoy puzzle-solving, and ways of using spare intellectual energy can and should be enjoyable – so it should not be impossible to discover a means of dealing with tension before it becomes positively damaging. Various physical relaxation techniques may be explored, from yoga to the simple alternative of country walks or quiet periods of reading or listening to music. Mars in Virgo makes the expression of sex somewhat cool, and certainly discriminating: those with this placing of Mars will not engage in casual pick-ups. Their partners should keep it in mind that they need careful coaxing if sexual parameters are to be extended – they are not necessarily eager to experiment.

Mars in LIBRA

The mind will be willing but the flesh may be somewhat weak: Mars is in a languid mood in Libra, and procrastination may well hinder achievement. Once motivated and encouraged by the appreciation of others, however, much can be achieved, probably helped by energy from the placing of the Sun, Moon or rising-sign. The appreciation and encouragement of friends and colleagues is important to those with Mars in Libra, and the desire to please and impress will be a strong motivation – not, however, in a self-aggrandizing way. The aggression of Mars will be toned down in Libra, though there will be a perverse tendency to provoke a quarrel simply because of the enjoyment of a good row. A positive element of this placing is the need for a happy permanent relationship, spiced by a naturally healthy and enthusiastic enjoyment of sex – though once again, however willing the mind, the desire just to lie back and enjoy the moment may mean that the partner has to work rather too hard.

Mars in SCORPIO

Both intellectual and physical energy will be high, and will constantly be challenged – in one way by the desire to rise in a profession or occupation, and in another, typically, by the enjoyment of sport and the positive need to win. Traditionally, Mars rules Scorpio, so the planet's influence from this sign is strong, and when positively expressed at work can be an enormous advantage – the sense of purpose and determination to get to the top is unparalleled. It will be important for the individual to have some way of expressing all his or her physical energy after work – sport is one obvious solution. Intuition is keen, and can be relied upon. A rewarding and fulfilling sex life is absolutely essential to those with Mars in Scorpio, and a partner who does not quickly realize that the insistent demands that will be made need to be met with equal enthusiasm will be in trouble. A possible masochistic tendency will need watching. There will almost certainly be an element of sexual jealousy, too easily aroused in either sex: that way danger lies.

Mars in SAGITTARIUS

Energy can be dissipated if the individual gives way to the attraction of versatility; a desire for experiment in various fields of endeavour can result in less positive results than if the energy is channelled into narrower fields. Challenge is important, especially physical challenge, and will be accompanied by a strong desire to succeed – this is an excellent placing for Mars in the HOROSCOPES of ambitious sportsmen and women. Again, however, ambition should be kept on track: the natural winner in one area of athletics should not give way to a sudden desire to excel in another area. Intellectual challenges will be met with equal enthusiasm; the same warning applies – a narrow field will be easier to command. There is a natural and happy tendency to enjoy life in all its aspects, with a breezy enthusiasm and a bright determination to look on the positive side of things. The sexual appetite will be voracious and enthusiastic, but the partner should avoid being too intense: for those with Mars in Sagittarius sex must above all be *fun*.

Mars in CAPRICORN

Martian energy is well controlled, disciplined and used from Capricorn; it will positively serve the will to succeed, especially when an ambition is clearly in view and progress towards it has been carefully planned. Individuals will meet difficulties with exuberance and almost with pleasure, knowing that their determination and mental strength are powerful enough to deal with most problems. These folk will excel in building up their own businesses, should the SUN- SIGN or RISING-SIGN suggest it. Promoted to a position of power they will react well, knowing that they have achieved it through their own abilities, and that a degree of personal isolation is the price to be paid. Physical energy should be positively used in sport or exercise, just as mental energy must be continually tested against any trouble that arises. Problems may arise in the bedroom because of a somewhat cool emotional level, and an apparently chilly attitude to sex, possibly together with a desire to dominate.

Mars in AQUARIUS

This placing of Mars encourages originality, experimentation and an eagerness to explore new ideas. The natural keenness to go into areas unexplored by others can become so engrossing that it leads to a degree of eccentricity, at least as seen by other people. The level of physical energy may be somewhat erratic, and is not likely to be especially high; there may be a high degree of nervous energy and a sort of tense excitability which will make true concentration difficult – especially since the individual is likely to want to experiment with many different aspects of life, exploring new ideas and attitudes. Those with this placing of Mars will be shown in a keen and eager desire to help others, often expressed in charitable work (sometimes in slightly strange ways). The word 'perversity', often associated with Mars in this sign, need not be taken too seriously in the sexual context, but sexual restlessness may lead not only to the need to experiment with different techniques, but with different partners.

Mars in PISCES

A rather low level of physical energy is countered by a rich well of emotion which, positively channelled, can help people with this placing of Mars to achieve much. It is a particularly good placing for those who enjoy physical activity linked to artistic expression – ballet, skating, dancing, for instance; such activities, if not professional, are very positive outlets of energy as simple hobbies. Consistency of effort and determination must be encouraged in a career, and it should be hoped that the SUN-SIGN, MOON- or RISING-SIGN will help by contributing a greater degree of determination than Mars is likely to contribute from Pisces. In partnership, there will be a beautifully sensual and warm attitude to sex, an instinctive sympathetic understanding of the partner's needs, and a deep desire to satisfy them. The only problem may be the low level of physical stamina – foreplay may turn out to be more enjoyable than the act itself.

Mars and the houses

Mars in the FIRST HOUSE

Mars acts strongly from the first house, and there will be a particularly assertive will to dominate. There will be little patience for anyone slower than the subject, and this can cause problems in relationships – just as self-ishness can. There will be abundant physical energy, and exercise will be important to help to use it and keep it under control. Undue haste and care-lessness can cause accidents; but if there is illness, the powers of recuperation are great.

Mars in the SECOND HOUSE

A preoccupation with wealth will in some way affect these people, who may work to acquire it or be impetuous in dispersing it, both for their own enjoyment and that of others. Sexual vigour will be directed at provoking an enthusiastic reaction from lovers, and if that is not forthcoming a relation-ship is unlikely to last, for these people need to enjoy expressing their sexuality as enthusiastically as they enjoy spending their money.

Mars in the THIRD HOUSE

Any kind of argument will be meat and drink to anyone with Mars in the third house: there will be a real pleasure in discussion, and the hotter it gets the more pleasure will be taken in joining in it. These people also enjoy making their own feelings and opinions known, and are very good at com-municating them and arousing others' interests. There will also be a positive pleasure in research: the answers to questions will be keenly and urgently sought. Urgency will communicate itself in sometimes undue speed on the roads: good driving skills are essential.

Mars in the FOURTH HOUSE

Interest in the home may express itself in almost continual redecoration, or sometimes a continual demand to move on to a house which at the moment seems more desirable. If this disturbs family life, it is connected with a desire to see the family comfortable and well housed. The importance of the family will be shown, too, in love of and care for children. The mother may be of well above average importance.

Mars in the FIFTH HOUSE

An emphasis on the love life will spring from enthusiasm for sex and an emphasis on sexual pleasure, which must be met with equal enthusiasm by a partner if there is to be a successful permanent relationship. The sex life will be fun rather than overintense, though this subject will want to take the lead. There may be an inclination for risk-taking, here as elsewhere; and an enjoyment of gambling which will match a natural enthusiasm, often shown in enjoyment of and achievement in sports.

Mars in the SIXTH HOUSE

The subject will work hard, with discipline and precision, though there may be impatience if the daily routine is too fixed and lacks variation. There may well be a critical edge to the responses to the work or attitudes of other people, though the assertiveness of Mars will probably not be as strong as when the planet is placed in other houses; indeed there will be a willingness to serve rather than lead. Physically there may be nervous reaction under stress, resulting in skin rashes or allergies.

Mars in the SEVENTH HOUSE

This placing of Mars can be helpful in personal relationships, for there will be real determination to make them work. There may be rather too much ambition to see the partner succeed, and it is possible that the subject may push a partner too hard. On the whole, however, relationships will be progressive and have a real sense of direction and purpose. Mars is never helpful where sudden quarrels are concerned, and a tendency to spark these should be watched. The sex life will be happily active.

Mars in the EIGHTH HOUSE

An unhappy and unfulfilled sex life will be a real problem for someone with Mars in the eighth house, for contentment in this area of life is essential for a balanced and happy life, and the lack of it will affect not only the partnership but other areas of life. There is likely to be an interest in business and finance, and certainly an interest in investment. There will also be a fascination with investigation of any kind – with police detective work, perhaps, but also with psychology.

Mars in the NINTH HOUSE

Intellectual challenge and adventure twin when Mars is in the ninth house; further education is almost a must, while travel – usually to places far from tourist routes – will be as essential to the psychological wellbeing of these people. Every kind of challenge will be accepted as a personal test, and great effort will be made to ensure success. If the opportunity for travel and adventure are in some way stifled, there will almost certainly be restlessness and frustration; if tension arises, relaxation techniques will offer some help.

Mars in the TENTH HOUSE

A sense of rebellion against authority, perhaps against society, may be an element when Mars is in the tenth house; on the whole, however, energy will be expended in the area of the professional life and the career, where success will be of above-average importance, and there will (or certainly should) be considerable emotional involvement. In the desire for success, hasty decisions may be made and lack of tolerance and displays of temper will be of no help with colleagues or competitors.

Mars in the ELEVENTH HOUSE

Friendship and companionship will be very important, but this will not be a particularly easy area of life, for the Martian tendency to aggression and argument can break bounds from time to time and cause problems. This may also be the case when the individual (as he and she almost inevitably will) takes the lead among a group of peers. In personal relationships great warmth should not be expected; there will be a strong desire for independence which can dampen down a real need for a partner who demands and supplies emotional closeness.

Mars in the TWELFTH HOUSE

A capacity for identifying with the problems and needs of others will often be expressed by those with Mars in the twelfth house, and this will be demonstrated either though sympathetic counselling or by actual physical or financial aid. In contrast, the individual may be rather secretive and unwilling to unburden personal problems on others. There will be a colourful inner life, often expressed through fantasy, and this will be a distinct advantage in personal relationships, for it will increase an otherwise somewhat cool emotional range.

* * *

masculine planets According to PTOLEMY the planets have both masculine and feminine qualities – for instance Mercury can be regarded as either masculine or feminine, according to whether it is linked to Gemini or Virgo (being masculine in the first case, feminine in the second), or, according to later astrologers, with another masculine or feminine planet. It has not been thought to extend this archaic idea to encompass the so-called MODERN PLANETS, but those who are interested assert that the Moon and Venus are the truly feminine planets; the Sun, Mars, Jupiter and Saturn are masculine, while Mercury is androgynous.

masculine signs The so-called masculine signs, as originally described by PTOLEMY, are Aries, Gemini, Leo, Libra, Sagittarius and Aquarius. They are also described as 'positive'.

Mashalla (ca. AD740–ca.815) A Jewish astrologer and astronomer (his full name Masha'allah ibn Atharī) who was one of the leading astrologers of his time. He wrote many books on astrology and is credibly said to have worked with other astrologers to calculate the most advantageous date for the founding of the city of Baghdad (AD762). His writing became known in the West only some centuries after his death, but little of it has survived, most in Latin or Hebrew translation.

MC *See* MEDIUM COELI or Midheaven. The abbreviation is invariably used by astrologers rather than the full title.

Mead, Richard (1673–1754) A leading physician, Vice President of the Royal Society, and author of *A treatise concerning the Influence of the Sun and Moon upon Human Bodies and the Diseases Arising Therefrom.* He asserted that the incidence of epilepsy, vertigo, hysteria and asthma were attributable to the phases of the Moon.

mean motion The speed at which a stellar body orbits another body.

mean time The problem of the irregular movement of the Sun, and thus of the difficulty of using it for precise timekeeping, was solved by a complex theoretical speculation resulting in the invention of an imaginary Sun which when it crosses the meridian above the horizon defines noon for any place on Earth: the local mean time is then 12.00.

medical astrology The association between medicine and astrology is ageless. In ancient Babylonia the study of planetary movements was used to predict plague and disease, while HIPPOCRATES and GALEN laid the foundations of the study of personal medical astrology. The four ELEMENTS or QUALITIES were represented in the human body by the HUMOURS, which indicated the balance of the four TEMPERAMENTS. The planets and their movements affected this balance. HORARY ASTROLOGY was used to diagnose illness and treat it, and individual BIRTH-CHARTS were studied to consider the possible astrological significators of sickness and cure. Physicians made a meticulous study of the association of various parts of the body with particular signs (*see* ZODIAC MAN). A doctor first set up a NATAL horoscope to discover the balance of the humours in his patient, then a chart for the beginning of the illness (or perhaps for the moment when he was summoned to attend the patient). The CRITICAL DAY (on which there would be a turn for the better or worse) was assessed, and within that, the critical moment at which the illness would be expected either to intensify or to begin to lose ground. Taught in medieval universities, the academic study of astrological medicine continued into relatively modern times (in Spanish universities, until the mid-18th century). Famous medical textbooks include Culpeper's *Complete Herbal*, which records the associations between specific herbs and the planets which govern them, while modern medical astrological encyclopaedias have been published. *See* PLAGUE, LILLY, FORMAN.

Medium Coeli or MC – the MIDHEAVEN or MERIDIAN. The southernmost point of the HOROSCOPE. A great circle of constant LONGITUDE passing through the celestial poles and a given place on Earth. The north and south poles will be on the horizon, and the ZENITH right above the observer.

Mercury ☿

One of the planets which has been observed for longer than history records, Mercury is the nearest planet to the Sun – between 29 and 43 million miles from it because of its eccentric orbit. It can therefore only either share a SIGN with the Sun or occupy the sign before or after the SUN-SIGN (for instance if the Sun-sign is Aries, Mercury can only be in that sign, or in Pisces or Taurus). It is the smallest planet in the solar system, with a diameter of only 3,000 miles; it has a year of 88 days, and a day lasting 59 Earth days. It has the shortest SIDEREAL period. Astrologically, Mercury RULES Gemini and Virgo, is EXALTED in Aquarius and in FALL in Leo. It has much to do with the way in which an individual communicates with his or her fellows, with everyday problems and the way in which they are solved. It can endow an individual with quickness of speech and intelligence, but also an inclination to deception, trickery and fraud.

Mercury and the zodiac signs

Mercury in ARIES

From Aries, Mercury will be a particular help at times when it is important to make decisions. It will encourage a thoroughly uncomplicated attitude to problems – to such an extent that other people may well not realize that the individual has any problems to solve. People with this placing of Mercury will not find it easy to pay due attention to detail, and their forthright way of coping with problems may leave the honing of fine points to other people. In argument they will be quick-witted and provocative, but capable of giving offence because of their impatience with slower-witted people, with whom that impatience may turn all too easily to anger. If Mercury is in Aries with the Sun, the thinking process will act with the speed of a computer; a Piscean Sun-sign tendency to dither and hesitate when decisions are called for will be very much mitigated with Mercury in this position, and there will be greater self-assurance and confidence than is usual with Pisceans. Working with a Taurean Sun-sign, Mercury will produce someone who is thoroughly assertive, punches home arguments with assurance, and is ready with an immediate answer to any situation.

Mercury in TAURUS

Those with Mercury in Taurus may well give the impression of tremendous stubbornness – to the extent that it may seem fruitless to argue with them. This is not necessarily the case, though such people may well get sly enjoyment from pretending to be far more inflexible than they really are. Working from Taurus, Mercury will encourage constructive and careful thought, though the process will be rather slow and deliberate: sometimes too much so. When a conclusion is reached and an opinion given, it will be practical, constructive, and succinctly expressed. In this sign Mercury can sometimes have a slightly worrying effect on children, who will be slower to make progress at school than one might hope. On the other hand their memory will be excellent and their powers of retention good; excellent foundations on which to build. With an Aries or Gemini SUN-SIGN Mercury will have an excellent effect on what might otherwise be undue hastiness of thought and action; those with a Taurus Sun-sign will be slow, steady, deliberate and extremely tactful and careful in offering their opinions.

Mercury in GEMINI

As the RULER of Gemini, Mercury's influence within the HOROSCOPE is much strengthened when it is placed in that sign, and the adjective *mercurial* might have been invented for them. They will be bright, quick, intelligent and able easily to talk themselves out of the most difficult or embarrassing situation. Able to cope with any number of problems at one time, they will frequently start out taking one side of an argument and end with a persuasive switch to the opposite view. Mercury's traditional association with the art of speech will be exemplified with this placing, and 'talkative' is scarcely a strong enough word to apply to those with Mercury in Gemini. They dislike being still, and a love of travel will be evident: they will be continually 'on the move' in everyday life. A sedentary office job is not for them. All this will be heavily accentuated if Gemini is the SUN-SIGN, and the mercurial aspect of their personality will be shown if the Sun is in Cancer, when there will also be enhanced rationality and logicality. With a Taurean Sun-sign Mercury will get traditionally slow, deliberate people moving more quickly, and discourage stubbornness.

Mercury in CANCER

A vivid imagination is encouraged and enhanced with Mercury is in Cancer. This can have advantages and disadvantages. If perhaps because of other influences in the HOROSCOPE, or for some other reason, the imagination is suppressed and not allowed to develop, it can run wild, and will turn inward so that small problems and fears assume disproportionate importance. This is not helped by the fact that the logical side of Mercury is not at its strongest when the planet is in Cancer. Clearly, then, it is important that someone with this placing of Mercury be encouraged to express his or her imagination in some way – and it really does not much matter how: an obvious way is through writing, painting, acting – none of these necessarily as a profession, but used to allow the imagination free range. This will be even more important if Cancer is also the SUN-SIGN, when the tendency to worry will be strengthened (though the quality of the imagination will also be enhanced). With Gemini as the Sun-sign the emotional level will be heightened – as will intuition and a tendency to sentimentality if the Sun is in Leo.

Mercury in LEO

Dogmatism and stubbornness may be linked to a rather conservative view of life, and a degree of pompousness. But the other side of this placing of Mercury is that it endows individuals with splendidly lucid planning ability and the capacity to work in an orderly and highly rational way. Strong powers of concentration will be allied to great enthusiasm and energy – these all the better for being well controlled and therefore applied to excellent effect. The Leo sense of drama will make these people capable of expressing themselves vividly and dramatically in speech, argument, discussion – they will be good at public speaking, though when it comes to question-time they must beware a tendency too easily to dismiss the opinions of others. Flexibility of thought should be encouraged. When Leo is also the SUN-SIGN big ideas will be grasped, marshalled and put forward to dramatic effect. There will alas also be a tendency to look down on those who seem less interested in advancing their own opinions, and who prefer a quieter style. With a Cancer Sun-sign there will be a positive outlook and less of a tendency to worry. Because Mercury rules Virgo, when that is the Sun-sign the Leo effect will be highly personal.

Mercury in VIRGO

Mercury rules both Virgo as well as Gemini, and in this sign has an additionally strong effect, making those with this placing capable of extremely demanding practical and constructive intellectual work. They may not always have the confidence to stand behind this work with sufficient stamina, often thinking themselves less competent than they are. Not properly displayed, their abilities can be lost on others. They have a great deal of nervous energy, and use it to the full – knowing precisely what they want to do and how and why they want to do it, they hate being unemployed, having no work on which to concentrate. In general they are not noted for their imaginative forces compared to those with Mercury in some other signs, but an abundance of common sense and practical ability, together with a sharp critical sense, are valuable and rewarding in other ways. They have excellent communication skills, are good conversational-ists, and with enquiring minds enjoy exchanging ideas and information with others. SUN-SIGN Virgoans are extremely critical, logical and rational; to a Leo Sun-sign, Mercury brings practicality; to a Libran, decisiveness.

Mercury in LIBRA

Those with Mercury in Libra may well tend to want to make the greatest possible effect with the smallest possible effort, and will be reluctant to undergo projects which seem likely to involve great concentration. Sympathetic, kind and considerate, they will express themselves rather languidly and slowly, and are not people to be ready with a swift response. Their thinking processes are leisurely, to say the least. They will also be indecisive – and finding it difficult to come to any conclusion in an argument, will keep away from controversy, and indeed from anything else that may tend to disturb their treasured peace and quiet, and the measured tranquillity that they love. Their outlook on life will be romantic, and they will be seriously disturbed if anything suggests that life may at any time turn unpleasant for them or their loved ones; they cling determinedly to the theory that in the end 'all will be well'. If Libra is also the SUN-SIGN, all these qualities will be emphasized. Sun-sign Scorpios will be lent a kinder and gentler quality by this placing of Mercury, and those with a Virgo Sun-sign will find it easier to relax than some of their compatriots. Mercury will also help them to be at ease in their emotional relationships.

Mercury in SCORPIO

An extremely interesting combination of influences, with the intensity and intuition of Scorpio combined with a more logical, rational approach to life – and with intense curiosity. Such people will have a clear sense of purpose, and be extremely eager to get to the bottom of any question or quandary that faces them. They will always want to know the reason for any statement or situation, and to find out every available fact about it. There is obviously potential for work as an investigator of any kind – whether that means as a private detective, a psychiatrist, pathologist, or simply an investigative journalist. The powers of observation will be extremely keen – but Mercury in this sign is not as communicative as elsewhere, and people with this placing of the planet are likely to be strong, silent types, able and even eager to keep their own counsel. They will be extremely purposeful and determined – even obsessively so, and indeed there is a danger that an obsessive character may emerge. Interest in mysteries in general could also lead to an interest in the occult. With a Scorpio SUN-SIGN Mercury's honing of the intellect and imagination will be intense. With a Libran Sun-sign those with a Scorpio Mercury will be additionally decisive, but must beware resentfulness and jealousy. Steady, productive enthusiasm and optimism will be characteristic of those with a Sagittarian Sun-sign.

Mercury in SAGITTARIUS

Those with Mercury in Sagittarius will share an extremely optimistic outlook on life, and an almost insatiable need for challenge. They will have breadth of vision and the ability very quickly to grasp even the most complicated concepts, and there will be a compulsion to study – but individuals must be sure to maintain their enthusiasm, for restlessness can impede the initial interest and slow down the impetus. They should consciously develop persistence of effort – there may well be a tendency to drop the current task or interest, should it become even slightly boring, for something more interesting and attractive (and, perhaps, less complicated). Versatility and a gift for languages will join a natural love of travel; and there will be a love of openness, both in landscape and in people – those with a stuffy, introverted view of life will not be their natural friends. With a Sagittarian SUN-SIGN Mercury can get somewhat out of hand, but enthusiasm and positivity will make for an extremely attractive personality.

A Scorpio Sun-sign with this placing of Mercury will encourage a very broad outlook on life; very few subjects fail to offer something interesting in the way of study – and the Scorpio intensity and emotion will be less emphasized. Those with a Capricorn Sun-sign will be less pessimistic than with other placings of Mercury – and the typical sense of humour will be enhanced and sharpened.

Mercury in CAPRICORN

This placing of Mercury will make for a cool, rather calculating, steady character – someone who will consider all options before making any decision, and with a sharp, incisive mind. Indeed, this will be a mind which will thrive on problems and delight in solving them, excluding emotion and employing a talent for weighing one fact against another, and for consider-ing not merely the present but the probable future. A high value will be placed on efficiency and practicality. If all this sounds like a recipe not just for self-assurance but for pomposity, there is no denying that that can be the case – these people can take themselves too seriously, giving a great deal of cautious thought to their own progress in life and the attainments of the objectives they have set themselves. When these have been attained, complete satisfaction may still not be achieved, for Mercury in Capricorn saps the sense of achievement, and tends to underestimate it. At least the planet will do something to encourage optimism and reduce the natural pessimism of the SUN-SIGN. If Sagittarius is the Sun-sign, Mercury will be a steadying influence, and blind optimism will be less likely; the character will be more practical and have a greater degree of common sense. If the Sun is in Aquarius, a love of tradition will be met by a desire for the uncon-ventional – with interesting and perhaps slightly comic results.

Mercury in AQUARIUS

From this sign Mercury exerts an influence which is enlivening, but can be somewhat confusing. The subject will be original and quick-thinking, but more than a little stubborn – brilliant and inventive, often with the capacity to take an unusual line of action. A difficult problem may be met by a seemingly eccentric action, a line of approach no one else would have considered – which will usually be effective. This is all very well and good, but an individual who relies on 'brilliance' to carry things through must cultivate persistence of effort to back up bright ideas. Communicating these ideas persuasively and clearly will not be difficult, and those with Mercury in Aquarius usually have a friendly personality which makes it easy for them to deal with colleagues and superiors. If Aquarius is the SUN-SIGN, the intense individuality, originality and independence of that sign will be intensified, and additional thought and control will be needed if things are not to get out of control: happily the ability to rationalize and take a detached view will also be encouraged. With the Sun in Capricorn, the serious Capricornian attitude will be lightened and enlivened; but inflexibility may remain a problem. The deep emotional content of a Piscean Sun-sign will be steadied by Mercury from Aquarius, and logic and a sense of detachment will be enhanced.

Mercury in PISCES

People with this placing of Mercury will be pleasant to know – nice, gentle, rather emotional, always willing to help, reluctant to rock any boat. Alas, these qualities contribute to the difficulties they may face in life, which include impracticality, forgetfulness, and such a strong desire to avoid trouble that they can fall into it without trying. They hate for instance to disappoint or hurt people, and as a result will often resort to little white lies – but with the natural characteristic of lies to grow and change colour, they sometimes end up in enormously complicated situations, and those they have been trying to placate are in the end offended by the very means by which the Mercurial characters have been trying to get out of awkward situations. Anyone with Mercury in Pisces should, from the very start, learn that while deceitfulness seems to provide an easy way out, this is very rarely actually the case. There is a tendency for these people to fail to grasp facts, and this can let them down when for instance they should be listening attentively to complex instructions – though on the other hand they have almost a photographic talent for retaining more general impressions. If the SUN-SIGN is Pisces, all Piscean characteristics will be strengthened, and there may be an interest in the occult. With an Aquarian Sun-sign, originality and individuality will be marked. When Aries is the Sun-sign, assertiveness and the need to win will be weakened, and there will be greater consideration of others.

Mercury and the houses

Mercury in the FIRST HOUSE

Mercury in the first house will make for a bright personality, talkative, quick-thinking and with a strong need to communicate. He or she will tend to act quickly and almost nervously, as though unsure of the consequences. The strong influence of the planet in the first house will vary according to the sign placing and the ASPECTS it received, but versatility will certainly be a hallmark. There may be a problem with superficiality and restlessness, and quick responses to questions or arguments will sometimes be tailored rather to the circumstances of the moment than to real consideration and thought. *Note* that the nearer Mercury is to the ASCENDING DEGREE, the more it will influence the ASCENDANT and the whole HOROSCOPE.

Mercury in the SECOND HOUSE

There will be a concentration on finance, with much energy spent in building up a secure financial base. It is not impossible that in anxiety to do this the subject may be taken in by insecure schemes which result in loss rather than gain. Bargaining ability will be an advantage, and will be much enjoyed – finding a bargain will make this man or woman's day. The ASPECTS present in the chart will be of importance where bargaining is concerned: positive aspects from Saturn will steady the nerves, while negative ones from Neptune will be more likely to confuse, and even lead to trickery and deception. It is not unlikely that two sources of income will be contrived.

Mercury in the THIRD HOUSE

The house of Mercury and Gemini ensure that Mercury will act strongly, conferring a need to communicate and a liking for the means of communication – emails, faxes, the telephone – even letters. The person with Mercury in the third house will be particularly concerned with how he or she expresses thoughts, ideas, suggestions – even if what is actually being communicated is not of the first importance. If Mercury is in an AIR SIGN, there may be a provocative tendency to turn a debate to the subject's advantage by reversing an opinion on a whim. Mental agility makes this easy, and striking powers of perception suit an argument to a circumstance, however much twisting and turning is needed. An interest in acquiring knowledge is unfortunately married to a somewhat superficial mind, which will use it and then forget it: these waters are shallow.

Mercury in the FOURTH HOUSE

The emphasis here is on home and family, and there may be a notable tendency to move from house to house, locality to locality, all because of a certain restlessness Mercury confers from the fourth house. Especially if Sun and Moon are in negative ASPECT to each other this may stem from uncertainty, some inner conflict which acts to weaken the feeling of security even in the most settled environment. The subject's attitude to the home will be linked to the sign in which Mercury is placed – on one hand there may be a relaxed attitude to family, on the other a tendency to worry about family members, or to feel subdued in their presence. Because this is the house of Cancer and the Moon, the influence of the mother may be strong – not merely in childhood, but throughout life.

Mercury in the FIFTH HOUSE

In the house of love affairs, Mercury will turn its attention to ensuring that emotions are expressed in a manner which will be most acceptable to the object of affection. Flattery will be employed if that seems likely to be profitable; if not, another course will be followed – one which will be most likely to get the desired response. The tendency to take risks, to gamble, which is also conferred by the planet from this house, could extend to the love life, particularly since there is likely to be some tendency to duality – the gambling being, of course, on the possibility of one woman – or man – finding out about the other. A desire for change and novelty will contribute to such a situation. Gambling will not necessarily be restricted to the love life; more safely, a lively intellect will find satisfaction in such games as chess.

Mercury in the SIXTH HOUSE

There will almost certainly be a preoccupation with diet – especially if the subject is prone to worry (not unlikely), when stomach upsets are likely to mean that care should be taken in this area. There will be an enthusiasm for vegetarianism or whole foods – not necessarily kind to a sensitive stomach.

These subjects often react well to homoeopathic and holistic medicine. But the problem can only be exacerbated by increased fretting about problems, imaginary or real, and learning to cope with this situation is important. Routine will be one solution (and in any case is encouraged by Mercury from the sixth house). There should also be an ability to entrust problems to others, and by talking them through, reduce tension and therefore worry.

Mercury in the SEVENTH HOUSE
Relationships, both personal and in business, are emphasized by Mercury from the seventh house. The former is based strongly on the necessity for friendship, even in the most intimate of relationships, while the latter usually indicates someone with a gift for selling – selling him- or herself, apart from anything else. In a personal relationship, the subject needs to be sure that, as well as a sexual bond, the partner reciprocates the desire for companionship. The desire for this can be so strong that there is an element of gullibility – a tendency to believe whatever is said or promised. The ASCENDING SIGN, or the sign position of Mercury, may balance this. In business, it should be easy for the subject to convey ideas persuasively to partners or clients. He or she will be an excellent negotiator.

Mercury in the EIGHTH HOUSE
There will be a serious side to anyone with Mercury in this house, to the extent that there may be a preoccupation with philosophy and the larger questions of life. The individual may be convinced that he or she has psychic gifts. This should be explored carefully, and if it proves to be the case, care should be taken before exploring them (especially if there are adverse ASPECTS between the Moon and Neptune. There should in any event be careful guidance from an expert. There may be an equally strong interest in the nature of sexuality, leading perhaps to a vibrant fantasy life. The individual will be interested in research of all sorts, and capable of it; any mystery will be fascinating – whether in a book or in real life – and solving it may take over every spare moment. There should be a good instinct for positive investment.

Mercury in the NINTH HOUSE
The ninth house is a sympathetic home for Mercury, for both are intellectually inclined. The minds of those with this placing of the planet will need

continual stimulation – some cerebral activity to keep them interested –
even to the extent of moving too quickly from one problem or preoccupation to another. The degree of ability to stay long with one subject and
really look into it will be indicated by the sign Mercury occupies. One
positive aspect of a continual interest in some subject or another is that it
will act against a tendency to daydream, which could otherwise weaken the
will to get on with life. Daydreams are likely to involve travel, the desire to
see the world, and there will be every attempt to make this a reality –
whether, when young, during a gap year, or when older in the temptation to
take long leaves, even if this means a loss of income.

Mercury in the TENTH HOUSE
Change is emphasized when Mercury occupies the tenth house –
particularly where the career is concerned, but in any case where thought is
being given to the general direction a life is taking, or the way in which
progress may be made. For a subject to be happy in a career, any occupation
should be able to allow for change – as much variety as possible. A job
behind a desk dealing with the same documents day after day will be
anathema and lead to extreme restlessness. Responsibility will help to
alleviate this, but mobility is perhaps the best answer, taking the person
concerned out and about. There is a connection here with the father,
whose influence may have been (may still be) considerable throughout life.
The father may speak through the lips of older friends or acquaintances,
apart from the parent himself.

Mercury in the ELEVENTH HOUSE
The person with Mercury in the eleventh house will be a social, gregarious
animal, who will want to move among a constant group of friends and
acquaintances. Deep one-to-one friendships may not be as attractive as
lighter, more ephemeral friendships – an easy, social environment is
however extremely important. The friends concerned may be working for
some common cause, and that will be specially gratifying, because this
subject will be interested in such things as alleviating hunger or poverty.
There may also be a need for solitary thought, peace and quiet, especially if
the Sun is in the twelfth house. If the Sun is in the tenth house the subject

may need to take life more quietly, for there will be a tendency to be involved all-out, day and night, either in the social round or for good causes.

Mercury in the TWELFTH HOUSE
Mercury's logical temperament may clash here with the intuitional, emotional atmosphere of the twelfth house (especially if Mercury is in a WATER SIGN). Rationality should be brought to the rescue, and the emotions channelled by Mercury towards well-established and positive objectives. There may be an equal conflict between the desire for peace and quiet and Mercury's love of the social round. If there is a talent for journalism, a critical mind can be brought to bear in the fields of popular communication – perhaps literary or perhaps social. A flair for technology can lead towards the technical side of communication – work as an engineer in radio, television or the internet, for instance. If there is a religious temperament, it will be strong, and there will be much confidence in the power of prayer – otherwise in the power of positive thought.

* * *

Meridian house system A system similar to that of REGIOMONTANUS, however with the east point taken as the ASCENDANT.

meridians In order to locate any place on Earth, two imaginary circles are used – the meridians of longitude and the parallels of latitude. Meridians of longitude are imaginary circles running north/south across the Earth's surface from one pole to the other. The meridian on which a particular place stands is that which passes through it. The prime meridian runs through Greenwich, and all LONGITUDES are measured from it, either east or west.

metals Ancient astrology associated gold and silver with the Sun and Moon. Much later, copper, iron and lead were linked to Venus, Mars and Saturn. The full list reads:

- Moon – silver
- Mercury – mercury
- Venus – copper
- Sun – gold

- Mars – iron
- Jupiter – tin
- Saturn – lead

meteorology There is a very long association between astrology and weather forecasting. Pre-Christian astrologers noted the connection between planetary movements and the cultivation of plants, especially the different effect of the Sun at different times of the day. From the earliest days until the mid-18th century innumerable astrologers specialized in this, and almanacs – particularly in America – devoted many pages to predicting the weather for the year ahead. The aphorisms of Jerome CARDAN were respected for at least two centuries – viz 'When about the beginning of winter Saturn shall dispose of [i.e. have more influence than] the Moon, expect unusual cold with a cloudy season and rain.' One of the earliest English astrological meteorologists was Robert of York, a friar who published in 1235 a work on weather prediction, with rules for predicting rain, frost, hail, snow, thunder, wind and tides. William Merlee, a fellow of Merton College, Oxford, who died ca.1347, kept detailed records of the weather for seven years, and published a discourse which discussed the signs of good or bad weather and interpreted them, using not only his own observations but those of farmers, seamen and others. A contemporary on the continent, Ennor of Wirtzburg, published a very similar work. Many astrologers also attempted to explain such occurrences as earthquakes and volcanic eruptions by movements and connections of the planets – notably Leonard Dygges, who in 1555 published *A Prognostication of right good effect, fructfully augmented containing playne, briefe, pleasant, chosen rules, to iudge the wether for euer* … There are few modern practitioners of astrological meteorology.

meteors Sometimes described as 'falling stars', meteors were anciently thought to be a sign of death. These are so frequent that it is futile to attempt to integrate them into the astrological theory; however recurrent meteor showers have sometimes been used, conjecturally, by astrologers.

mid-day chart Some astrologers set a chart for mid-day when the day but not the time of birth of a subject is known.

Midheaven or MC. The point of the HOROSCOPE at which the MERIDIAN intercepts the ECLIPTIC. In most systems of HOUSE DIVISION this is also the CUSP of the TENTH HOUSE, but in the oldest, the EQUAL HOUSE system, it can fall in any house from the 9th to the 11th.

midpoints The midpoint between the positions of two planets is claimed to influence the subject of a horoscope by TRANSIT or PROGRESSION. This theory has been known since the 16th century, but was developed in the 1920s in Germany as Uranian astrology (at the Hamburg school) and Cosmobiology. Midpoints can easily be discovered by counting the number of degrees between two planets and dividing by two. These points are activated when a planet occupies one or more of them. There is a total of 78 midpoints between the traditional planets, the Moon's NODE, the ASCENDANT and MIDHEAVEN. Clearly using all these would be to make the chart difficult to interpret (*see* BLACK CHART). Astrologers determine which of the midpoints are most important, according to the research of such researchers as EBERTIN and ADDEY, and their own experience. COSMOBIOLOGISTS also consider indirect midpoints to be of importance.

minor aspects The aspects which did not appear in PTOLEMY'S original list – i.e., the SEMI-SEXTILE (30°), SEMI-SQUARE (45°), SESQUARE (135°) and QUINCUNX (150°). Among those added by later astrologers are the QUINTILE (72°), bi-quintile (144°), SEPTILE (approximately 50°), and nonile (40°).

Mithraism The most potent of all rivals to CHRISTIANITY, the mystery cult of Mithraism spread through the Roman Empire and by the 4th century reached as far as Britain. The god Mithra, whose birth was celebrated on 25 December, was a force for good in the eternal struggle between good and evil. The slaying of a bull, a pantomime of Mithra's killing of the cosmic Bull of Creation and the conquest of evil, was a focus of the ceremonies. There was a strong emphasis on astrology and Sun-worship. Sixteen of the known Mithraic temples show the complete zodiac.

'modern planets' The term sometimes (of course, inaccurately) used to describe the OUTER PLANETS, Uranus, Neptune, Pluto and Chiron.

moiety Ancient astrologer believed that each planet was surrounded by an invisible aura of light, whose radius was known as its moiety. In HORARY astrology this is used to calculate the extent to which one planet could be regarded as in ASPECT to another (not to be confused with the system of ORBS used in natal astrology).

month The amount of time it takes the Moon to complete an orbit of the Earth – that is, about 29? days. The *sidereal month* is the time it takes the Moon to return to its precise position among the FIXED STARS, which has been measured as 27 days and some 7 hours and 43 minutes.

Moon ☽

The Moon is described, in astrology, as a planet, though of course it is no more a planet than is the Sun. It is a satellite of the Earth, orbiting at an average distance of 238,840 miles once every 27 days, 7 hours, 43 minutes 11 seconds. When between the Sun and Earth it is unseen, and called *new*; it increases until it is half-full. Its increase (while it is three-quarters full, or *gibbous*) continues until it is *full*. This period takes 14.5 days. It then passes through its phases in reverse order until it is once more obscured by the shadow of the Earth. The Moon RULES Cancer and is EXALTED in Taurus. There is a tradition that the characteristics of the Moon-sign are the ones one inherits from parents. Modern astrologers claim that it will show how one instinctively reacts and responds to situations in life. It is concerned with love and personal relationships, with art and fashion, and with the feminine side of one's nature. It encourages friendship, gentleness and the social graces, but under stress can make one indecisive, careless, over-romantic and overdependent on others.

The Moon and the zodiac signs

Moon in ARIES

The instinctive reactions of those with the Moon in Aries are swift, leading to immediate action. If this is sound, excellent; if unsound, there can be extreme difficulties. On the whole however, quick decisions are right for these individuals, and any tendency to succumb to impulsive and premature action will in time be controlled by experience and very possibly with the help of the characteristics of the RISING-SIGN or SUN-SIGN, direct, forthright, uncomplicated Aries qualities will come positively into play. The Moon in Aries can help individuals to inspire and motivate action in others, but a tendency to respond selfishly under pressure means that care is needed to ensure that this aspect of Aries does not mar relationships; inconsiderateness can be a distinct possibility.

Moon in TAURUS

The Moon works very strongly from Taurus. Though reactions to situations may be a little slow, there will be no doubt at all about the individual's opinions: after thought, these will be expressed pungently and firmly, and there will be little opportunity for discussion. The need for security will be emphasized, but will be an immediate reaction rather than a lasting and essential factor in life. For instance, once a situation has been thought through and a decision made, there will be no hesitation about taking risks if this seems necessary. When emotional security seems threatened, typical Taurean possessiveness will be a basic reaction, and a tendency to conservatism may make itself felt (though the individual will fight against this; it seems almost an imposed rather than a natural reaction). Stubbornness should be resisted.

Moon in GEMINI

Reactions will be so quick they will seem almost instantaneous; responses will be succinct, unemotional and straight-to-the-point, relying on logical, intellectually orientated reasoning and an immediate grasp of a situation. There may be a failing however, to grasp the full implications of a situation, for these people may be restless and in need of continual change, and this tendency extends to obstructing the deep consideration of a subject. Individuals with the Moon in Gemini can give the impression of lacking real interest and concern for other people and their problems, and there may be something in this. Irritatingly, and sometimes insultingly, they can while talking to one person be looking over her shoulder in search of someone who might be more interesting. Concentration is something that can lack real intensity; one must hope that support from other planets' influences and that of the RISING-SIGN will help out.

Moon in CANCER

Because the Moon RULES Cancer it will emphasize all the Cancerian qualities when it is in its home sign. Instinct and intuition are so strong in people with this placing of the Moon that it is really necessary to be aware of their strength and be prepared to rein them in if and when reason demands it. In particular, if the individual feels himself or herself to be psychic or to have a 'sixth sense', it is extremely important that they treat this seriously, and while not smothering it, seek proper training if they wish to use it. Cancerian tenacity too is emphasized, as are persistence of effort and strength of will. This is a placing that is specially good for parenthood, but mothers with the Moon in Cancer tend to treat their children as infants up to the eve of their marriage and are given to worrying unduly about them. Sweeping changes of mood are frequent and sometimes immediate.

Moon in LEO

Anyone with the Moon in Leo will be capable of seizing a situation, however difficult, and coping with it, to the admiration of others. This is a strong response and a powerful one, and must be treated with care; it should not be used as a tool to show how superior these people are to those around them. Decisive and effective action, a fine show of enthusiasm and emotion, are characteristic and impressive, and those with this placing of the Moon tend to impress and influence people. But they do often have an inherent feeling that their proper place is at the top – whatever that may mean in a particular situation – and there is a tendency to dogmatism and authoritarianism which can embarrass and at worst disgust other people. Humility should not be treated as a dirty word. But when all is said and done, the Moon in Leo capacity to cope in tricky situations and to do so with determination and speed, is a welcome characteristic and will no doubt be extremely useful in shaping a career.

Moon in VIRGO

From Virgo the Moon will help a person to react to situations logically, practically, and speedily. He or she will be sharp and intelligent in debate, and will check and cross-check every fact before putting forward what will often seem an unanswerable argument. The need to care for and help others will be strong. People with this placing of the Moon often work in nursing or other areas of medicine; they are down-to-earth, sensible and reliable – and the epitome of the successful ward sister who will stand no nonsense from anyone in their determination to see that rules are followed. On the personal side, the emotions may be a touch cool and clinical, which can be a distinct disadvantage in forming a close personal relationship. Extravagance will not be a fault – which can conflict if other areas of the HOROSCOPE suggest it.

Moon in LIBRA

The most dominant factor with those who have the Moon in Libra is the air of peace that surrounds them. Their immediate response to a situation will very possibly appear lackadaisical and hesitant, and it is certainly the case that they will probably wait for instructions before doing anything; but this in itself can be an advantage as a calming influence. There will be an appearance of complete serenity, and in a crisis these people will be at a distinct advantage, for there will be no panic and no rush into sudden, possibly rash action. A sympathetic ear is always ready to listen to the problems of others, and these people are paramount peacemakers, who are excellent at reconciling opposite views and calming warring factions. They are unlikely to take an extreme view in any argument, but rather steer a diplomatic course as close to the middle ground as possible.

Moon in SCORPIO

Though someone may not have any of the more extreme characteristics of those with a Scorpio RISING- SIGN or SUN-SIGN, and have a more equable and quiet nature, it is more than likely that there will be occasional outbursts of emotion and the sudden expression of more extreme feelings than one might credit. In a fairly peaceful and apparently unimpressive character this can have the effect of making people sit up and pay attention to them. These are in fact likely to be people of action who will respond energetically and strongly when energy and strength are required. They will take time out to influence other people powerfully but subtly, so that their persuasion is scarcely noticed. In personal life, any situation that provokes jealousy is likely to arouse them to a characteristic explosion – in a way illustrative of the inner strength which when it is used, is extremely powerful.

Moon in SAGITTARIUS

A straightforward, no-nonsense reaction to every situation is characteristic of people with this placing of the Moon; there will be no obfuscation, but a steady consideration of the facts followed by a considered and measured response. If suggestions are invited, they will be equally measured, thoughtful and always practical. There is no shortage of emotion in the character, but it is emotion that will be expressed in ways dominated by the positions of the Sun and the nature of the RISING-SIGN. Considerable attention will be paid to the way in which other people react to this individual – and this is important in youth, for undue criticism of someone with the Moon in Sagittarius is likely to affect them considerably, deflating them and robbing them of some self-assurance. One result of this with young people is that later in life they will tend to toss their heads and ignore justified criticism. Potential for development is, however, strong and will be well expressed.

Moon in CAPRICORN

A cool, calm response to even the most difficult situation will be character-istic with this placing of the Moon; indeed, the reaction will be so cool that there may be an impression of remoteness. There will also be a decided tendency to grumble when anything goes wrong – even insignificantly. However, other characteristics of the full HOROSCOPE should ensure that the individual will almost immediately criticize himself for this, and turn his or her attention to making progress – and progressing towards an objective, which is usually a position in command, very possibly one of authority. It will be important to recognize the characteristics of Capricorn as they are brought out by the Moon – the temptation for instance to look down on other people who seem socially or for any other reason less prominent. The Moon can, from this sign, make people somewhat fearful and oversensitive when others put ideas to them – sometimes because they see them as some sort of attack. This tendency should be fought, and fought strongly. Self-confidence should be kept at a decently formidable level.

Moon in AQUARIUS

The moon shines clearly and brilliantly from Aquarius, whatever the SUN-SIGN or ASCENDING-SIGN. It will contribute a glamorous sheen to a

personality, and an atmosphere of somewhat mysterious attraction. On a
personal level this is of course of enormous benefit – though real warmth
and affection are somewhat at a premium, and will have to be contributed
by other areas of the complete HOROSCOPE – though people with this placing
of the Moon tend to show unexpected traits of sentimentality and romanticism from time to time. They will be quickly responsive, especially if they
are asked for help, and there will be no lack of affectionate kindness. They
will be moved by human suffering and will wish to work to alleviate it.
They will tend to act in unexpected ways, sometimes without due thought,
and must be prepared to suffer from the occasional silly mistake. But the
Moon donates splendid potential from this sign, and backup for any
inherent talent will be generous – the uniquely original talent of Aquarius
will come through.

Moon in PISCES
Pisceans have a high emotional and intuitive level, and the Moon in that
sign will contribute both to the personality of people with other Sun-signs.
Especially when the individual comes into contact with suffering or cruelty,
the emotions will be readily and deeply stirred; but it will not stop there, for
they will wish to express these emotions practically and constructively, and
will find ways of doing so. The imagination will be stimulated, and at best
used positively. The major problem however, a tendency to deceive – to
take the easy way out of difficult situations by prevarication and dishonesty,
to give a quick answer which is not precisely true, or in a difficult situation
to respond with a completely false reply or action. This is a fault contributed by the Moon in this position, and other levels of the personality
will despise it; conscious awareness of it is the beginning of disposing of it
– and if this is not the case, the continual difficulty and confusion that will
inevitably result should effect a cure.

The Moon and the houses

Moon in the FIRST HOUSE
'Protection' is a keyword when the Moon is in the first house of the BIRTH-
CHART. There is a strong feeling with these individuals that they should
protect their families and loved ones – and, not least, themselves. If the

Moon is close to the ASCENDING degree, this urge will be extremely strong. The personality will be lent a warm, gently caring quality which will be greatly admired. The vitality may be variable, and diet should be carefully considered; in women, the reproductive system may be sensitive.

Moon in the SECOND HOUSE

Those with this placing of the Moon are often in an almost continual state of concern about their financial situation – sometimes quite irrationally. This no doubt has something to do with an innate sense of insecurity, often emotional as well as financial. Any sign of a change in the money market can worry them, even if their investments are minimal. There is the added difficulty that if they are spiritually or creatively bent, money can slip through their fingers with astonishing ease – until from time to time they realize just how much they have spent or given away, when the brakes will be applied and concern will mount. There is an acquisitive instinct, which again has much to do with the need for security – in this case to surround themselves with familiar, loved objects.

Moon in the THIRD HOUSE

There will be a need to collect facts, to search out the reason for the actions of others; but the knowledge gained will be rather superficial, for these people will not have the real talent to observe, to absorb what they discover; they will have an enormous amount of superficial knowledge. This sounds like a journalistic trait, and indeed the need to communicate what they have found out is almost as strong as their desire to uncover it. They will also have a shrewd, almost cunning streak which will emerge in difficult situations, or when they are searching out a good story. It is important for them to move among other people – they are by no means lone wolves, and need to be in continual touch with others. They make interesting parents, for they are excellent at communicating with younger people.

Moon in the FOURTH HOUSE

The creation of a secure home in which a family can feel safe and at ease will be an important motive for those with the Moon in the fourth house. If there is any question of domestic uncertainty or anxiety there will be an immediate reaction, and the personal and working life will be affected. A claustrophobic atmosphere is possibly a result of a shrinking away from outside influences, which may seem to threaten the carefully nurtured security. There is sometimes an introverted, nervous quality which can affect these people's relationships with others – criticized or attacked, they can retire within themselves and simply refuse to respond. There is also a possibility that nervous reaction may give rise to (often imaginary) illness.

Moon in the FIFTH HOUSE

This is the house of children, and also the house of sexuality. As far as children are concerned, it highlights the pleasure one receives from them, and also underlines an instinctive knowledge of how to act and react to them as they grow and mature. The demonstration of love through sex indicated when the Moon is in the fifth house is more complex than simple enjoyment of making love; this will always be linked to the creation of closer bonds between the two people involved, with concern not merely for sexual satisfaction but for a deepening and strengthening of the relationship itself. There can be a tendency to showiness and flamboyance, countered by a sudden dislike of oneself for this; similarly, there can be financial risk-taking, followed by the feeling that the action has damaged one's security.

Moon in the SIXTH HOUSE

There is an emphasis on health with the Moon in this house, and it is best to avoid such risks as drug-taking, smoking or drinking too heavily; these will all have an even more adverse effect than common. A steady routine of work and creative exercise is advisable; this and a regular daily rhythm to life will help to counter any tendency towards risk-taking where health is concerned. If the Moon is in an EARTH SIGN, this will be easier. Attention to the diet, also ruled by this house, is necessary: when there is any tension in the life, there may be a tendency to consume comfort food in larger quantities than is wise. Anorexia is not out of the question.

Moon in the SEVENTH HOUSE

Working from the seventh house, the Moon deepens the need to respond to a partner. This can be excellent, sensitively expressed and helpful in building a sound relationship. However, reliance on the partner can become too highly stressed, with a need always to live in the other's pocket, to go everywhere and do everything together, so that a sense of individuality is damaged or lost. Someone with this placing of the Moon can give way too often and too completely to the other's wishes – or in other cases provoke disagreement in order to be able to show devotion by giving way, later, thus also giving the other partner the opportunity to express devotion, for this action can stem from a basic feeling of inadequacy and inferiority, when reassurance is badly needed. There may in this way be an imbalance and uncertainty at the heart of what seems a settled relationship, which in the end will become damagingly overt.

Moon in the EIGHTH HOUSE

Strong emotional forces will be at work, and these may well include jealousy and suspicion, so that a strong sense of security will be vital in a relationship if there is not to be a steady and inevitable erosion of trust. A strong degree of sexuality can be a great help, given that the partner's tastes and inclinations match those of the subject – for this too can be a danger area if one partner's sexual enthusiasm is not matched and met by the other's. There are generous emotional resources in this placing of the Moon, but once again they need to be supported and expressed without any feeling of mistrust or hesitation about the commitment of the other partner.

Moon in the NINTH HOUSE

The main problem with the Moon in this house is procrastination. There may be a strong desire to study, to travel, to take a particular decision, but the almost inevitable reaction will be to put off, for one reason or another – usually spurious. Emotion may be the problem, clouding the issue and making hesitation almost inevitable. A strong sense of reality will help, and the subject may reach a decision after initial hesitation. The sign in which the Moon is placed will be important in determining how the problem is best approached and solved. Moral problems may be treated in this way; but in that case decisions will be taken instinctively, and probably much more quickly. There will be a love of travel, and if this is not physically possible it will be expressed in the reading of travel books, watching TV travel programmes, and so on.

Moon in the TENTH HOUSE

The Moon seems, from this house, to shine almost like a spotlight on those people in whose BIRTH-CHART it is shown, for a great number of those who are at the centre of public life have this placing – often actors, film stars, but also politicians and those in positions of authority, for there is an ability to preside over large organizations employing many people. An understanding of how to deal with groups of people is inherent, and people with the Moon in the tenth house are often highly regarded and even loved by those under their control. Intuition and emotion are expressed in the care of the people whose wellbeing they have at heart. People with concern for the world environment and care for it are often found to have the Moon in this house.

Moon in the ELEVENTH HOUSE

It is very often the case that those with the Moon in the eleventh house are happiest when involved with others, in a group of those with like interests. The satisfaction and reassurance they gain from this may stem from the fact that they had difficulties in relating to their contemporaries when they were young, feeling themselves in some way to have been 'outsiders', and now determined to compensate. A result may be overcompensation, so that other people begin to feel smothered, or too heavily depended upon. Coming to terms with this, and learning not to rely too profoundly on others, is important if independence is not to be sapped.

Moon in the TWELFTH HOUSE

However gregarious one may be, the Moon working from the twelfth house makes it important that time is regularly spent alone in retrospection and thought. This can be done in different ways: from joining a religious retreat to spending a set time each day listening to music, or in meditation. Withdrawal of some sort is really necessary to the wellbeing of those with this placing of the Moon. A danger is that this need may lead to negative escapism. An instinctive feeling that one is a 'loner' may lead to secretiveness and even deception when someone else, perhaps a prospective partner, attempts to discover more about the personality than these people feel able to allow. This can obviously, if taken too far, be a bar to a satisfactory relationship.

* * *

Moon ruler *see* PERSONAL PLANETS

Moon's nodes *see* DRAGON'S HEAD AND TAIL

Moore, Francis (1657–ca.1715) Born at Bridgnorth, Shropshire,
Moore learned his astrology as an assistant to John PARTRIDGE, and
obtaining a licence to practise medicine set up shop as doctor, schoolmaster and astrologer in Lambeth. His first publication seems to have
been an almanac of weather forecasting; but in 1700 he published the first
of his annual almanacs, *Vox Stellarum*, for which he became famous.
By 1738 it was selling 25,000 copies a year, and was continued by
various astrologers after Moore's death. In 1768 its sales reached
107,000 and by the end of the century, 353,000. Its success rested on its
catholicity – it dealt with politics, the weather, famous men and women,
wars, earthquakes – and there were also lists of current and coming events.
Old Moore's Almanac is the sole remnant of the 17th-century almanacs
still to be annually printed.

Morin, Jean-Baptiste (1583–1656), was born at Villefranche, in France,
and studied philosophy and medicine, becoming astrologer to the Bishop of
Bologne in 1613, and then advising the Duke of Luxembourg and later the
duke d'Effiat. He was also an eager student of astronomy, and was
professor of mathematics at the Collège Royal from 1630 until his death –
an appointment of the King, Louis XIII. In Paris, he became court
astrologer to the King, who ordered him to attend the *accouchement* of the
Queen in order to be sure of recording the precise moment of birth of the
child, the future Louis XIV. Later, he was concealed behind a screen in the
wedding chamber of the Dauphin in order to note the moment when the
marriage was consummated, so that he would have the time of conception
of any future child. Morin also served Cardinals Richelieu and Mazarin,
who relied on him for advice in ecclesiastical matters.

     Apart from advising members of the Church and court, Morin worked
on various aspects of astrological theory. He devised a system of HOUSE
DIVISION based on the equal division of the equator; and known as the
Morinean system. He also began work on a reliable system of producing
lunar tables, but never completed it. His one substantial work, *Astrologia*

Gallica – 26 books on natal, judicial, mundane, electional and meteorological astrology – was published in Latin in 1661, and was a serious attempt to bring the most recent astronomical discoveries into the astrological theory and modernize it. From a rational point of view, he failed spectacularly, claiming (among other things) that scientific astrology was revealed to Adam by God, that the planets, though solid objects, were also celestial beings, and that the Star of Bethlehem was neither a comet nor two stars in conjunction, but an angel in a radiant cloud.

Morrison, Richard James (1795–1874) Born in Edmonton, UK, Morrison served in the Royal Navy between 1806 and 1817, rising to the rank of Lieutenant Commander. After retiring on half-pay, he studied astronomy and astrology. He had somewhat eccentric views on the former, but treated the latter with respect, and in 1831 set up in opposition to *Raphael*, publishing his own annual almanac, *The Herald of Astrology*, under the name Zadkiel – the Cabbalistic name for the angel of Jupiter. He later changed the almanac's title to *Zadkiel's Almanac*, under which it became extremely popular. In 1833 he published *The Grammar of Astrology*, a textbook, and later edited LILLY's *Christian Astrology*.

In the 1840s there began a number of prosecutions of astrologers for 'fortune-telling', under the Vagrancy Act. Morrison, with the aid of sympathetic solicitors, began a series of attempts to change the law in order to make such prosecutions impossible. Success evaded him. He received much publicity in 1861, when in his almanac for that year he suggested that people born on or near 26 August would suffer from health problems; these included the Prince Consort (whose birthday was on that date). On 14 December that year Prince Albert died. A number of fierce attacks on Zadkiel in several newspapers followed the apparent accuracy of his forecast; one of them in an anonymous letter which proved to have been written by a retired Rear-Admiral, Sir Edward Belcher. Morrison decided to prosecute him for slander.

Morrison vs Belcher was heard in June 1863 before the lord chief justice. The evidence concentrated as much on the spiritualism which Morrison also used as a means of prognostication, as on astrology. Belcher was found guilty, but damages of only 20s were awarded, and Morrison had to pay his own costs. The publicity however, resulted in a greatly increased circulation for the almanac. Morrison died in 1874; his almanac was carried on under Zadkiel's name, by A J Pearce.

Moulton, Thomas (fl. ca.1540) A Dominican monk, celebrated for one book: *This is the Myrour or Glasse of Helthe necessary and nedefull for every persone to loke in that wyll kepe body frome the Syckness of the Pestilence. And it sheweth howe the Planetts reygne in every houre of the daye and nyght with the natures and exposicions of the xii signes devyded by the xii monthes of the yere, and sheweth the remedyes for many divers infirmities and dyseases that hurteth the body of man* (1539) which went into nine editions.

Mukherji, Asit Krishna (1898–1977) A Jewish Bengali Brahmin astrologer, Mukherji took a doctorate in history at London University, and travelled to the USSR. Disillusioned with Communism, he became an enthusiastic supporter of the National Socialist movement in Germany, and *The New Mercury*, a magazine he started in England with a collaborator, Sri Vinaya Datta, was vociferous in its support of Ayrian supremacy and the Nazi race laws. In 1940 he met and married Savitri Devi, a fellow Nazi sympathizer, in order to save her from internment. When the British government closed *The New Mercury*, Mukherji set up *The Eastern Economist*, publication of which was sponsored by the Japanese legation in London. After the war he took no further part in politics, merely practising as an astrologer.

Mul_apin A famous set of Babylonian astronomical tablets, written in about 700BC, summarizing the result of observations going back to about 1300BC; study of the tablets has enabled us to recognize over 70 stars catalogued in Babylonia during the great period of astronomical observation. The name means Plough Star, and refers to the constellation Triangulum, which lies between Aries and Andromeda, and includes the Pleiades. The tablets are the source of much of what we know about the methods of calculation of the early Babylonian astrologer-astronomers.

mundane astrology Though nothing is known about the origins of astrology, so ancient is the subject, it can safely be conjectured that from very early times the movements of the planets against the pattern of fixed stars, together with such phenomena as ECLIPSES and COMETS, were used to attempt to predict national and political events. It is the examination of such matters that the term still describes, though its definition is vague and broad.

music KEPLER believed that there was, or certainly should be, an association between the planets and musical harmony, and the phrase 'harmony of the spheres' has an ancient parentage, originating with PYTHAGORAS in the 6th century BC. His fascination with the relationship between the musical note produced by a plucked string and its length was basically mathematic, and it followed that the musical notes produced by the planets, humming in a particular frequency as they moved through space, must relate to their speed and orbit. A number of composers, interested in astrology, have produced works based on the planets, the most famous being that written by Gustav HOLST.

mutable signs The mutable signs of the zodiac are Gemini, Virgo, Sagittarius and Pisces. These, when the Sun occupies them at birth, produce adaptable folk who are flexible enough to change with the prevailing wind, if they see that change to be to their advantage. They are versatile and resourceful, sympathetic and grateful for assistance. Diplomatic, they are generally liked, though if accused of duplicity they are often guilty. The mutable HOUSES are the third, sixth, ninth and twelfth. Planets in these houses will contribute a mutable flavour to the HOROSCOPE..

mutual reception Two planets are in mutual reception when each is in the sign ruled by the other – i.e., Mercury in Sagittarius, Jupiter in Gemini. *See* RULERSHIP.

– N –

nadir The lowest point at which the PRIME VERTICAL and the MERIDIAN intersect – the point of the CELESTIAL SPHERE opposite the ZENITH.

Nakshatras *see* LUNAR MANSIONS

Napier, John (1550–1617) Scottish mathematician and astrologer who invented logarithms, invaluable for the manual calculation of HOROSCOPES, and promulgated the use of the decimal point.

Napier, Richard (1559–1634) Born at Exeter, Napier was ordained after leaving Exeter College, Oxford, and studied astrology under William LILLY before becoming Rector of Great Linford, Buckinghamshire, where he remained for 44 years. He was an extremely devout man (his knees were 'horny from praying', the gossip John Aubrey wrote – at the same time noting that Napier claimed to be a personal friend of the angel Raphael). He continued to practise astrology, and Lilly so admired him that he left him all his manuscripts. He taught himself medicine, and in addition to his Church duties practised as doctor and astrologer, making a fortune from innumerable clients. He took every opportunity of advising his Church colleagues to study astrology, lending them books from his large and comprehensive astrological library.

natal astrology Astrology relying on the BIRTH-CHART as opposed to HORARY ASTROLOGY, which employs a chart drawn up for the moment a question is asked.

natal chart A BIRTH-CHART or HOROSCOPE calculated and drawn for the moment and place of an individual's birth.

Naylor, R H (1889–1952) English astrologer credited with inventing the modern SUN-SIGN newspaper column. For this *see* SUN-SIGN ASTROLOGY. He also had a considerable private practice.

Nechepso One of the kings of Egypt, said to have succeeded Stephinates, the founder of the 26th Dynasty. Little is known of him, and he is associated with astrology only in that PETOSIRIS is alleged to have written an astrological text for him. *See* Egypt.

Nectanebus *see* ALEXANDER THE GREAT

neo-Porphyry house system A system of HOUSE DIVISION similar to PORPHYRY, but modified so that the difference in QUADRANT sizes is equalized. First published in 1994.

Neptune Ψ

Discovered in 1846, Neptune orbits the Sun every 165 years, and therefore spends about 14 years in each of the zodiac signs. In astrological terms, though it works individually in every HOROSCOPE, it therefore has a 'generation influence'. The dates given below are approximate.

Neptune and the zodiac signs

Neptune in GEMINI

(1888–1901/2) Those born during this period seemed on the whole to have a mistrust of the pace at which new scientific developments took place, though inquisitive about them. About the developments themselves however, there was no marked scepticism or suspicion. In global terms this was a period that seemed allied to the Geminian interest in communication, with the invention of the telephone and the development of easy travel by road and train.

Neptune in CANCER

(1901/2–1915) As the sign of home and family, Cancerian values were affected by violence and suffering, a feature in the lives of almost everyone born during this period, either experiencing the First World War as children, or the second as adults. In general and personally, however, sensitivity and a vivid imagination seem to have been stimulated; but so does the capacity for anxiety.

Neptune in LEO

(1915–1928/9) Glamour played a remarkable part in the lives of these individuals, despite the problems of the inter-war years and the economic depression. The cinema and the period of classical musical comedy seemed to marry the influence of Neptune and the panache and creativity of Leo, and in particular stimulated those with creative potential.

Neptune in VIRGO

(1928/9–1942/3) The generation born during this period has taken a strongly critical view of established religions and of entrenched social attitudes: the question 'Why?' has been asked with an insistence reminiscent of the Age of Enlightenment. There has been a growth of idealism, and the period saw the beginning of the swift growth of an interest in conservation.

Neptune in LIBRA

(1942/3–1956/7) The peaceful influence and tendency to take the easy way out, characteristic of Neptune, married to the beauty-loving and relaxed attitude of Libra produced the characteristic 'flower people', with their interest in escapism – through drug-taking, for instance. Those with an Aries Sun tended to be inspirational but forgetful and vague, while otherwise healthily strong personal characteristics of those with a Capricorn Sun-sign were somewhat weakened by this position of Neptune.

Neptune in SCORPIO

(1956/7–1970/1) This influence seems best reflected in the edgy and seemingly brutal appearance of punks, who also often possessed a somewhat bafflingly mysterious character. The generation seems to have an increased emotional intensity. The combination of Neptune and Scorpio seemed equally strongly reflected in the popular music of the period, with its insistence and intensity.

Neptune in SAGITTARIUS

(1970/71–1984/5) The steady growth of interest in social justice and conservation, even before the concern about global warming, seem an inevitable result of the combination of Neptune and Sagittarius, with the former working inspirationally. Many of this generation are attracted to vegetarianism, and have a special concern with the wellbeing of animals.

Neptune in CAPRICORN

(1984/5–1998) The effect on universal concern for the wellbeing of Earth itself is obvious, with a cautious determination to meet the challenge. On a personal level, there is often a flair for the creative use of natural materials, but too often a tendency to negative escapism – the problem of drug-taking as a means of escaping the tensions and overwork of modern life is far from over.

Neptune in AQUARIUS

(1998–ca.2010) It is considered that the temperate qualities of Neptune should marry well with the compassionate elements of Aquarius, though the isolated, independent Aquarian traits are foreign to the sensitive, perceptive emotions of Neptune. On a personal level the marriage of the two should not be incompatible.

Neptune and the houses

Neptune in the FIRST HOUSE

A tendency to look for the easy way out when faced with problems or predicaments is common with this house placing of Neptune, and similar excuses may be found for a disinclination to make the most of potential. Quite apart from the dreamy, other-worldly attitude to life that this planet encourages, it may also work from the first house to undermine self-confidence.

Neptune in the SECOND HOUSE

Feelings of generosity may run riot to the extent that those with Neptune in the second house can almost bankrupt themselves to help others. Similarly, they can bankrupt themselves of time and emotional vigour; and a certain natural gullibility makes them easy targets for those who want to milk them either of time or money. Professional advice is highly advisable when thinking of investment. A free outpouring of love and affection is attractive.

Neptune in the THIRD HOUSE

Primary education may be difficult to instil, for day-dreaming will be a habit difficult to shake off. The imagination which will find this outlet in childhood will hopefully prove an advantage in adult life, especially if the HOROSCOPE as a whole shows imaginative flair. In family life, a child with this house placing of Neptune may tend to be difficult to reconcile to the presence of a younger sibling; confusion and jealousy may feature.

Neptune in the FOURTH HOUSE

This position of Neptune often reflects on the childhood of a subject, which may have been bewildering and confused, generally because home circumstances were chaotic and undisciplined. Not, however, unhappy; the imagination will have been stimulated (particularly perhaps by the mother). There may have been little attempt to instil a moral sense, and some confusion about the difference between right and wrong may take time to resolve.

Neptune in the FIFTH HOUSE

From the fifth house, Neptune tends to encourage a highly romantic and almost equally highly unrealistic attitude to love: those with this placing will fall in love all too easily, and the conviction that the loved one is not only beautiful and good, but equally loving and romantic, will inevitably sometimes be disappointed. Sex as an ingredient of romance will not however be neglected, and a touch of fantasy will add colour and adventure. But the heart will unquestionably rule the head, and while caution is necessary, it will rarely be exercised.

Neptune in the SIXTH HOUSE

A concern, even overconcern, with the health can be the result of this house placing of Neptune. Hypochondria is a distinct personality. There may be a poor reaction to prescribed drugs, and alternative medicine may be an excellent compromise. A steady routine at work is advisable, but will be difficult to attain; work will eventually be done, but in the subject's own time and manner, which may lead to difficulties with colleagues or employers.

Neptune in the SEVENTH HOUSE

High expectations of partners may cause problems in personal relationships – both before and after commitment. Attitudes may be confused, with both procrastination and sudden decisions featuring – neither of which will necessarily commend themselves to happiness. There is however a talent for romance which can be extremely tempting – though impracticality may mean that paying for romantic circumstances may be forgotten or long delayed. Real partnership must mean shared practical commitment.

Neptune in the EIGHTH HOUSE

Sensuality is emphasized when Neptune is placed in the eighth house, and the individual will have strong powers of attraction. Since there will be a heightened interest in sex, which will need to be satisfied, this may seem a dream combination; however (especially if Neptune is in Scorpio) there may be elements of confusion in the attitude to sex, which in the extreme may need professional help to revolve. A gullible attitude to finance may centre on the partner, and the possibility of deception should prompt a degree of caution and care.

Neptune in the NINTH HOUSE

An idealistic personality and a philosophical outlook on life will combine, and a degree of wisdom will result in a remarkable character, with a studious disposition and perhaps a religious bent, or at least an interest in the mystical elements of life. A healthy degree of scepticism should also be present, however, and while the intelligence will range at will over every possible area of spirituality, a sense of logicality will keep fantasy at bay.

Neptune in the TENTH HOUSE

There is likely to be a greater than average number of changes of direction in the life of someone with this house placing of Neptune. Both the career and the personal life are likely as a result to be fairly colourful. If Neptune is CONJUNCT the MIDHEAVEN there will be a very strong impetus to achieve whatever objectives the individual has set. The imagination will be heightened, and there will be a romantic outlook on life; both these, carefully controlled, will assist progress.

Neptune in the ELEVENTH HOUSE

The social life will be much enjoyed, among a large group of friends and acquaintances. These, however, must be tried and tested, for there is a tendency to gullibility which will allow someone with this placing of Neptune to be easily deceived. The subject will be too easily persuaded to accept a position that may become a trial: the chairmanship of a group at a particularly sensitive time, for instance. His or her initial hesitation to do this will be the right approach.

Neptune in the TWELFTH HOUSE

An excellent position of Neptune for anyone with creative potential, for it will underline whatever talent is displayed. At the same time there will be a strong tendency to pursue aims in seclusion; there will be reclusive and secretive tendencies which from time to time must be satisfied. The subject will allow his or her work to speak for them. There will be strong sympathy with the sick and suffering, and work in the caring professions will be highly satisfying; empathy and understanding are underlined.

* * *

neutral planets Mercury and Neptune, said to be helpful when well aspected to the BENEFICS, and unhelpful when aspected to the MALEFICS.

new moon *see* FULL MOON

newspaper astrology *see* SUN-SIGN ASTROLOGY

ninth house The ninth house of the HOROSCOPE is the house of Sagittarius and Jupiter, and is concerned with higher education, long-distance travel, dreams and challenge. The focus is on the way in which a person enlarges and expands his or her mind, on language skills and the ability to communicate what is learned. This house should be consulted when considering how a person should pursue higher education. There is an emphasis on the philosophical outlook, the personal moral code, conscience and a sense of vocation (strong aspects to Jupiter would firmly indicate the latter). Literature is also connected with the ninth house, and those areas of the media connected with foreign countries. Dreams and the inspiration received from them are a matter for this house. If the indications within the house are positive there will be good encouragement for someone who might wish to work in the travel industry or live abroad.

nocturnal *see* DIURNAL

nocturnal arc The distance travelled by a planet during the night.

nocturnal chart *see* DIURNAL CHART

nodes The two points at which the orbit of a celestial body intersects the plane of the ECLIPTIC or the CELESTIAL EQUATOR. When a planet intersects the plane while travelling north, the point is called the *ascending* or *north node* (its traditional name is the *Dragon's Head*); when travelling south, the *descending* or *south node* (the *Dragon's Tail*). Ancient astrologers used only the Moon's nodes – modern astrologers often take all nodes into account. It is claimed that in a horoscope they show how a subject relates to other people. Some astrologers assert that the Moon's north node has the quality of Jupiter and its south node that of Saturn, in which case the north node will be expected to show how potential may be used, and the south the limitations placed on us by our backgrounds – themes of expansion and restriction.

northern signs Aries, Taurus, Gemini, Cancer, Leo, Virgo, in which the Sun has northern DECLINATION.

Nostradamus (1503–66) Although Michael de Nostradamus is often referred to as an astrologer, his famous prophecies were almost entirely the product of other alleged means of foretelling the future. After a brief period of study at the University at Avignon, cut short by an outbreak of plague, he began studying medicine at Montpellier, but was expelled because he had worked for a time, in the intervening years, as an apothecary, a forbidden practice. In 1550 he wrote his first ALMANAC, so successful that a series followed containing almost innumerable prophecies. Requests for astrological consultations proliferated; he welcomed them, though was apparently unable to calculate HOROSCOPES and expected his clients to supply them, themselves. His collection of a thousand verses foretelling future events – for which even today he is remembered – was a success from its first publication; after reading it, Queen Catharine de Medici summoned him to court to construct horoscopes for her children. His quatrains have been examined and re-examined over the years since his death, and he has been credited with foretelling almost every major event from the French Revolution to the Second World War and the attack on the New York World Trade Centre in 2001. Though he claimed that his prophecies were rooted in astrology, they seem in fact to have been entirely psychic – though some are alleged to have been stolen from previously published books of forecasts.

numerology The use of numbers to predict the future. Mystical values are given to particular numbers – notably seven, which has religious significance in many traditions. Calculations based on the numerical values assigned to the letter of a name or the numbers of a birthday are used to produce a single number believed to have special power. ST AUGUSTINE, that inveterate enemy of astrologers, believed that numbers could be used to unlock the meanings of the more obtuse ancient biblical books, and PYTHAGORAS asserted that numbers had metaphysical significance. Charles CARTER used numerology in tandem with astrology, though he did not publish on the subject, and the manner in which he worked is obscure.

– O –

obliquity of the ecliptic The angle of 23° 27′ between the CELESTIAL EQUATOR and the ECLIPTIC.

occidental Planets placed in the western half of the HOROSCOPE are described as occidental; those in the east as oriental. A planet that is 'oriental' is therefore near the ASCENDANT, one that is 'occidental' is near the DESCENDANT. Occidental planets are visible in the evening, oriental ones in the morning. PTOLEMY claims that when planets are oriental they are masculine in influence, and when occidental, feminine, and that oriental planets therefore have the most powerful influence. The latter he believed to influence the personal appearance of a subject.

occultation As the Moon moves eastward across the sky, it from time to time *occults* or covers a star, hiding it from Earth. It moves at about half a degree an hour, and so while it seems to snuff out the star instantly, in fact it takes some time to cover it. Occultations of bright stars or planets are fairly rare.

Oken, Alan (b.1944) Professional American astrologer, teacher and lecturer, working at the Quiron Centre for Astrology and the Esperito do Sol, Lisbon. A former director of the Wisdom School in Santa Fe, he also works with the Australian Institute for the Development of Consciousness. Among his books are *Soul-Centred Astrology* (1990) and *Houses of the Horoscope* (1999).

Old, Walter Richard (1864–1929)) Old renamed himself W Gorn Old, but was best-known as Sepharial. An astrologer and theosophist, he studied medicine, but became interested in astrology and numerology. Working so furiously at astrology, Old suffered a nervous breakdown by the time he was 21, and arriving in London (from Birmingham) in 1889 became much involved with Anne Besant, Madame Blavatsky's successor in the British

Theosophical movement. He took the nom-de-plume of Sepharial, edited three magazines, wrote a textbook and a number of others, including *The Birthday Book of Destiny*, and a column of astrological advice in a monthly magazine, *The Society Times*. He worked to discover a means of predicting the winners of horse races and the movements of shares on the stock exchange (he was perhaps the first 'business astrologer'). Madame Blavatsky called him 'The Astral Tramp' because, she said, he 'roamed about in his astral body at night'.

Omarr, Sidney (1926–2003) American astrologer and numerologist, a prolific writer of SUN-SIGN books and well-known performer on television. Said to have been privately consulted by President Franklin D Roosevelt. He was also for some time a journalist, which assisted him in the writing of newspaper Sun-sign columns, notably for the *Los Angeles Times*, but widely syndicated.

Ophiuchus A constellation – one of those listed by PTOLEMY – which has never been a part of the zodiac, but was sometimes referred to as the 'thirteenth sign'. It stretches from about 17° Scorpio to 27° Sagittarius. Ptolemy believed that it had an influence similar to that of Saturn, though mitigated by Venus; but traditionally it attained the reputation of having an evil, poisonous influence.

opposition Two planets are in opposition when they are separated by 180°, and are therefore exactly opposite each other across the HOROSCOPE. An orb of 8° is allowed – but up to 10° when the Sun, Moon or RULING PLANET is concerned. The opposition is generally considered a negative ASPECT.

orb An ASPECT is only considered if it is 'in orb' – that is, if the planets are aligned to each other within a certain number of degrees. For the orbs allowable in each case, *see* the individual aspects.

orbit The path taken by a planet or moon as it orbits (circles around) a star or planet.

oriental *see* OCCIDENTAL

outer planets The four planets of the solar system most recently discovered, sometimes referred to, eccentrically, as the 'modern planets'. *See* URANUS, NEPTUNE, PLUTO, CHIRON. *See also* RULERSHIPS.

out-of-sign Said of an ASPECT which is not 'in ORB', and therefore not considered (or, exceptionally, only considered as having an extremely weak influence) when interpreting a HOROSCOPE.

– P –

Pallas Athene Often simply known as Pallas, this was the second
ASTEROID to be discovered, in 1802. As with the other asteroids, astrologers
consider the name given to it (however arbitrary this may seem). Though
there are a number of Pallas in myth, astrologers seem to associate it most
with the Titan Pallas, god of healing, intelligence and wisdom, and the sign
in which Pallas falls is said to indicate the area of life in which battles will
be fought and won in order to achieve ambitions. It strengthens the will to
overcome disappointments and turn them to positive account.

palmistry Many astrologers have had an interest in palmistry as a parallel
means of exploring personality and the possible future of a subject, and
indeed the association between palmistry and astrology has been insufficiently researched. It is an ancient practice, dating certainly from before
1500BC in India; Aristotle wrote about it at length, and it was taught in
German universities in the 17th century. The mounts, or fleshy pads on the
palm of the hand, are named after the planets. The few astrologers who
have taken a serious interest in palmistry have found that as a delineator of
character, and where prediction of the patterns of life are concerned, it is the
only other system which is as accurate as their own.

parallel aspect Planets which have the same degree of DECLINATION on the
same side of the EQUATOR are said to be in parallel aspect, and to share the
same indications as the CONJUNCTION. Planets in contra-parallel are
similarly placed but on opposite sides of the equator, and are said to share
the indications of the OPPOSITION aspect.

paran When two transiting planets are ANGULAR as one of them contacts the
ASCENDANT, MC, DESCENDANT or IC, it is said to be paran. For instance,
any stars or planets rising, culminating, descending or on the IC at the same
time that Venus was also in any of those positions, would be paran of
Venus, and believed to have an influence on its authority.

Parker, George (1651–1743) A high churchman, Parker was a keen and able mathematician, occasionally employed by Halley. After keeping a tavern, he set up as an astrologer in London, and in 1690 began publishing an annual almanac, *Mercurius Anglicanus; or the English Mercury*, which later became *Parker's Ephemeris*. For including the name of the Old Pretender in a list of monarchs, he was heavily fined and forbidden to publish any more almanacs. He had a long and contentious relationship with PARTRIDGE, violently attacking him in a pamphlet entitled *Flagitiosus Mercurius Flagellatus; or the Whipper whipp'd*. Partridge enthusiastically reciprocated.

pars fortunæ *see* PART OF FORTUNE

part *see* PART OF FORTUNE

partile An aspect is partile when it is precise (within 60′ of ARC and in the same degree). Traditionally the planets concerned had also to occupy the same degrees of LATITUDE and LONGITUDE. A planet is not partile when merely in ORB, but not in the same degree as another.

part of fortune A point which is as far from the ASCENDANT (in LONGITUDE) as the distance between the Sun and Moon. It is traditionally said to indicate an area of life in which a subject will find contentment and fulfilment and where he or she can fully express the personality. The modern astrologer Robert Hand sees it as a prime indicator of prosperity and of the relationship between the body and health.

Partridge, John (1644–1715) Originally a cobbler in East Sheen, Partridge studied Latin, Greek, Hebrew and astrology. Moving to London he lived first in Covent Garden then in Blackfriars, and began issuing an annual almanac in 1678. He was an enthusiast for the astrology of Ptolemy, and denounced his colleagues for unnecessary reform of the methods laid down in the *TETRABIBLOS*. He attacked LILLY especially for his HORARY work, which he considered an aberration. A natural combatant, Whig and Dissenter, he attacked the monarchy, the Church and most contemporary astrologers. When James II succeeded to the throne, he left England for safer ground in Holland, whence he continued to issue almanacs forecasting the downfall of the King and popery. When William and Mary took the throne, he returned to London, probably the most famous astrologer in England, and as such bitterly satirized by Jonathan Swift who, as 'Isaac Bickerstaff', published a fake almanac in which he predicted Partridge's death and later another in which the astrologer's death was actually reported, together with an elegy beginning:

Here five feet deep lies on his back
A cobbler, starmonger and quack.

Partridge had some difficulty in proving that he was still alive; he lived for another seven years; a rich man, he retired to Mortlake in Surrey, where he died.

Pearce, Alfred James (1840–1923) The son of a homoeopathic doctor himself interested in astrology, Pearce failed to qualify as a doctor, but acted as an assistant to his father, calculating the BIRTH-CHARTS of patients before Dr Pearce prescribed for them. He became an acquaintance of R J MORRISON, and when the latter died the family invited him to become the editor of *Zadkiel's Almanac*. He agreed, and edited the magazine for 47 years, until his death, raising its circulation very considerably. Unlike Morrison, he eschewed any form of spiritualism, and concentrated on 'pure' astrology, which he viewed as a mathematical science. In particular he insisted on using PRIMARY DIRECTIONS as a means of prediction, rather than the simpler SECONDARY directions. He violently attacked theosophical astrology, describing its magazine, *Modern Astrology*, as 'superstitious nonsense'.

peregrine A planet without essential DIGNITIES is described as peregrine.

perigee The point in the orbit of a planet when it is nearest Earth.

perihelion The point in the orbit of a planet when it is nearest the Sun.

personal planets The 'personal planets' are the Sun, Moon, the planet ruling the ASCENDANT sign (also known as the chart ruler), the planet ruling the SUN-SIGN (the Sun ruler) and the planet ruling the sign occupied by the Moon (the Moon ruler).

Petosiris (otherwise **Ankhefenkhons**) *(*fl. ca.300BC) Said to have been a high priest of Thoth at Hermapolis during the epoch of Persian rule in Egypt. He wrote an astrological book for King Nechepso of Egypt. He is buried at Tuna el-Gebel. *See* EGYPT, NECHEPSO.

Pisces ♓

The twelfth sign of the zodiac. SUN-SIGN period 19 February–20 March.

It should be remembered when reading of the characteristics of the Sun-signs that these will always be affected by the effects of the rising-sign, the planets in various other signs and houses, and the relationships the planets make to each other.

General characteristics

Often referred to as the poets of the zodiac, those people born when the Sun is in Pisces are deeply emotional and usually not afraid to show it. They are very susceptible to the emotions of others, and often ready to subdue their own feelings, sometimes deceiving themselves in order to do so – ready for instance to lie rather than hurt the other person. Deceiving others, they often deceive themselves, donning rose-coloured spectacles and seeing situations in a rosy glow which glamorizes hard facts. They have a strange almost self-destructive tendency, seeing what needs to be done, and even knowing what they should do – but for some often obscure reason taking a line of action completely counter to their best interests. The following confusion seems almost to satisfy some psychological need in them. Extremely charitable, they are always ready to help others, sometimes putting their own interests aside in order to do so (perhaps because they find their own lives difficult to control, and devote their time to other peoples' lives as a way of escape). They make warm, affectionate lovers, and express their love generously – in the case of their children, perhaps overgenerously.

The growing child

Even when small, Piscean children will be ready to tell white lies to get themselves out of difficult situations. If this is not gently but firmly corrected at a very early age, it can lead to a habit of deceit difficult to break in adolescence and adulthood. Even when being truthful, the young Piscean may not be strictly so, for he or she will enjoy embroidering the truth with their own often fantastic imagination. Children with the Sun in Pisces are usually extremely creative, begin to draw at a very early age, and very soon become devoted to the digital and video camera. Encouragement in this area can give them self-confidence, which they often lack – every Piscean knows someone who is better than them at any task they are performing.

Education

Sun-sign Pisceans may appear lazy at school, and given to day-dreaming; this may impede study and lead to poor performances in examination – on the other hand they will be brilliant at the social side of school life, in school plays or concerts, for instance. They may be easy prey to school bullies and/or insensitive teachers; the development of a straightforward, no-nonsense attitude, putting their dreams aside during school hours, will help guard them from this – and increase their powers of concentration. If they are interested in science, it will be in those areas which allow a free rein to imagination – space exploration is certainly one. They will need to learn to concentrate, and to allow their fantastic imaginative powers to give way to, or at least be informed by, real facts.

Friendship, romance and sex

Kind and generous friends, Pisceans tend to shrink from any praise given them, tending not to believe that the compliment which is being offered can possibly be an honest opinion. Their genuine shyness can be mistaken for equivocation, for they will often wait for decisions to be made for them. When they fall in love, they do so with all their romantic hearts, and often with an idealized version of the prospective partner which can lead straight to disaster. They will woo with passionate intensity, and if there are differences of opinion between them and their lovers these will simply be ignored. The partners will also be seen as perfect, their faults also ignored:

another way of courting disaster. Sexually, they are warm and ardent, but they can crave emotional excitement, which can lead to promiscuity (Pisces is a dual sign).

Permanent partnership and family
Pisceans are tender and caring partners, but in a permanent partnership their generous emotions, the expression of which probably seems charming at first, can become cloying and irritating emotional sense-lessness. Under pressure they can sometimes be petulant and irritable, and when things go wrong extremely evasive, vague and deceptive. Both in major and minor domestic upsets, they can lie, telling them-selves that it is to prevent the partner being hurt. They believe this, and it will no doubt be true – until of course the reality comes to light, when the situation is made ten times worse. Shared interests will do much for the partnership, and Pisceans do have a real intuitive talent for 'know-ing' what their partners – or children – think or need. Often too easy-going, their children can take advantage of them; they can sometimes see in their children the opportunity to achieve their own ambitions, and pressure them in inappropriate directions.

Occupation
When the Sun is in Pisces it often encourages people to work in some way behind the scenes, sometimes leaving others to take the credit which should be theirs. The kindly, emotional Piscean works well in the caring professions – nursing is a good example, and in other branches of the medical profession. A profession which demands hours of work in a confined, claustrophobic space – for that matter requires very strict timekeeping – will not be ideal; it may provide security, but the Piscean will find it stifling. On the other hand discipline is welcomed (avoiding the necessity to make too many decisions!). There is a strong traditional link between this Sun-sign and the Church, and a vocation for the priesthood (or a similar position in some other creed) is not unlikely. Pisceans enjoy 'showing off'; the 'theatrical' side of Church ritual will appeal – but so will the theatre proper. Actors frequently enjoy hiding their own personalities behind those of the characters they portray, and this suits Pisceans admirably.

Health

The Piscean body area is the feet, and these sometimes give trouble (especially to women who wear fashionable shoes, ignoring the fact that they cause pain). But the imaginative, rather sensitive Piscean system is well suited to hypochondria, which is always a possibility with those of this Sun-sign. On the other hand, even physically nonexistent illness has an effect, and stress can show itself in headaches, slight digestive problems, or even the conviction that they are somehow not completely well. The temptation to take even the 'safest' drugs is usually resisted; Pisceans react poorly to them, in particular to antibiotics, even something as simple as aspirin. The reaction to alcohol is similarly likely to be extreme. Every one of the many 'social' drugs are likely to cause severe problems, while if everyone is better avoiding cigarettes, Pisces is top of the list. Yoga is excellent for them, as is noncompetitive exercise.

Finance

The Piscean who hands all his or her money over to a wiser partner, or straight into the hands of a financial adviser, is extremely wise. What is known as 'an easy touch', these Sun-sign people are financially rash and gullible: Pisces and his (or her) money is soon parted. It is extremely rare to find a Piscean who has made a fortune through wise investment, by seeing 'a good thing' and putting money into it. If this is the case, a strong influence from some other area of the HOROSCOPE has surely been at work. They are best at making money by the exercise of their creative, imaginative powers – usually backed by wise advisers. They will be wise to reject any attempt to get money out of them: indeed, the advice 'neither a borrower nor a lender be' may have been addressed to a Piscean.

Growing older

Poor organizers, and reluctant to look at the future with an eye to shaping it in any way, Pisceans will shrink from the idea of the change brought by retirement; the very thought of having to go through it will confuse and worry them. Their imaginations will have them in the workhouse the moment their regular income ceases, and they will have no idea how to go about organizing their lives once their days and weeks are no longer planned for them by the conditions of their employment. Those who enter retirement with a strong interest in some hobby will be less likely to worry than others, for they will be delighted at the opportunity to widen and broaden that hobby; if there is no such interest, the desert of free time stretching ahead will appal them, and they will have no idea what to do with it. Acquiring an interest of some sort will be vital.

Pisces as rising-sign

When Pisces is rising, everything that has been said above as characteristic of Pisces will be emphasized, with resulting stress on the nervous system. There will in addition be a very strong critical sense, which when applied to a prospective or permanent partner will be capable of doing the relationship real harm. These people will not suffer fools gladly; while they may be polite enough to restrain their comments in the company of that fool, their opinions will be very firmly expressed indeed to anyone else who will listen. The influence of Pisces when it is the rising-sign will, interestingly, soften and mitigate some of the harsher edges of other Sun-signs – but every Piscean fault itself will be exacerbated and magnified.

Traditional associations

- Ruling Planet – Neptune (formerly Jupiter)
- Triplicity/Element – water
- Quadruplicity/Quality – mutable
- Colour – soft sea-green
- Gemstone – moonstone or bloodstone
- Metal – tin or platinum
- Flower – water-lily
- Trees – willow, fig, trees growing near water
- Herbs and Spices – saccharum, succory, lime, mosses
- Foodstuffs – cucumber, pumpkin, turnip, lettuce, melon
- Animals – mammals that like water; fish
- Countries – Portugal, the Gobi and Sahara deserts
- Cities – Alexandria, Bournemouth, Jerusalem, Santiaga de Compostela, Seville, Warsaw
- US States – Florida, Maine, Nebraska, Ohio, Vermont, Washington DC

* * *

places A traditional name for the HOUSES.

Placidus house system One of the two most popular systems of HOUSE DIVISION (the other being the EQUAL HOUSE system). Though it has been attributed to the 17th century Placido de Titus (1603–68), he clearly relied on an earlier method devised by PTOLEMY, and/or an 8th-century Arabian system, and the Placidus system was in fact first published in 1602 by Giovanni Antonii MAGINI.

plague The scourge of the various waves of plague which swept across Europe exercised astrologers, particularly those who were either physicians or interested in MEDICAL ASTROLOGY. The notorious Black Death, for instance, estimated to have killed 25 million Europeans between 1342 and 1351, prompted not only speculations as to its cause but as to its treatment. Geoffrey of Meaux is said to have predicted the approach of the Black Death, connecting it to the appearance of a notable comet in 1315, followed in 1345 by the conjunction of three superior planets in Aquarius and a total lunar eclipse. He suggested that because at that time there were few stars of magnitude in Aquarius, the plague attacked the peasantry more than the nobility. The astrologer Gentile da Foligno, a severely practical astrologer, held that it was a sickness caused by planetary dispositions – he and most astrologers suspected eclipses of the Sun and Moon and conjunctions of Saturn and Mars as prime movers, especially when they occurred in one of the 'human' signs of the zodiac, when the planets produced a kind of rotting of the air which was poisonous when drawn into the lungs. He suggested the drinking of potable gold as a possible specific; he himself died of the plague shortly after publishing his views at the commission of the University of Perugia. Astrologers were united in claiming that the coming of plague was signalled by God through the movements of the planets (though they disagreed about which particular movements were most indicative); this and their advice on the treatment of the disease – which again varied wildly from one to the other – had the effect of confirming the stature of medical astrology, and the fact that many astrologers remained closely in contact with the sick, nursing as well as advising them, added to their reputation.

Much the same effects occurred during later plagues. The plagues which decimated the population of London in 1603, 1625 and 1665 equally exercised the minds of such astrologers as FORMAN, LILLY and GADBURY.

planet The bodies which, like Earth, circle the Sun and from Earth appear to travel through the zodiac. Recently some astronomers have attempted to redefine the word, one of the results being the reclassification of Pluto as a 'dwarf planet'. The general public has so far ignored this, and for astrologers it has no significance whatsoever.

planetary hours Traditionally every hour of the day is supposed to be ruled by one of the planets. However, the conventional modern 24-hour clock is *not* used, and to calculate the time at which each planet is ruling one must divide the hours of daylight and those of darkness by 12. For instance, if the Sun rises at 6.15 a.m. and sets at 7.43 p.m. (19.43), the length of the day – calculated for the hours of daylight – is taken as 13 hours 27' 52''. This is divided by 12 to give 12 hours of 1hr 7' 11'' each. Remember also that the planet that rules the first hour of daylight is the one that rules the day: i.e., the Sun on Sunday, the Moon on Monday, and so on.

The complete table is as follows:

Hour	Sunday	Monday	Tuesday	Wednesday	Thursday	Friday	Saturday
1	Sun	Moon	Mars	Mercury	Jupiter	Venus	Saturn
2	Venus	Saturn	Sun	Moon	Mars	Mercury	Jupiter
3	Mercury	Jupiter	Venus	Saturn	Sun	Moon	Mars
4	Moon	Mars	Mercury	Jupiter	Venus	Saturn	Sun
5	Saturn	Sun	Moon	Mars	Mercury	Jupiter	Venus
6	Jupiter	Venus	Saturn	Sun	Moon	Mars	Mercury
7	Mars	Mercury	Jupiter	Venus	Saturn	Sun	Moon
8	Sun	Moon	Mars	Mercury	Jupiter	Venus	Saturn
9	Venus	Saturn	Sun	Moon	Mars	Mercury	Jupiter
10	Mercury	Jupiter	Venus	Saturn	Sun	Moon	Mars
11	Moon	Mars	Mercury	Jupiter	Venus	Saturn	Sun
12	Saturn	Sun	Moon	Mars	Mercury	Jupiter	Venus

The same rule applies for the hours of darkness:

Hours	Sunday	Monday	Tuesday	Wednesday	Thursday	Friday	Saturday
1	Jupiter	Venus	Saturn	Sun	Moon	Mars	Mercury
2	Mars	Mercury	Jupiter	Venus	Saturn	Sun	Moon
3	Sun	Moon	Mars	Mercury	Jupiter	Venus	Saturn
4	Venus	Saturn	Sun	Moon	Mars	Mercury	Jupiter
5	Mercury	Jupiter	Venus	Saturn	Sun	Moon	Mars
6	Moon	Mars	Mercury	Jupiter	Venus	Saturn	Sun
7	Saturn	Sun	Moon	Mars	Mercury	Jupiter	Venus
8	Jupiter	Venus	Saturn	Sun	Moon	Mars	Mercury
9	Mars	Mercury	Jupiter	Venus	Saturn	Sun	Moon
10	Sun	Moon	Mars	Mercury	Jupiter	Venus	Saturn
11	Venus	Saturn	Sun	Moon	Mars	Mercury	Jupiter
12	Mercury	Jupiter	Venus	Saturn	Sun	Moon	Mars

planetary man Similar to the ZODIAC MAN, associating the planets with specific areas of the body, which they are supposed to affect. PTOLEMY introduced the idea in his *TETRABIBLOS*, with the following list: Saturn is Lord of the right ear, the spleen, the bladder, phlegm and the bones; Jupiter of touch, the lungs, the arteries and the seed; Mars of the left ear, the kidneys, the veins and genitals; the Sun of sight, the brains, the heart, the nerves and all the right side of the body; Venus of smell, the liver and the muscles; Mercury of speech and thought, the tongue, the bile and the buttocks; and the Moon of taste, drinking, the mouth, the belly, the womb and the left-hand side of the body.

Plato (427–347BC) Greek philosopher. Plato taught (in his *Timaeus*) that the *demiurge*, or craftsman who had formed the universe, had made the human soul from the same material as the stars, and that each human soul had originated as a star, and then been translated into animal form. It was man's destiny eventually to return to the stars. He writes of the movements of the planets as 'the dance of the gods', and was aware that the pattern they made – especially OPPOSITIONS and CONJUNCTIONS – caused men to fear for the future. He did not write specifically about astrology, but was clearly aware of the existence of astrologers, and his theories strongly influenced the development of their theories.

Plotinus (ca. AD205–270) A philosopher and writer, the founder of the Neoplatonic school of philosophy, Plotinus opposed fatalistic astrology, but believed that the stars and planets were divine, and considered the Christians to blaspheme when they held that mankind might be superior to these heavenly gods, in whom there could be no evil.

Pluto ♇

Pluto was discovered in 1930. It takes about 248 years to travel round the Sun, and therefore stays in each sign of the zodiac for as long as 30 years – though because of the eccentricity of its ORBIT, it remains in others for as few as 15. Astrologers have connected the sign with violence, extreme action and reaction. It has been assigned to rule Scorpio (previously ruled by Mars). Because of the long period of time it stays in one sign its influence is on whole generations, though it can also have a dynamic influence in individual HOROSCOPES.

Pluto and the zodiac signs

Pluto in GEMINI
(1883/4–1912/3) There was a certain amount of mental restlessness (depending on the influences of other planets). The generation as a whole seemed inclined to make drastic changes: in England the reign of King Edward VII considerably loosened restrictive moral standards.

Pluto in CANCER
(1913/4–1937/8) The disruptive effects of Pluto on family life were exacerbated by the two worlds wars which fell during this period. Sun-sign Cancerians with this placing of Pluto tend to hug problems to themselves rather than share them with others who can help.

Pluto in LEO
(1937/8–1956/7) There has been a distinct spread of petty and major dictators during this period, and the protection of the interests of the general

mass of people has come under pressure. The domineering aspect of Pluto has been emphasized, and marginally fanatic tendencies have been demonstrated by SUN-SIGN Taureans, Scorpios and Aquarians born during this period.

Pluto in VIRGO

(1956/7–1971) Those born with Virgo as their Sun-sign, MOON- or RISING-SIGN tend to be leaders of their generation in whichever area they move, making dynamic changes which affect not only their own lives but those of people around them. Everyone with Pluto in Virgo possesses a personal idiosyncratic power to use in their individual way.

Pluto in LIBRA

(1971–1983/4) The Libran sense of justice does, or should, possess those born during this period. The invention of the birth-control pill freed women, in particular, from previous inhibitions, and 'opting out' of convention was a feature of many areas, from sexual behaviour to personal refusal to take part in warfare. On another personal level, obsessive tendencies are possible.

Pluto in SCORPIO

(1983/4–1995) Intensity and sense of purpose are features of those with Pluto in this sign. If Scorpio is the Sun-sign, Moon- or rising-sign there will be a very strong emotional drive which will need to be governed and positively channelled. More generally, the Scorpio influence is seen in the overwhelming appearance of black in fashion, and in the more frenetic pop music. As Pluto entered Scorpio in 1984 the AIDS virus first became prominent.

Pluto in SAGITTARIUS

(1995–2017) Pluto and Sagittarius are in general opposing influences – freedom-loving and independent on one side, secretive and intense on the other. Clearly this can lead to problems – though Pluto may act as a sort of purging influence, prompted by Sagittarius to free up overcautious behaviour and reveal what has previously been hidden.

Pluto in CAPRICORN

Pluto first entered Capricorn in January 2008; its major influences are being discussed.

Pluto and the houses

Pluto in the FIRST HOUSE

Pluto (which may well also be in the ASCENDING SIGN) will shade the personality with an emotionally intense quality. There may be obsessional tendencies, and certainly an enjoyment of research, of discovering hidden or obscure facts. A need to release emotional energy through sex can be positively or negatively expressed – or sometimes sublimated and directed towards achieving ambitions – important, since a strong sense of purpose will be present, and need to be satisfied.

Pluto in the SECOND HOUSE

Excellent potential for success in business can be encouraged by a keen interest in making money; if this becomes obsessional, damage can result. There will be ample determination and will to succeed, and possessions (illustrating a degree of success) will be important. The emotional and sexual life will be healthily passionate, and Pluto in this house actively encourages the study and practice of sexual techniques.

Pluto in the THIRD HOUSE

Keen observation will be used to satisfy continual curiosity about what makes everyone and everything tick. Investigative journalists are greatly helped by Pluto working from the third house, and the communicative skills encouraged by the third house is characteristic. Children with this placing of Pluto will be as interested in gaining information as adults, and will not be put off by superficial or insufficiently clear answers.

Pluto in the FOURTH HOUSE

A degree of frustration during youth is not uncommon among those with Pluto in the fourth house; parents may also have inhibited growth by the exercise of too much restrictive power. Intuition, determination and tenacity are excellent weapons, however, and lessons (even learned the hard way) will be heeded. This is not an easy placing for the planet; fortunately those who suffer it also often have a strong sense of self-analysis, which aids them to look for positive results.

Pluto in the FIFTH HOUSE
The sex life will be intense, rich and possibly varied, but those with Pluto in the fifth house expect a great deal from their lovers, and are inevitably sometimes disappointed; there will be more than the usual amount of moving on, seeking perfection and (naturally) failing to find it. Creative work will be important; again perfection will be sought, and with determination. The tendency to take financial, emotional and physical risks can sometimes result in disaster.

Pluto in the SIXTH HOUSE
Routine and discipline are extremely important when Pluto inhabits the sixth house – to an extent which can become obsessional. But the powers of concentration are extremely good, and the results of careful work are impressive. A concern with health can centre on bowel problems (Pluto's constipating effects becoming all too literal); when suffering from emotional problems, comfort-eating can contribute to this.

Pluto in the SEVENTH HOUSE
A great deal of emotional energy will be expended on personal relationships, which are likely to be stormy if the person with this placing of Pluto does not curb the desire always to be in control, always to dominate, always to be on top. In extremis, he or she may purposely look for a partner with a weaker will, who will be content to be dominated. Imbalance in the relationship will not be positive. In business the problem is not so destructive; a partner still needs to be consulted, but in the end there is probably the need for only one driver, and that will be the individual with Pluto in the seventh house.

Pluto in the EIGHTH HOUSE
A shrewd business sense will be a distinct advantage, and the strong intuition with which this position of Pluto generally endows a person will mean that a combination of the two elements will make for an excellent

businessman or woman (especially if Pluto is in either Cancer or Virgo). The emotional level will be high, but there may be some difficulty in expressing it, especially sexually; counselling may be needed – perhaps also in connection with a possible preoccupation with an alleged psychic ability.

Pluto in the NINTH HOUSE

Willingness – indeed eagerness – to accept any mental challenge can be expressed too strongly, with tension and strain resulting. A striving for perfection will drive someone with this placing of Pluto to extremes, performing a task again and again in an attempt to improve the result. Discontent and frustration will be common if the challenge is actually beyond the subject's abilities. This can be worsened if it means throwing over a course of study on which high hopes had been placed.

Pluto in the TENTH HOUSE

With Pluto in the tenth house, here must be a strong involvement with the career, or at least with some important personal goal, especially if the planet CONJUNCTS the MIDHEAVEN. A sense of power may be too predominant. The expenditure of all this emotional energy on something concrete and achievable is vital if there is not to be psychological trouble; there is great potential, and it must be positively expressed.

Pluto in the ELEVENTH HOUSE

This is a somewhat mild influence, which tends to be exerted in the area of life concerned with friends and acquaintances, who may become of too much importance in the mind of the subject; there can be quarrels over extremely small alleged offences. Indeed the attitude of society in general will be important; there will be a continual preoccupation with the opinions of others, at the expense of personal relationships.

Pluto in the TWELFTH HOUSE

Not an easy placing of Pluto. Introspection may become a problem when what can be a powerful unconscious affects everyday behaviour, in a mysterious and incomprehensible way. Reclusive, secretive tendencies are common, and an inability to discuss even everyday problems with family or friends. There can also be the possibility of seeking an escape through drugs

– whether such 'innocent' ones as tobacco or alcohol, or more dangerous illegal substances. Even tranquillizers can be addictive.

* * *

polar charts In setting up astrological charts for polar regions astrologers meet with severe difficulties – at each pole half of the ECLIPTIC is permanently below the horizon and at certain times of year the Sun fails to rise. Most systems of house division are then inoperative, EQUAL HOUSE being the only reliable one.

polarity The *polar* signs are Aries/Libra, Taurus/Scorpio, Gemini/Sagittarius, Cancer/Capricorn, Leo/Aquarius and Virgo/Pisces. Opposite each other across the zodiac, they share a special relationship. Far from their influences opposing each other, these pairs of signs complement each other, sharing a special rapport and understanding. Polarity is of considerable importance when considering personal relationships between two people: those who share an emphasis on a pair of polar signs are likely to find it easy to understand each other's point of view, while not necessarily being always in agreement.

Poole, William (fl.1600–50) Describing himself as 'a nibbler at astrology', and claiming to have worked in 17 professions, Poole left an unpublished manuscript and a large library to his friend the astrologer Dr Ardee with strict instructions that 'if he give my wife anything that is mine, I wish the Devil may fetch him body and soul'. Ardee gave the books to Poole's friend William LILLY, who passed them on to Mrs Poole. Poole was at one time accused by a magistrate, Sir Thomas Jay, of stealing a silver cup. Hearing later that Jay had died, Poole visited his grave, defecated on it, and left a note:

> *Here lieth buried Sir Thomas Jay, Knight,*
> *Who being dead, I upon his grave did shite.*

popes, the, and astrology Many popes had a strong interest in astrology, saw no reason to suppose it was the work of the devil, and used it in

216

various ways. Sixtus IV (1471–84) was himself a noted astrologer, while Pius II (1458–64) accepted it at least to the extent that he imprisoned a man for predicting his death (the astrologer, as it turned out, was correct). Paul III (1534–49) was particularly enthusiastic, and his court became a positive university for astrologers, headed by Luca GAURICO, who would specify the precise moment when important works (such as the laying of the foundation stone of a new church) should be undertaken. Alexander IV (1492–1503) commissioned the artist Pinturicchio to paint mythological astrological scenes in his private rooms in the Vatican, including a portrait of Hermes. Adrian IV (1154–59, the only English Pope), Julius II (1503–13) and Leo X (1513–21) were also either enthusiasts for the subject or at the very least encouraged astrologers to make predictions relevant to themselves and their times. It is however fruitless to search the *Catholic Encyclopaedia* for information on this subject; it has been carefully censored.

Porphyry (Malchus) (ca.234–ca.305) A student of philosophy under Plotinus, whose work he later edited, Porphyry wrote a life of Pythagoras and commentaries on Euclid and Aristotle. He published work on philosophy, philology, vegetarianism and religion. He was a violent opponent of Christianity, claiming that 'The Gods have proclaimed Christ to have been pious, but the Christians are a confused and vicious sect'. Among his work on astrology, he developed his own system of HOUSE DIVISION. But *see* ANTIOCHUS.

Porphyry house system A system of HOUSE DIVISION in which each QUADRANT of the ECLIPTIC is trisected between the four ANGLES.

precession The gradual movement of the VERNAL EQUINOX westward at the rate of 50″ a year. *See* AGES.

prediction There is sensitivity among astrologers about the use of the word 'prediction'. Some, especially those troubled by theological arguments or by the apparent lack of basis of the means of prediction (and *see* SECONDARY PROGRESSIONS) take the view that it is impossible to predict events, and that astrological prediction can best be compared to widely recognized predictive techniques such as weather or financial forecasting.

Others claim that accurate prediction is possible, and that a competent astrologer should be able to predict the major events in the life of any person whose BIRTH-CHART is studied. It must be said that there are, both in historical and modern times, spectacular examples of accurate predictions of both personal and national events; whether to a degree which excludes the possibility of coincidence is arguable. It is also the case that when accurate predictions have been made, they have often been insufficiently detailed: the accurate prediction, to the day, of maritime disaster illustrated by the sinking in 1987 of the car ferry *Herald of Free Enterprise*, with great loss of life, was impressive – yet unless in such a case the astrologer could produce such detail as even a rough estimate of the position of the disaster or the type of vessel involved, his prediction is more or less useless.

Astrology was only one – though probably the most sophisticated – of many means of prediction which have been used throughout history. They include – apart from the work of mediums and prophets – prediction through the use of:

- a red-hot axe – *axinomancy*
- the smoke from burning poppy leaves – *capnomancy*
- the sound of neighing horses – *hippomancy*
- the noise of a waterfall – *hydromancy*
- the examination of the entrails of a fish – *ichthyomancy*
- the crackling made by roasting a donkey's head – *kephalomancy*
- the sound of stones being struck together – *lithomancy*
- the behaviour of rats or mice – *myomancy*
- the texture of fig tree leaves – *sycomancy*
- the reflections in the oiled fingernails of a young male virgin – *onychomancy*

Dreams have also frequently been thought to predict the future. The Tarot and the I Ching are perhaps the only two systems of prophecy that can be compared to astrology as far as complexity and sophistication are concerned.

prenatal eclipse An eclipse occurring within twelve months before the birth of the subject of a HOROSCOPE.

prenatal epoch An alleged CONCEPTION CHART, calculated for the day about nine months before birth, on which the Moon is in the opposite position to its position at the time of actual birth, or was on the ASCENDANT or DESCENDANT degrees.

primary directions Prediction from the birth-chart of an individual is based on the idea that each 24-hour period of Earth time is equivalent to one degree in the Sun's movement around the zodiac, so that a movement of one degree equals one year in the life of the subject. Predictions are made after examination of the ASPECTS between the planets in their new positions. *See* PROGRESSIONS.

prime vertical A vertical circle passing through the ZENITH and NADIR and the east and west points of the horizon is called the prime vertical. Its plane corresponds to the points of intersection of the horizon and the equator.

progressed chart *see* SECONDARY PROGRESSIONS

progressions When forecasting the possible future pattern of a life, astrologers use a Ptolemaic system called 'a Day for a Year'; the positions of the planets 24 hours after birth are taken to symbolize the circumstances of an individual's life trends during the second year; those shown 5 days after birth are taken to symbolize the trends between the ages of 5 and 6; those 20 days after birth will indicate the circumstances of life between 20 and 21 – and so on.

Ptolemy, Claudius (ca. AD100–ca.178) Greek astronomer, mathematician, geographer and astrologer. Ptolemy's *Almagest* was the most important astronomical text of his time. His astrological text, the *Tetrabiblos*, is of equal weight. Its real title accurately translated is *A Mathematical Treatise in Four Books*, and it was for over a thousand years the most important of all astrological texts. Many of the terms used in it are still employed by 21st-century astrologers. In historical times, when there was no problem with the proposition that a distinguished astronomer should also have written on astrology, there was no question of Ptolemy's authorship; with the Age of Enlightenment astronomers attempting to distance themselves from astrology disgracefully pretended that the text could not have been by its true author. More modern scholars however have shown it to be genuine.

The *TETRABIBLOS* had an enormous effect not only on astrology but literature (Ptolemy is for instance the originator of the seven ages of man attributed to Jacques in Shakespeare's *As You Like It*). Ptolemy speculates on the possibility that the time of conception may be as important, astrologically, as the time of birth; he sets out in full his theory of correspondences between Earth and heaven, listing the zodiac signs which RULE various countries; for medical purposes he relates the planets to specific parts of the human body (thus enlarging the theory which already pointed out a relationship between body areas and the zodiac signs).

Pythagoras (ca.580BC–ca.500) A Greek philosopher said to have been a personal pupil of Zoroaster in Babylon, whose main beliefs influenced later philosophers such as Plato and Aristotle, and thus the whole course of philosophical thought. While his arguments and discoveries have been confused with those of his disciples, he is generally believed to have been the first to examine the theory of numbers and their significance (including, for instance, the idea that odd numbers are masculine and even numbers feminine). It is the development of this theory that is the main significance of his work as far as astrology is concerned.

– Q –

quadrants The four quarters of a HOROSCOPE or BIRTH-CHART.

quadratures The changes, phases or quarters of the Moon; the SQUARE aspect.

Quadripartium, The *see* TETRABIBLOS

qualities Fire, earth, water and air are said to be composed of different qualities: fire is hot and dry, earth cold and dry, water cold and moist and air hot and humid. The signs that are hot by nature, the fire and air signs, exude energy, are animated and considerate, draw on the energy of others. The dry signs, the fire and earth signs, are edgy and tense, carefully considering the implications of every action and breaking quick to act. The cold signs, the earth and water signs, are more thoughtful, slow, everything down to its component parts. The wet signs, the air and water signs, and are calm and supple in their minds, good at relating to others, and at lateral thinking, never accepting things at face value.

quartile Traditional name for a SQUARE aspect.

querant The term used in HORARY ASTROLOGY to describe a person who asks a particular question not applying to a personality: i.e., the place where a lost object may be found, the circumstances of a theft, the conditions likely to apply to a journey, etc.

quincunx A quincunx ASPECT is formed when two planets are 150° apart. An ORB of 2° is allowed, or up to 3° with the Sun, Moon or a PERSONAL PLANET. This is considered a somewhat strenuous negative aspect.

quindecile An ASPECT of 24°. *See* KEPLER.

quintessence *see* ELEMENTS

quintile An ASPECT of 72°, or one-fifth of the zodiac. *See* KEPLER.

– R –

radix The basic birth-chart or HOROSCOPE from which all astrological work begins.

Raleigh, Sir Walter (1552–1618) English courtier, pirate and poet. In his *History of the World*, written when he was imprisoned in the Tower of London, he argued elegantly in favour of astrology:

> *If we cannot deny but that God hath given virtue to springs and fountains, to cold earth, to plants and stones, minerals and to the excremental parts of the basest living creatures, why should we rob the beautiful stars of their working powers? For, seeing they are many in number and of eminent beauty and magnitude, we may not think that in the treasury of his wisdom who is infinite there can be wanting, even for every star, a peculiar virtue and operation …*

Raman, Bangalore Venkata (1912–98) The Indian author of many books on VEDIC ASTROLOGY, Raman was well known worldwide as a lecturer. He was the President of the Indian Council of Astrological Sciences, and edited *The Astrological Magazine* between1936, when he founded it, and his death. He took particular pride in the accuracy and efficacy of his predictive powers.

Raphael *see* SMITH, ROBERT CROSS

rasi The Hindu term for a BIRTH-CHART, drawn up using the equal house method of HOUSE DIVISION.

Recent Advances in Natal Astrology Published in 1977, a book compiled by Geoffrey Dean and Arthur Miller, with contributions by many distinguished astrologers, attempted to survey every area of astrology and to look at the work done by the most notable astrologers in the field of NATAL ASTROLOGY and published between 1900 and 1975. Its aims were

> *to review impartially but critically as much as possible of the literature of natal astrology published since 1900; to review briefly the relevant scientific literature; to summarize the findings [of astrological literature] clearly, concisely and in sufficient detail to be useful [and] to provide a guide to research methodology and worthwhile areas of research.*

An epoch-making publication, the book was widely unpopular with astrologers, the examination of most of their theories and assertions being too rigorous to produce any other conclusion but that they were incapable of scientific proof.

reception When a planet is in a sign it does not rule, it is said to be 'in reception' or to be 'received by' the ruler of the sign. When it is in ASPECT to a faster-moving planet, it is said to 'receive' that aspect. *See also* MUTUAL RECEPTION.

rectification The adjustment of a horoscope by altering the time for which it is set up. The argument is that birth times are very rarely entirely accurate, and that by adjusting the time by perhaps only a few minutes the chart can be made to 'fit' the personality more closely. The astrologer takes a number of significant events in the life of the subject, and looks to see how these may have been signalled, astrologically. This allows the chart to be 'rectified' or altered so that it appears to be more accurate. The effect is usually most radical on the RISING-SIGN.

rectify *see* RECTIFICATION

Regiomontanus, house system A system based on the equal division of the equator into twelve sections, which are projected onto the ECLIPTIC in great circles that embrace the north and south points on the horizon. *See* HOUSE SYSTEMS.

Regiomontanus (Johannes Müller von Kœnigsburg) (1436–76)
Astrologer and mathematician who abbreviated his Latin name, Joannes de
Regio monte, and is known in history simply as Regiomontanus. An
astrologer from his youth, he published a famous series of ALMANACS at
Nuremburg between 1475 and 1506. It is claimed, on some authority, that
one of his ephemerides was used by Christopher Columbus to predict a
lunar eclipse, thus impressing the natives of Jamaica, where he was
marooned. A builder of ASTROLABES and sundials and a translator of
PTOLEMY, Regiomontanus built in 1471 the first German astronomical
observatory. He travelled to Rome in 1475 to work for Pope Sixtus IV on
the reform of the CALENDAR, and seems to have died by assassination the
following year. *See* HOUSE DIVISION.

Regulus A fixed star at 30° Leo, one of the four Royal Stars. Believed to
have a violent and 'evil' influence except when culminating.

Reinhart, Melanie (b.1949) Professional astrologer, lecturer and teacher,
born in Zimbabwe but practising in the UK. Trained in a number of
humanistic therapies and interested especially in meditative experiential
work, among her books are *Chiron and the Healing Journey* (1989) and
Saturn, Chiron and the Centaurs (2001).

relocation astrology *see* ASTRO*CARTO*GRAPHY

retrograde When a SUPERIOR PLANET near OPPOSITION is overtaken by the
Earth, moving at a higher relative speed, it can become retrograde,
appearing to move backwards. The simplest way of visualizing this is to
imagine oneself in a car travelling down a motorway. When another car is
overtaken, it appears to move backwards relative to one's own car, though
in reality it is merely travelling at a lower speed. Modern astrologers
generally pay somewhat less attention to the alleged unfortunate influence
of a retrograde planet than was once the case.

returns Each planet, as it makes its imaginary journey around Earth's sky,
returns in due course to the position it was in when one was born.
Astrologers describe this *cycle* as the planet's 'return': an individual will

experience his or her Jupiter return at the age of 12, Saturn return at about 29, the Uranus half-return at just over 40, Chiron at 50, the second Saturn return when approaching 60; the long-lived will experience a full Uranus return at 84, and perhaps a third Saturn return at 90. These influences usually mark times of change and reassessment. Other cycles, so long that no human will live to see them, are said to instigate changes in the affairs of countries, changes in climate (making a contribution, it has been suggested, to global warming) in the rise and fall of religious philosophies.

Rhetorius (fl.6th/7th c. AD) Little is known of this astrological writer, referred to as Rhetorius of Egypt, except that he apparently wrote voluminously about astrological techniques, and is responsible for what we know of the work of ANTIOCHUS. Relatively little of Rhetorius' work has survived, but he is an important link between the work of VETTIUS VALENS, PTOLEMY and others, and later medieval astrologers.

Richard of Wallingford (1292–1336) An English astrologer and cleric – Abbot of St Albans. He had studied at Oxford before entering the Church as a monk, after which he returned to Oxford for more study before being appointed to St Albans in 1326. There, he designed an astronomical clock (later built but destroyed at the Reformation) and a mechanism that could be used to calculate longitude and predict eclipses.

right ascension The celestial equivalents of LATITUDE and LONGITUDE are DECLINATION and right ascension. Right ascension is a system of measurement expressed in degrees of declination eastwards from the first point of Aries, within the plane of the celestial EQUATOR. It is in fact the interval in SIDEREAL TIME between the TRANSIT of the EQUINOX and that of the object from which measurement starts.

Righter, Carroll (1900–88) An American astrologer and attorney, Righter became interested in astrology as a critic determined to prove it nonsensical. Convinced of its probity by Evangeline ADAMS he became, however, an influential proselytizer. He is said to have written the first syndicated SUN-SIGN column in America, his column appearing in over 500 US newspapers.

In Hollywood he became a consultant to many prominent movie stars, and claimed to have been a personal adviser to Ronald Reagan for over 45 years (he was not, however, the sole claimant to that privilege – *see* DIXON, JILLSON). He is said to have employed Robert Mitchum as his press agent, before Mitcham became a success in films. He founded the Carrol Righter Astrological Foundation. A friendly soul, he was known as 'the gregarious Aquarius'.

rising-sign *see* ASCENDANT

Robson, Vivian (1890–1942) English astrologer and curator of geology and paleontology at the British Museum. Editor (with Bessie Leo) of the magazine *Modern Astrology*. Author of a number of books, including *Astrology and Human Sex Life*.

Rodden, Lois (1928–2003) An American astrologer who studied with the Church of Light. Rodden became a well-known astrological consultant to Hollywood film stars. She was one of the first American astrologers to concern herself with the use of computers, and provided the data for perhaps the first monthly computer forecasts. She wrote a great number of SUN-SIGN books and published five volumes of astrological data, noted for their accuracy. She subsequently founded AstroDataBank with the purpose of making accurate data widely available to colleagues.

Rome Astrology came to the Roman world when Greek textbooks on the subject began to be translated and published in the city. Immediately, scholars began to take sides. Cato and Ennius were hostile to astrology, but later Sulla, Posidonius and Varro were enthusiasts. Vitruvius, Propertius and Ovid were all supporters, and from the 1st century almost every intelligent person subscribed to a belief in the subject – if not in every detail, at least to the extent that they believed in fate and in the powers of the planets for good and evil. Even the most enthusiastic critics, such as Plotinus and Origen, while they insisted that the movements of the planets could not determine the future, believed that they indicated the course general events would take.

During the heyday of the Roman Empire astrology played an enormously important role in state politics, and from time to time astrologers were banned from the city, while an attempt to use astrology to influence events often resulted in the death of the astrologer – especially if it was suspected that he was using the Emperor's horoscope to plan a coup. The most powerful of all Roman astrologers was THRASSYLUS, Tiberius's astrologer.

In the 4th century Augustine violently denied that astrology could in any way be a valid subject for study by a Christian, and it was officially banned – though this had no effect on the ordinary person's addiction, which continued enthusiastically.

Rosicrucianism The Rosicrucian Order is considered by its followers as a 'College of Invisibles' formed to help the spiritual development of humanity. Though its followers assert that it was formed in ancient times, the association known as the 'Brethren of the Rose Cross' seems to have originated in Germany in the first two decades of the 17th century, when a literature proposed the 'universal reformation of mankind'. There has been from the earliest times a close association with astrology, studied and used by many of the Brethren.

Royal Stars A title given to the four stars now known as ALDEBARAN, REGULUS, ANTARES, and FOMALHAUT. They were regarded by ancient Persian astrologers as Guardians of the World, also called the Watchers. Their RIGHT ASCENSION being about six hours apart, they mark the four angles of the heavens. In order, they were known as the Watchers of the East, North, West and South, and ruled the VERNAL EQUINOX, SUMMER SOLSTICE, AUTUMNAL EQUINOX and WINTER SOLSTICE.

Rudhyar, Dane (1895–1985) Born in France – his natal name was Daniel Chennevière – Rudhyar was a respected if relatively little-performed classical composer as well as an astrologer. He has claims to being the first transpersonal astrologer. His *The Astrology of Personality* (1936), though somewhat opaque and knotty, was an epoch-making book in astrological terms, asserting that prediction is a relatively unimportant part of astrology, and that the chief value of the BIRTH-CHART is in guiding the astrologer through intuition to insights into a subject's personality.

ruler/rulerships It seems to have been PTOLEMY who first matched particular planets with particular signs; modern astrologers have brought the so-called MODERN PLANETS into the scheme. Traditionally a planet was said to be lord of its sign; it is now said to 'rule' – that is, have a special relationship with, and a strong influence in – the sign with which it is allied. When it is in the sign that it rules, a planet is said to be in its own sign, and is of ESSENTIAL DIGNITY. When in the opposite sign it is in DETRIMENT, and has decreased strength. The generally accepted modern list is:

- Mars – rules Aries
- Venus – rules Taurus and Libra
- Mercury – rules Gemini and Virgo
- Moon – rules Cancer
- Sun – rules Leo
- Pluto – rules Scorpio
- Jupiter – rules Sagittarius
- Saturn – rules Capricorn
- Uranus – rules Aquarius
- Neptune – rules Pisces

Various astrologers have disparate views about rulership, some swearing that the traditional rulerships always work, others that the theory is unsubstantiated.

– S –

Sabian symbols A set of DEGREE SYMBOLS published by the astrologer Marc Edmund JONES. These – one for each degree of the ECLIPTIC – were dictated to him in 1925 by a medium, Elsie Wheeler, in Balboa Park, San Diego, Miss Wheeler secreted in some bushes in order that no outside influence should influence her. Mr Jones was aided by 'a Brother on the invisible side of life' in compiling the symbols into a book. They include 'A tiny nude miss reaching into the water for a fish', 'A large hat with streamers flying, facing east', and 'An old man attempting vainly to reveal the Mysteries'. Perhaps against the odds, the Sabian symbols are still taken seriously by some mystical astrologers.

Sacrobosco, Johannes de (1195–ca.1244) An English astrologer and astronomer educated at Oxford, who taught mathematics at the University of Paris. In 1230 he published *Tractatus de Sphaera*, in which he asserted that the world was round. He worked on the CALENDAR, pointing out that the Julian calendar was faulty and should be corrected.

Sagittarius ♐

The ninth sign of the zodiac. SUN-SIGN period 23 November–21 December.

It should be remembered when reading of the characteristics of the Sun-signs that these will always be affected by the effects of the rising-sign, the planets in various other signs and houses, and the relationships the planets make to each other.

General characteristics
Freedom and challenge are two keywords which apply to a person with the Sun in Sagittarius. They need to face a challenge of some sort every day of their lives – however large, however small. Sometimes these challenges

may seem lowering and depressing; but the Sagittarian will rise to meet them, and seek out ways of making them interesting. As to freedom – these are enthusiastic, positive people who need to be able to express themselves without feeling confined by convention. Versatile, their energy is sometimes sapped by their desire to experience every aspect of life, thus diffusing their vigour – they tend to be restless souls. However, their versatility is usually marked by achievement in a number of different areas of their lives. They need exercise, and turn to sport as readily and enthusiastically as anyone else, and possibly enjoy it more. Their dislike for claustrophobic conditions is marked, and shown in their attitude to emotional relationships, within which, characteristically, they need a certain amount of freedom.

The growing child

Typical enthusiasm can make children with the Sun in Sagittarius extremely boisterous and excitable. Encouragement of their favourite interests should focus on steadying their approach, remembering that they can find an intellectually demanding hobby as fascinating as a more physical one – a boy interested in sport will for instance find the history of the sport he favours almost as fascinating as the activity itself; the same would apply to a girl studying ballet (or vice versa). Catering for both the active and passive aspects of their interests prevents the Sagittarian from obsessing, which can be a danger. From an early age, discipline should not be a problem, provided it is reasonable and the Sagittarian can *see* the reason for it.

Education

There may be a problem with discipline unless the school is particularly enlightened, making it perfectly clear why each rule has been devised and why it is necessary. This done, the Sagittarian child will obey with perfect grace; but rules made at some entirely unnecessary whim will simply be ignored – if not actually resisted. Sagittarians usually have very considerable creative potential, often including a talent for languages. This should obviously be encouraged. They may find the classroom somewhat claustrophobic, and do their best work away from it – similarly, the daily routine at school will not be popular with them, for they do not care to have the same thing happening at the same time every day, and will try in some way to ameliorate this, perhaps by volunteering for tasks which will take them in a slightly different direction from the usual habitual timetable.

Friendship, romance and sex

Sagittarians are naturally friendly and easy-going, and usually have a lot of charm; their company is generally great fun – one is certainly never likely to be bored. Their enthusiasm prompts one's interest in *their* interests, whatever they are – they are eternal students who never stop seeking enlightenment and information, and are happy to share it. Despite their natural informality, they tend to begin a friendship rather seriously, perhaps seeking some common interest which will lead to informal chat and discussion, before starting a flirtation – and that will probably be rather off-hand and casual. People with the Sun in Sagittarius are not among the world's great romantics, partly because of their deep commitment to personal freedom – the last thing they want is to give the impression that they are seeking a permanent relationship. Once a relationship has started, however, they will be eager to make it sexual, for they are naturally passionate, and their plentiful physical energy will keep any partner happy as far as sex is concerned. But it must always be remembered that permanence, let alone marriage, is not high on their list of objectives

Permanent partnership and family

When a Sagittarian does commit to a permanent relationship, the need for a high degree of personal freedom is not rejected; restraint and restriction are dirty words to him or her. The partner may, then, have to be reconciled to extramarital interests – and should remember that jealousy will be anathema to the Sagittarian – a quick and easy way of ending a relationship. On the other hand, Sagittarians have a vein of orthodoxy and conventionality, and pride may prevent them from straying seriously, restricting themselves to flirtation (they love to be admired, which strengthens the possibility of straying). The sexual side of the partnership should be fine, but warm affection may be in shorter supply. Shared interests will do much to cement the partnership, and mutual challenge will keep both on their toes – an element of competition will be valuable. As parents, Sagittarians are close to ideal, with children responding to their enthusiasm and zest for life.

Occupation

With the emphasis on 'freedom' which is important in every area of a Sagittarian life, it is obvious that employment is best sought in an occupation which allows the employee the greatest possible degree of latitude. A job that offers travel opportunities is perhaps ideal; it is important to get away from the possible claustrophobia of the office and the predictability of a daily routine. Sagittarians are good at planning as far as a broad sweep of ideas is concerned; detail is best left to others. Involved at the early stages of a project, they will grasp the overall conception immediately, but will not be good at crossing the t's and dotting the i's. Professional sport seems to attract many Sagittarians, and with natural determination success can result. They make enthusiastic salespeople. Traditionally, the law and the Church are associated with Sagittarius, though the strict disciplines of both do not necessarily make them easy grounds for freedom-loving men and women.

Health

While regular exercise is valuable, and to a degree essential for everyone, Sagittarians need it more than most. First deciding what form of exercise is best for them, they ideally make it a part of their everyday lives, perhaps as members of a good gymnasium or health club – the competition of other members, the social life, and the various machines which enable them to avoid a regular routine, will be attractive. Their sports interests too will ideally change with the seasons, so that one does not preoccupy them long enough to become routine or boring. The Sagittarian body area is the hips and thighs, and this can relate both to a tendency to put on weight around the waist and thighs and to the possibility of trouble with the hips in old age, if exercise is not kept up. Sagittarius also governs the liver, which means (since Sagittarians enjoy their food and drink) that it can suffer if there is overindulgence. Dieting may be recommended from time to time, but will probably not be maintained.

Finance

Sagittarians are not generally very much interested in money. They may be excited by a particular investment, but it will be because of its nature rather than because of the money to be made. Many people with the Sun in this sign find the whole idea of money deeply boring; a few will find a challenge in making it work for them. There is usually a natural gambling instinct buried somewhere, which will emerge from time to time if there is a little spare cash doing nothing. If it surfaces, it will be for its entertainment value, as a counter to a boring stretch of work, or if there is a difficult problem which is proving intractable. When this happens care must be exercised lest the habit really takes hold. As for investment, if a particular stock appeals, caution is again needed that too much money is not invested in that particular direction. In business, Sagittarians are versatile enough to want to handle everything themselves; however a good accountant is a necessity, leaving the Sagittarian free to concentrate on enthusing about and selling the product.

Growing older

Given a certain amount of care in vulnerable areas of health (*see above*), Sagittarians will remain themselves, with all their adventurous versatility in good condition, well into old age. Spare-time interests will always have played a part in the life, usually balancing work – so that if the career calls for adventure, spare time will be spent in a more thoughtful way; and vice versa. When the time comes for retirement, the hobby, whatever it is, will continue to take a great deal of time – but it will prove difficult to drop completely the area in which the career has been spent. Sagittarius is the hunter of the zodiac, and while this may not mean hunting in the conventional sense, it may well mean hunting down antiques, old books, or contributions to collections of whatever kind. Study will continue into old age, too, with new subjects springing up from time to time, to be as thoroughly explored as possible – 'a little knowledge' does not appeal to these people; the fuller and more complete a course can be, the better Sagittarius will like it.

Sagittarius as rising-sign

A Sagittarian rising-sign has an excellent effect on the Sun-signs: those with an earth Sun-sign will find the heavier aspects of their characters lifted and given a freer, more imaginative strand; those whose Sun-sign is in air will have more enthusiasm and strength of will than otherwise might be the case; while with the other FIRE SIGNS a tremendously positive and vital influence will be felt. Those with WATER SIGNS might tend to be more emotionally relaxed. The tendency to spread talent, time and energy too thin may also have an effect, however, and there may be a difficulty with the expression of Sagittarius' deep-seated need for freedom, which may run counter to indications from elsewhere in the HOROSCOPE, and it will certainly be the case that there will be no easy agreement to be confined within a permanent relationship.

Traditional associations
- Ruling Planet – Jupiter
- Triplicity/Element – fire
- Quadruplicity/Quality – mutable
- Colours – dark blue, purple
- Gemstone – topaz
- Metal – tin
- Flowers – pinks and carnations
- Trees – lime, birch, mulberry, oak
- Herbs and Spices – sage, aniseed, balsam
- Foodstuffs – bulb vegetables, grapefruit, currants, sultanas
- Animals – horses, animals that are hunted
- Countries – Austria, Hungary, South Africa, Spain
- Cities – Budapest, Cologne, San Diego, Sheffield, Stuttgart, Toledo, Washington DC
- US States – Alabama, Delaware, Illinois, Indiana, Mississippi, New Jersey, Pennsylvania

* * *

San Miniato Zodiac The church of San Miniato al Monte in Florence contains, set in the pavement in the centre of the basilica, a marble intarsias, the largest zodiac to be found in any European church. Highly sophisticated symbolism was involved in the building and decoration of the church, and as with certain Egyptian temples, it was planned so that the beams of the sun should strike into its interior on particular days and at special times.

Saros cycle A cycle of eclipses first observed by Chaldean astrologers in ancient times. It occurs over a period of some 19 years, during which there are 10 solar eclipses, 29 lunar eclipses, 14 partial eclipses and 17 annular eclipses (which occur when the Moon is sufficiently far away to appear smaller than the Sun). The most recent research suggests that each Saros cycle possesses its own qualities, which should be studied when its eclipses occur. Some modern astrologers claim that there are 'good' and 'bad' Saros cycles.

satellitium *see* STELLIUM

Saturn ♄

Saturn is the sixth and outermost major planet, orbiting the Sun every 29.5 years. It originally ruled both Capricorn and Aquarius, but now rules only the former. Its influence is considered serious and sober and linked to one's destiny (though in Western astrology there is no emphasis on fatalism). The planet is important in the way in which it relates to others through the aspects it receives. Its KEYWORDS are restriction and limitation, but also control and stability. If it can indicate a cold personality, restricted in outlook and rather gloomy, it can also point to common sense and patience, discretion and honesty.

Saturn takes two and a half years or so to travel through one sign of the zodiac, and is therefore in the same sign for everyone born during that time. Since it travels through all the zodiac signs during 29–30 years, as we approach 30 and then again at about 60, we receive the Saturn RETURN. Many people find that those times mark important periods in life, during which reassessment can lead to practical or psychological change.

Saturn and the zodiac signs

Saturn in ARIES

When facing challenging situations, the individual with Saturn in Aries may feel some conflict: the urge to accept the challenges and move forward may be obstructed by a certain amount of inhibition. This may lead to a 'stop-go' attitude which will inevitably hold things up. If such a negative stance can be overcome, and caution is allowed to take the place of any lack of self-confidence, the individual will be able to make use of the positive side of the Saturn influence, which will bolster ambition and the desire to make progress in life. The influence of Mars may well be crucial in such a case.

Saturn in Taurus

Saturn will in many ways be sympathetic to the characteristics of Taurus, so this is normally a good position for the planet. It will make for someone who is ambitious for material progress, but who will take his or her time, patiently building a careful scaffolding up which it will be safe to climb towards whatever goal is proposed. This will be the right approach, for progress by leaps and bounds will not be right for these characters. Their confidence will be bolstered most effectively by slow progress in building a material lifestyle which will include property and a good bank balance. This kind of security is psychologically important to them, though it may involve more than a hint of complacency. Routine could become a master.

Saturn in Gemini

The quick and versatile Geminian mind will be steadied, and the logical and rational approach controlled and channelled with this placing of Saturn; deep, rational thought will lead to sound and reasoned decision-making. Psychologically, however, there may be an element of restlessness – light-hearted Geminian wit and the more serious Saturnian cast of mind can clash. At times the youthfulness of Gemini will predominate; at others the maturity of Saturn will place a firm hand on the shoulder of impulsive-ness. The individual will have to devise his or her own way of coping with this possible conflict, especially when it comes to the formation and expression of opinions. There will sometimes be scientific ability.

Saturn in Cancer

Traditionally, Saturn in Cancer prompts thoughts of one's family history and heritage, which will be influential in forming the character. What is learned in early life will almost stand in stone, and is unlikely to be greatly modified by age or even by experience. There may be a certain amount of shyness and inhibition to be overcome when these people are young, and when they are challenged the typical Cancerian defensiveness will be an immediate response. Anyone with Saturn in Cancer will certainly be courageous, but the instinct for self-preservation will be equally strong, and caution will rule: these are not risk-takers. If other planets' positions show a high level of emotion, the Saturn influence may dampen it and hold it down.

Saturn in LEO

The fiery, exuberant, enthusiastic character of Leo conflicts strongly with the serious, practical, constructive nature of Saturn. However, the conflict is not complete, for both have a need for quality in everything, and perfection will always be sought in any area of life, whether at work, at home or at play. Thoroughness, ambition and determination are other qualities which will be characteristic, and the attitude towards life will be rather formal, ceremonious and almost regal – even at the extreme, pompous. This placing makes for convention, within the nature of the generation to which the individual belongs – there will be no clinging to the past, but past standards will inform present behaviour. There will be an ability to carry responsibility, and powers of leadership will emerge if other planets support it.

Saturn in VIRGO

Someone with Saturn in Virgo will be critical, but extremely practical and with plenty of common sense. They will take an almost clinical attitude to the way in which they live and behave, and have a somewhat serious attitude to life and a tendency to worry. They will express themselves with discrimination and a lack of careless overemphasis. However, self-confidence will not be a strong point, and may have to be cultivated – the praise of colleagues and friends will help to put an end to the tendency to underestimate performance. Look for a boost to the self-confidence in the position of the Sun, Moon and Ascendant.

Saturn in LIBRA

Traditionally well placed in Libra, Saturn gives those with this position of the planet a well-balanced attitude to life and an ability to recognize any psychological problems they may have, and instinctively know how to make adjustments that will in the end resolve them. There is a need to see that other people are treated fairly – for instance by employers – and while there is no lack of ambition, these are not the people to tread down colleagues as they pursue their own ambitions. They respect other people's views and feelings. The attitude to emotional relationship will be serious, and loyalty and faithfulness are characteristic. Sometimes people with Saturn in Libra commit themselves to older partners.

Saturn in Scorpio

It may be quite difficult for those with this placing of Saturn to express their emotions, which can be a problem since emotional intensity is also characteristic. It is often the case that they keep emotional problems to themselves, and are unwilling – even, it may seem incapable – of sharing them. However, they have extremely powerful resources with which to fight this; they also contribute toughness, determination and the will to succeed. These resources need to be tried and tested and must find positive expression; challenges will be welcomed, and are an excellent means to this end. Repression will lead almost inevitably to stagnation and discontent, which will spoil progress. A preoccupation with the unknown is a strong possibility.

Saturn in Sagittarius

It may take quite a long time for those with Saturn in Sagittarius to come to terms with the combination of effects this will have: breadth of vision joined by single-mindedness of purpose. There will be a distinct temptation, especially during the early years, to swerve from the set purpose of the time in order to enjoy new experiences and challenging situations. Inwardly however, these people will know the right course to take and in the end will take it. There will be swings of mood, from optimism to pessimism, sometimes to the point at which the individual will at the same time be extremely happy about one aspect of life, and desperately miserable about another. Fortunately Saturn is a great source of common sense, and it is upon this that they can reliably depend to ensure that life isn't one constant series of dramatic changes of mood.

Saturn in Capricorn

Saturn rules Capricorn and its influence from this sign is demonstrably stronger than when it is placed elsewhere. It will enhance the individual's ambition and determination to succeed. There will be an ability to carry responsibility, and there should be no problem in coping with the loneliness that sometimes accompanies promotion to a position of power. This indeed will probably be a person who distinctly enjoys working alone, although that will in the end depend on the placings of the Sun, Moon and rising-sign. A preoccupation with the career and with material matters may give the impression that socially this is a rather distant and unapproachable individual. That need not always be the case. There will be a strong sense of humour, and if there are psychological problems they will be solved by self-analysis.

Saturn in AQUARIUS

Saturn works in a rational, logical and positive manner when in Aquarius. If there are problems, particularly psychological ones, the individual with Saturn in Aquarius will be able to take a detached view of them and, while there will not be a great deal of flexibility in the nature, be able to come to terms with what is wrong, and deal with the difficulty by using the stronger side of the nature. Individuality will be marked, and a tendency away from conservatism – these are not people to be attracted to convention or the establishment. Saturn's mood when in this sign is positive and optimistic, with faith in the future and a firm conviction that the best his or her generation has to offer is worth fighting for.

Saturn in PISCES

Those with Saturn in Pisces will be in control of their emotions, which will be useful should a high emotional level be contributed in other areas of the birth-chart – through the positions of Sun, Moon and rising-sign for example. This faculty will help to steady and anchor the personality. A certain shyness and inhibition is possible, and should be overcome. This is not always easy, for Saturn in this position can make people rather quiet and with a tendency to keep their talents under wraps. Creativity is to be encouraged. Religious faith may be strong, and a wonderfully kind and charitable disposition. But in the main, the thing to remember is that those with this placing of Saturn must learn not to underestimate themselves.

Saturn and the houses

Saturn in the FIRST HOUSE

When Saturn is placed in the first house of the horoscope it is almost certain in some way or another to have an inhibiting effect on the personality. The way in which it does so can be discovered by looking at the planet's sign placing, but shyness and lack of self-confidence, a pessimistic outlook and the feeling of simply not being able to cope with life are among the possibilities. The outlook will be conservative and conventional, and where health is concerned vitality may be low; there is also likely to be a tendency to hypochondria.

Saturn in the SECOND HOUSE

Hard work and application will be necessary to build whatever resources are held by someone with this placing of Saturn; easy money will not play any part in the financial life, and it will be extremely unwise to take part in any financial gamble – investments should only be made in the most gilt-edged of stocks. Saturn may also inhibit the natural flow of emotion in these subjects, which may delay commitment and thus the normal outlet for romantic and sexual emotions.

Saturn in the THIRD HOUSE

With the third house's alignment to the mind, Saturn is likely to make for a sensible, practical individual with the ability to make long-term plans based on clear thinking. There is the possibility that in some way education may have been interrupted or disrupted. The subject should retreat from any idea that this is necessarily inhibiting; indeed it may have taught valuable lessons in overcoming obstacles on the way to a position of authority.

Saturn in the FOURTH HOUSE

Some tensions in early family life are suggested by this placing of Saturn – a lack of warmth between parents and the subject, perhaps, or even the absence of a father. It is possible that in adulthood there may be a struggle to escape the influence of parents when this proves inhibiting to a free expression of emotions and opinions. Intuition will be a valuable tool, and may be trusted.

Saturn in the FIFTH HOUSE

The fact that Saturn may have made the subject's relationship with his or her father strained and difficult will have the result that he or she will make an excellent parent, ready to give plenty of time to the children, and to spend freely when that is necessary. The tendency to see a child as someone who can be shaped to become the person the parent failed to be, must be carefully watched; a child should not become the clone of the parent. An extremely serious attitude to love may well delay commitment by women; many will fail the ultimate test of comparison to the father.

Saturn in the SIXTH HOUSE

A reluctance to change may trap the person with Saturn in the sixth house in a dull, repetitive, routine job which does not fulfil any ambition except a desire for security, which they will pursue with dogged determination. Personal achievements will be downplayed, and real satisfaction at work may be evasive – yet these people will often resign themselves to their positions simply because the idea of taking any risk is frightening. The health may be somewhat vulnerable: rheumatism may become a problem – but not so much a problem as lack of self-esteem and self-confidence.

Saturn in the SEVENTH HOUSE

This is an excellent position of Saturn where the construction of a lasting emotional partnership is concerned. Personal relationships will be taken extremely seriously, with a heavy emphasis on faithfulness and constancy. The most serious effect of this placing is if there is an OPPOSITION between Saturn and the ASCENDANT. A real commitment may then never be made, sometimes for psychological reasons, sometimes because a family will be regarded as a burden, financial and emotional. There may however be a desire to marry for money and prestige; love will not enter the equation

Saturn in the EIGHTH HOUSE

A splendid placing of Saturn for anyone working in business, for determination and excellent powers of concentration will be joined by a seriousness of character which will make these people totally trustworthy: banking and insurance spring to mind as ideal occupations. However, it should be noted that Saturn working from the eighth house can provoke depression and sometimes obsession – and is likely to obstruct the sex life, bringing possible inhibition or deviancy (not necessarily, of course, criminal). Suspicion and jealousy may outweigh trust in personal relationships.

Saturn in the NINTH HOUSE

Caution and convention will make anyone with Saturn in the ninth house unlikely to be adventurous or inventive, and while they will have a real commitment to self-education, which will be pursued with great determination, any challenge will be approached with extreme prudence. Fear of flying is common – and travel of any kind is likely to be nervously undertaken. This attitude can extend to any proposition which seems to offer the possibility of danger, of any kind. Saturn's traditional companions, inhibition and apprehension, are again at work.

Saturn in the TENTH HOUSE

From its own house, Saturn will pile burdens of responsibility upon the person born with this placing of the planet – but at the same time give them the stamina and power to deal with them. Ambition will be a powerful force, and aspirations will be high. This may mean that attention is drawn away from the personal and family life, with problematical results. There is a distinct possibility that preoccupation with problem-solving and the pursuit of material success may deprive these subjects of much that is good in life.

Saturn in the ELEVENTH HOUSE

There is an emphasis on the social life – but not in the sense that someone with Saturn in this house will be always ready to rush out with friends and have a good time. On the contrary, friends may be made for the reason that they may be able to advance the career, or because they are socially desirable. Even with genuine friends, there will be little time for frippery and flippancy – having fun will be a serious matter. Committee work will be attractive and will be well performed, and a strong humanitarian streak in the character will lead to work for 'good causes'.

Saturn in the TWELFTH HOUSE

This is an isolating position for Saturn, and those affected by it will feel the need in some way to withdraw from other people. Work with others will be competently done, and there will not be such withdrawal as to offend; but after work there is unlikely to be any socializing. Hobbies will be those that do not involve others – reading, listening to music... Too much introspection can result in hypochondria. Creative exercise is advisable, and some contact should be made with the outside world if Saturn is not to create a complete reclusive.

* * *

Saturn return *see* SATURN

Schöner, Johannes (1477–1547) German astrologer, astronomer and editor of astrological manuscripts, who published the work of REGIOMONTANUS.

Scorpio ♏

The eighth sign of the zodiac. SUN-SIGN period 24 October–22 November.

It should be remembered when reading of the characteristics of the Sun-signs that these will always be affected by the effects of the rising-sign, the planets in various other signs and houses, and the relationships the planets make to each other.

General characteristics

Scorpio has the reputation of being the strongest of the twelve signs, with the greatest resources of emotional and physical energy. These must be positively used, or the person with the Sun in Scorpio will be unfulfilled. The career should be truly engrossing, and important enough to the subject to employ much of their vigour. The more a Scorpio has to do, the better. The emotional intensity of the sign is immense, and needs to be expressed in a satisfactory sex life. The general view of Scorpio as obsessed with sex is an overstatement, and in some cases sexual energy is sublimated and expressed in other directions – notably through the career and the desire for achievement. Drive and determination can become obsession if other outlets are not found – exercise and sport, for instance. But there is no question that stagnation and restlessness are the greater evils. The area of the body traditionally ascribed to Scorpio is the genitals, and there is an above-average susceptibility to sexually transmitted diseases. Though generally slim and wiry in build, with their great love and enjoyment of life, Scorpios are among those who can put on weight if there is not regular exercise and care about diet.

The growing child

Sport and exercise will almost inevitably be an important part of the Scorpio child's life from a very early age; they will also be physically active in every other way – and if this is not the case, ways should be found of making it so, for they need to be kept busy. If this is not the case a child can become introspective and give the impression of being troubled, and since it is never easy to prise private thoughts from a Scorpio, parents may become worried. If these moods are not accompanied by physical stagnation, it is probably the case that the Scorpio child is working on some scheme which needs careful consideration – perhaps to do with schoolwork. However, it is essential for parents to discover just what is going on in the Scorpio mind, for if the child is slipping into a negative mood it may be difficult to turn round. Discipline should be sparingly, calmly and fairly administered – the Scorpio child will bitterly resent what is perceived as injustice.

Education

Scorpio pupils and students need strict discipline, and on the whole thrive on it – a predictable, constant routine is best for them, giving them a sense of security which makes it easy for them to fit in. The discipline, however, must be founded on a fair set of rules, fairly applied – Scorpios hate injustice and muddled thinking, and any rules which have outrun their sell-by date or are improperly administered will receive short shrift from them. It is highly advisable for them to choose carefully which courses they decide to study, for it is necessary for them to be able to involve themselves completely in their work and pour their energies into it. They do not find study difficult or too taxing, and know that their best work is done steadily and without taking short-cuts. Their ability to work hard is an advantage to them, and they are likely to recognize it, and not shirk even what may seem at the time to be unnecessarily detailed curricula.

Friendship, romance and sex

Scorpios are enthusiastic and lasting friends, and it takes quite a serious disagreement or quarrel to damage the friendship. In courtship they are determined, and express their emotions with real feeling; if there is no immediate response, persuasion will be applied with a colourful enthusiasm quite difficult to resist. The popular view of Scorpio as the sexiest of the signs is perhaps related to the fact that the sign rules the genitals; all the same there is a strong sexual charge in most Scorpios – which, however, they are quite capable of controlling, for their self-control is as strong their capacity for enjoyment. If they are rejected by a lover, they can descend into gloom, brooding and depression, and even feel that they are being persecuted in some way – so it is difficult to end an affair with a Scorpio, who will cling on with all his or her might. Once the affair *is* ended, however, there will be no prospect of ever renewing it. Jealousy is a major problem when it arises (which can sometimes happen for no good reason).

Permanent partnership and family

The proud Scorpio nature does not naturally acclimatize itself to a permanent relationship or marriage. He, or sometimes she, will frequently contract a marriage which offers a financial advantage, or is seen as socially advantageous. In such cases there can be a lack of that strong sexual relationship which Scorpio needs, and he or she will look for it elsewhere – though being careful not to let this disturb domestic life, which is kept apart from everything else. It is a mistake not to assume that the Scorpio woman is every bit as strong in character as the male; both have a strong sense of justice and the capacity to love and hate with equal intensity. It follows that marriage with a Scorpio can be either very happy or the reverse. Jealousy, in either event, is likely to raise its head – and will be even more dangerous to a happy marriage than to an unsuccessful one. This jealousy will not necessarily be sexual – it may occur when Scorpio feels the need to cultivate interests outside the home. Scorpio parents will encourage their children in all their interests; they sometimes take discipline to extremes, but are otherwise generous parents.

Occupation

Emotional involvement with their work is essential for those with the Sun in Scorpio. This can often be taken as read, for whatever they do as adults probably stems from a lifelong interest which started when they were very young. They are thorough and efficient learners, and will not take long to get on terms with the running of any business with which they become associated. Once acquired, knowledge remains securely in their heads and is ready for use at any moment. Their career should provide sufficient interest for them in one way or another, and often this will be associated with finance – they find the financial markets fascinating, and the process of money-making equally so. When placed in charge of a department, or gaining control of a business they will treat employees with respect, but with a strict eye to discipline, making sure that work is not skimped, slow to give way when there are disputes, and so intent on obedience and maintaining their own authority that they can become authoritarian to a distasteful and even damaging degree.

Health

Physical exercise must take a high priority when it comes to maintaining the health of someone with the Sun in Scorpio. At whatever age, some kind of physical activity will form an important part of their lives – boxing and the martial arts are common with men, swimming and diving with men and women. Any sport which allows a certain amount of aggression can also be valuable in getting rid of excess physical and emotional energy. The body must have no greater chance of stagnating than the mind – Scorpio illnesses are often rooted in psychological or physical blockage of some sort. Scorpios who do not have the opportunity for regular exercise may have bowel troubles – typically, constipation or haemorrhoids – and need to take medical advice in dealing with them. (A characteristic disinclination to 'see the doctor' can be a mistake). The genitals are the Scorpio body area, and can be susceptible to sexually transmitted diseases, especially when always ready physical passion overrules caution. Varicose veins can also be a problem. There may be a greater than average number of minor throat infections.

Finance

As has already been pointed out, Scorpios take a keen interest in finance, and it is usually safe for them to follow their intuition when it comes to money matters; their excellent business sense and natural shrewdness and caution will serve them well. They take pleasure in handling their own financial affairs, and invest with care but with an eye to steady profit. Any risks they take will have been carefully calculated. They make good business partners, and their common sense is second to none – though their tendency to be secretive can be damaging, for they may tend to keep from a partner information which is essential to the good of the business. Differences over money, which can raise themselves in marriage, can also be a setback in a business partnership. Privately, the Scorpio is likely to take pleasure in building a collection of some sort – from wines to antiques – which will represent good value in terms of investment, both capital and in appreciation.

Growing older

Assuming that a Scorpio takes care of his or her health, and maintains a reasonable exercise regime into old age (taking care however to tailor it to physical ability) there should be no real problem. Retirement as such will not appeal, and the Scorpio is likely to be as busy, to expend energy in much the same way, when 80 or when he or she was 18. As to occupying the mind – many have good singing voices and enjoy being members of choirs; there is also often an interest in research, sometimes into criminal matters (in some ways Scorpio makes an ideal criminal, though we hesitate to suggest this as either a full-time or spare-time career). Any hobby which requires quiet hours of concentration will be enthusiastically pursued. It might also be said that Scorpios will never quite lose their appetite for flirtation and conquest, and whether exercised platonically or otherwise, this will be an amusement that will never cloy.

Scorpio as rising-sign

As a rising-sign, Scorpio is very valuable as an energizer, endowing an individual with enormous vigour which be directed to the characteristics of the Sun-sign, whatever that may be. It will do a great deal to strengthen the powers of concentration. It will tend to work on the surface – that is, it is unlikely for instance to disturb the deepest characteristics of the Sun-sign. Those with Scorpio rising are likely to be even more demanding lovers and partners than if Scorpio is the Sun-sign: the passion which needs to be expressed through sex will be extremely challenging, and anyone to whom it is directed will need to have almost equally strong appetites if they are not to be overwhelmed and overcome. An equal partnership will be wonderfully well expressed.

Traditional associations

- Ruling Planet – Pluto (once, Mars)
- Triplicity/Element – water
- Quadruplicity/Quality – fixed
- Colours – dark red and maroon
- Gemstone – opal
- Metal – steel or iron
- Flowers – geranium, rhododendron
- Trees – blackthorn and thick bushy trees
- Herbs and Spices – aloes, witch-hazel, catmint
- Foodstuffs – most strong-tasting foods
- Animals – crustaceans, most insects
- Countries – Austria, Morocco, Norway, the Transvaal, Algeria
- Cities – Denver, New Orleans, Fez, Milwaukee, Liverpool, Halifax, Hull
- US States – Montana, Nevada, North Carolina, North Dakota, Oklahoma, South Dakota, Washington

* * *

Scot, Michael (1175–1234) After studying at Oxford and in Paris, Scot travelled to Toledo, and after studying Arabic (and translating several astrological works from the Arabic) went on to Italy, where he became astrologer at the court of Frederick II at Palermo, and published *Liber Introductorius*, a textbook of astrology based on older authorities such as PTOLEMY, Euclid and Aristotle, and condemned the use of 'magic' or the occult in astrology. He also claimed that astrology had been revealed to the patriarchs of the Bible, and had been take by the giant Atlas from North Africa to Spain, and thence to the rest of Europe. On his advice, it is said, Frederick II refused to consummate his marriage until the propitious hour. Scot found favour with Pope Honorius III and his successor Gregory IX. In 1230 he reappeared at Oxford, where he lectured on Aristotle, using texts he had translated from the Arabic at the behest of Pope Gregory. It was rumoured that he died in England and was buried in his native Scotland, but it is more probable that he returned to Italy before his death. In his own time he was enormously famous (Dante in the *Inferno* placed him and Guido BONATI among the damned magicians in Hell) and was said to have made many successful prophecies – including that of his own death and that of Frederick II.

secondary progressions Predictions are made on the basis that the positions of the planets on certain days after birth represent the circumstances of the life of the subject during certain years of his or her life. Looking at the planets' positions for the 50th day after birth, for instance, the astrologer can hope to estimate the circumstances during the subject's 50th year. The system of secondary progressions is based on the movements of the planets around the ecliptic, and estimated at the rate of one day for every four minutes of time; it is therefore a more accurate system than that of PRIMARY DIRECTIONS (the Ptolemaic system recommends allowing one degree as representing one year). The chart drawn up with the planets in their positions for this method of interpretation is known as the PROGRESSED CHART.

second house The house of Taurus and Venus, the second house of the HOROSCOPE (sometimes called the House of Money) in some respects represents a subject's partners and possessions – love between partners is a matter of the FIFTH HOUSE). This house can indicate whether a partner is thought of as simply another possession, or is treated as an individual. A planet placed in this house or a planet on the cusp can reveal the answer. The link between emotional and financial security makes the second house important in both areas, often revealing the degree of importance a subject gives to both. The second house rules the throat and larynx. In MUNDANE ASTROLOGY the second house represents a nation's wealth, taxation and general financial state.

sect In ancient astrology the word 'sect' was used to describe the way in which the seven then observable planets were grouped into three DIURNAL and three NOCTURNAL planets. The Sun, Jupiter and Saturn were diurnal, and were at their most powerful when they appeared in HOROSCOPES in which the Sun was above the horizon, while the Moon, Venus and Mars exerted most power when the Sun was below the horizon, and were therefore described as nocturnal. Mercury, as in so many other areas of early astrology, was considered hermaphrodite, and had no sect – or rather changed sex depending on whether it rose and set before or after the Sun.

semi-decile An ASPECT of 18°, considered as mildly beneficial.

semi-quintile An ASPECT of 36°, considered mildly beneficial. *See* KEPLER.

semi-sextile A semi-sextile ASPECT occurs when two planets are 30° apart. It is regarded as weakly negative. An ORB of 2° is allowed.

semi-square A semi-square ASPECT occurs when two planets are 45° apart. It is negative. An orb of 2° is allowed.

separation As a planet moves away from an ASPECT it is said to be in separation, the aspect becoming gradually weaker while the aspect remains in ORB. In HORARY ASTROLOGY, separation is taken to indicate an event that has just taken place, or to a supposed event that will not take place.

Sepharial *see* OLD, WALTER

septile An ASPECT of 51.4° (one-seventh of the zodiac circle) said to be mildly beneficial. Used chiefly in HARMONICS.

sesquare A sesquare ASPECT is formed when two planets are 135° apart. An ORB of 2° is allowed. This is considered a weakly negative influence.

sesquiquadrate *see* SESQUARE

sesquiquintile An ASPECT of 108°, believed to be favourable. *See* KEPLER.

seventh house The house of Libra and Venus, the seventh house focuses on personal relationships, and is sometimes called the house of marriage. It will strongly indicate the kind of partner for whom the subject will seek, and what he or she will need from that partner (though the FIFTH HOUSE, the house of love affairs, and the SEVENTH HOUSE, the house of partnerships, will both have much to say on the same subject). The seventh house will show the extent to which the partnership will be a true one in the sense of genuine sharing and harmony – it can indicate not only this, but also possible conflict because of selfishness or attempts to dominate (the house of conflict is another traditional name). It also comments on working relationships and attitudes to colleagues, especially in a business setting. It is useful in choosing a secretary or PA. In MUNDANE ASTROLOGY it rules the plaintiff and lawyers in law suits, courts and disputes at law, international disputes, and the social conscience of a people.

sex, astrology and General indications of the effect the planets have on sex life and love life will be found under the planetary headings, as will the general sexual indications suggested by the SUN-SIGNS. The wide interest in sexuality which began to be frankly expressed in the second half of the 20th century has led to considerable speculation about how far astrology can discover indications of sexual orientation or preference, or can be used to help to solve sexual problems. However, this is nothing new: one of the earliest known horoscopes to have survived (ca.200BC) suggests that the subject will die 'from an excess of love-making', while in Elizabethan times and subsequently astrologers such as William LILLY and Simon FORMAN were extremely frank in recording and discussing their clients' sex lives, and in Forman's case participating in them. Individual astrologers have been as successful, or unsuccessful, in dealing with their clients' sexual difficulties as with any other area of difficulty in their lives. There have been few statistical studies that have attempted to discover significators of, for instance, paedophilia, sadism, masochism; perhaps predictably attempts to discover any reliable indication of homosexuality have been based on studies of the charts of individual homosexuals (in one early case, the charts of Oscar Wilde and Tchaikovsky), and have revealed only that the charts of such men or women are as individual and as difficult to read as those of heterosexuals. *See also* under individual SIGNS.

sextile Two planets form a sextile ASPECT when they are 60° apart. An ORB of 4–6° is allowed. This is a positive aspect.

Sextus Empiricus (fl.3rd c.) Greek philosopher and historian who attacked personal astrology on the grounds that an accurate birth- or conception-time could never be accurately recorded, but also that the placing of the CUSPS between the signs was inaccurate, and that astrology was based upon a hopelessly inadequate set of observations.

Shakespeare, William (1564–1616) Unsurprising, considering the age in which he lived, there is no play of Shakespeare's without astrological references, some more important to plot or characterization than others. Astrologers claim him as an ally; others as an unbeliever. What can at least be said with confidence is that he clearly knew the basics of astrology, was able to joke about technical aspects of the subject (cf. *Twelfth Night*), and use it as an indication of character. It has been conjectured that he may have learned something about the subject from FORMAN (who attended plays at the Globe theatre) or from his landlady, Mrs Mountjoy, who was one of Forman's clients. It has also been pointed out that the antagonistic references to astrology in the plays are inevitably made by the villains (cf. *King Lear*, I, ii, 115ff.) while the more intelligent of his characters took the view of LILLY – i.e. that 'astrology does not compel' (*see Julius Caesar* I, ii, 138–40 and IV, iii, 217–23ff.)

short ascension *see* ASCENSION

Sibley, Ebenezer (1751–99) Born in Bristol, after studying surgery in London and graduating in medicine from King's College, Aberdeen, Sibley became more and more preoccupied by astrology. He took an intelligent interest in the subject, in which he was well read; he believed that modern science should be informed by ancient knowledge. His *A New and Complete Illustration of the Celestial Science of Astrology* (1784–8) was the first serious book published on the subject for three generations: 'The science which we call Astrology is no more than the study or investigation of this frame or model of Nature, with all its admirable productions and effects.' In 3 volumes and over 1,000 pages it went into 12 editions within 30 years. Sibley edited CULPEPER's herbal. In 1787 he predicted the downfall of the French monarchy and the success of the American Revolution.

sidereal month *see* MONTH

sidereal time Sidereal time is based on the rotation of the Earth related to the celestial sphere, the imaginary sphere of the heavens above us. As the Earth turns, one sidereal day is the time it takes for a star to pass twice above a given observation point. The sidereal day is about four minutes shorter than the SOLAR DAY – one mean solar day equals 1.0027379093 sidereal days.

sidereal zodiac The sidereal zodiac begins at 0° sidereal Aries. There is some controversy about the exact point of TROPICAL Aries at which this occurs – the difference between the two may be as great as a whole zodiac sign. Both tropical and sidereal systems have worked together in India, the original sidereal zodiac giving way to a TROPICAL ZODIAC following the Greek invasion by Alexander the Great in 327BC, but today most Indian astrologers use the sidereal zodiac, and most Western astrologers the tropical.

Sieggruen, Friedrich (1877–1951) German astrologer and nautical scientist, one of the founders of the Hamburg School and promoter of URANIAN ASTROLOGY. He invented the HYPOTHETICAL PLANETS Apollon, Admetos, Vulcanus and Poseidon.

sigil The written symbol that represents, in astrology, the signs, planets, aspects and so on. More usually known by astrologers as GLYPHS.

sign Astrologically, the word 'sign' indicates one of the 30° sections into which the zodiac circle is divided, and which bear the twelve familiar names – ARIES, TAURUS, GEMINI, CANCER, LEO, VIRGO, LIBRA, SCORPIO, SAGITTARIUS, CAPRICORN, AQUARIUS and PISCES.

significator In HORARY ASTROLOGY the word 'significator' is used to describe the strongest planet in a HOROSCOPE, which is taken to represent – or *signify* – the QUERANT, or person consulting the astrologer. It is usually, but not always, the RULER of the ASCENDANT. The term is also used to indicate the subject or characteristic represented by a planet or a house – so, for instance, Venus would be the significator of love, or the sixth house of charity and care.

sinister aspect 'Sinister' in this context means *left*, and the reference is to an ASPECT which is read from the left, or clockwise, in the natural order of the SIGNS.

sixth house The sixth house of the HOROSCOPE is the house of Virgo and
Mercury, and is related to the way we look after our bodies – to health, diet
and exercise – but (contrary to the influence of the FIRST HOUSE) more with
the general effect these disciplines have on the general wellbeing of the
subject than with the actual physical effort we may make to keep fit and
well. The house relates too to our daily routine of work, whether in the way
of a career or as the person who runs a house and cares for a family. The
sixth house will have much to say about a person's reaction to routine –
whether this will be natural, or is more likely to disintegrate into anarchy.
Traditionally called the house of work, and considered the house of
'servants', in our own time it refers rather to those we employ: electricians,
plumbers, mechanics, decorators and such. It rules the bowels, and in
MUNDANE ASTROLOGY governs civil servants, police and the health
service.

slow in course A planet whose movement is slower than its MEAN MOTION.

Smith, Robert Cross (1795–1832) Born at Abbott's Leigh, near Bristol,
Cross was self-educated, and worked at first as a clerk in London. Not long
after his marriage, he became interested in astrology, and collaborated with
George Graham (a balloonist and student of the occult) on *The
Philosophical Merlin*, published in 1822 as a translation of a manuscript
once the property of Napoleon (but in fact plagiarized from an earlier book).
Smith then became editor of *The Straggling Astrologer*, a weekly magazine
one of whose contributors was H.R.H. the Princess Olive (who claimed to
be an illegitimate daughter of the brother of George III). The magazine
rapidly collapsed. There were more disappointments, including the short-
lived *Astrologer's Chronicle and Mystical Magazine*. But *The Prophetic
Messenger*, first published in 1826, and containing astrological forecasts for
every day of the year, was an immediate success. Cross began, when contributing, to call himself 'Raphael', and within a few years published a
number of popular books, including *Raphael's Sanctuary of the Astral Art;
Being a Book for the Boudoir, Drawing-room Table, and Evening Parties*.
He died, before actually making a fortune, at only 36 years of age.

solar arc A system of PROGRESSION in which the difference between the
position of the progressed Sun and natal Sun on any particular day is added

to every planet and point in the chart. The arc is approximately equivalent to the individual's age.

solar chart A HOROSCOPE or BIRTH-CHART set up with the Sun placed on the CUSP of the FIRST HOUSE. This is usually done when the birth-time of a subject is not known. The writers of SUN-SIGN columns also use this convention. *See* SOLAR RETURN.

solar eclipse *see* ECLIPSES

solar return In lay terms, one's birthday: the day on which the Sun, each year, returns to the point in the sky it occupied at one's birth – but in astrological terms this is calculated to the degree and minute of its longitude. The chart is used to suggest a course of events during the coming year. *See* SOLAR CHART.

solar time Solar time is based on the apparent movement of the Sun around the Earth, and a solar day is the period of time which elapses between two transits of the Sun across a particular MERIDIAN. The apparent movement of the Sun, however, is not regular, and even if it were the ecliptic is inclined to the EQUATOR, so its movement would be uneven.

solstices The highest points of the ECLIPTIC, which the Sun reaches when it enters the *tropical signs* CANCER and CAPRICORN in June and December. At the time of the June solstice in the northern hemisphere the Sun traces out the imaginary circle known as the tropic of Cancer, and in December the tropic of Capricorn.

solsticial signs The signs indicating the summer and winter SOLSTICES – i.e., Cancer and Capricorn.

square A square ASPECT is formed by two planets when they are 90° apart – that is, at right angles within the HOROSCOPE. An orb of 8° is allowed. The square is a negative aspect.

standard time Standard time is the time set for a particular area of the Earth's surface, adopted for the sake of clarity and good timekeeping. The zones are measured from Greenwich: i.e., New York, which is placed on the 75th meridian west of Greenwich, is five hours slow compared to Greenwich time; Tokyo uses the 135th meridian east of Greenwich, and is nine hours in advance of Greenwich time – so when it is noon in Japan, it is 3 a.m. GMT. There are, however, endless complications for the astrologer attempting to discover how a local time relates to Greenwich: at the turn of the century seven European countries and most of the countries of South America were still refusing to accede to GMT; others changed to GMT, then changed back. There was, in addition – and continues to be – local adaptation of summer time, and sometimes in emergency double summer time. *See* GREENWICH MEAN TIME, DAYLIGHT SAVING TIME.

star-sign *see* SUN-SIGN ASTROLOGY

stationary planet A planet is said to be stationary when it appears to be standing still between RETROGRADE and DIRECT MOTION.

stationary direct A stationary planet at the moment when it returns to DIRECT MOTION after being RETROGRADE. This is believed to indicate a good time at which to make decisions or implement projects.

stationary retrograde A stationary planet at the moment when it is about to turn RETROGRADE. This is believed to indicate a time for reconsideration of plans and projects.

stellium A group of three or more PLANETS gathered in one SIGN or HOUSE of the zodiac; sometimes a multiple CONJUNCTION. This is sometimes, but not necessarily, a stressful sign in a HOROSCOPE, and will dominate the personality traits or affairs of the sign or house the stellium inhabits. In MUNDANE astrology there is some suggestion, unsupported by statistical evidence, that stelliums can signify earthquakes.

Stöffler, Johannes (1452–1531) Most notable, at a time when it was almost impossible accurately to time events, for his work on clocks and astronomical instruments, mainly at the University of Tübingham, where he taught. A parish priest (at Justingen) he made clocks and celestial globes, but also set up and interpreted horoscopes. In 1499, with astronomer Jakob Pflaum, he published an almanac, and in 1512 a book on the use of the ASTROLABE. He became Rector of Tübingham University in 1522.

summer time *see* DAYLIGHT SAVING TIME

Sudines (fl. ca.240BC) A Chaldean astrologer and astronomer, one of those who was prominent in the movement of astrological knowledge from Babylonia into Greece and thence to Rome and the Western world. An expert in the properties of pearls and stones, onyx, crystals, amber, chrysophal, he is believed to have computed tables of the Moon's motion, and is the first astrologer known to make a connection between gemstones and the zodiac signs.

Sun ☉

An ordinary star that is at the centre of our solar system. The ancients believed it to be a glowing hot stone or ball of fire about two feet in diameter. In fact it has a diameter of 864,000 miles and it at an average distance of 93 million miles from Earth. From the inception of astrology it has been at the centre of the theory, though in terms of the personal BIRTH-CHART the ASCENDANT has traditionally been as, or more, important (*see* SUN-SIGN ASTROLOGY).

> *NB For the astrological effect of the Sun in different zodiac signs, see under the relevant sign – i.e., Aries, Taurus, Cancer, etc. For the effect of the Sun in different houses, see below.*

The Sun and the houses

The Sun in the FIRST HOUSE

Anyone born with the Sun in the first house will have been born near sunrise, and it is very likely that the Sun- and ASCENDANT signs will be the same. This means that the characteristics of the sign in question will be very strongly stressed in the personality – the person in question will be very typically Cancerian or Sagittarian or Scorpion. The effect of the planet which RULES the Sun- and Ascending sign will also be very strongly emphasized. It is very probable that the individual concerned will to a degree be self-centred, even egocentric. There will be a strong competitive streak, and a desire – even a need – to be the victor in any situation.

The Sun in the SECOND HOUSE

A pride in possessions and a delight in showing them off is characteristic of someone with the Sun in the second house. There will be no modesty, no silent enjoyment of a work of art, a bank balance, even a partner: 'Look what I have!' will be the reaction. Care is clearly needed that this does not look like boastfulness in the case of the former, and in the case of a partner that he or she does not begin to feel like just another possession. Hard work will have been done in the interests of building a satisfactory lifestyle, and generally speaking there is likely to be generosity, and enjoyment of the good things of life.

The Sun in the THIRD HOUSE

Education, education, education – those with the Sun in the third house see its importance, and whatever the mental capacity it will be tended and used to the full. If the necessity to make a living gets in the way, high academic achievement may come late in life; but generally speaking it will come, for the individual will feel that something is lacking in his or her life, and will be eager to fill the gap. Communication skills will be notable, especially if Mercury shares this house with the Sun, which may well be the case. The area in which these skills are shown will depend on the nature of the sign the Sun occupies.

The Sun in the FOURTH HOUSE

The Sun's influence will warm and enrich the family life. Parenthood is a main concern of the fourth house, and the nature of the Sun-sign will dictate the way in which a father and mother with this emphasis on the fourth house will act in relation to the children: i.e., from a sensitive sign such as Pisces the Sun will contribute a high degree of sensitivity, while in a more

exuberant sign such as Aries the emphasis will be more extravert and enthusiastic. A sense of security will be important, and those with the Sun in the
fourth house are never particularly eager to stray far from their home patch.

The Sun in the FIFTH HOUSE

This is the house of the Sun and of the Sun's sign, Leo, and as one might
expect the effect is on the whole extremely strong and positive. There will
be powerful ambition, and on the way to achieving it the individual will not
be averse to demonstrating his or her best points, especially in the creative
field (any creative urge should be satisfied). The sex life is well in focus,
and the need for fulfilment in this area of life will be considerable. Both
emotional and physical risks are likely to be taken, and there may be an
inherent taste for danger, perhaps demonstrated by enjoyment of high-risk
sports. There may also be a taste for gambling which can get out of hand.
This is the house of children; parents with this placing of the Sun may tend
to push them too hard.

The Sun in the SIXTH HOUSE

This is the house to which to look for indications affecting the health. The
Sun should animate every positive aspect of the health of the individual,
focusing on general wellbeing. But illnesses too, and vulnerability to ill
health, will also be in focus – look to the nature of the Sun-sign to
illuminate this. People with this placing of the Sun can be overconcerned
about their health, and see signs of illness where none exist – or worry too
much about their diet. If the Sun receives some good ASPECTS from the
Moon or Mars there should be excellent powers of recuperation. Elsewhere
in the personality, the need for routine is emphasized and the sense of duty
underlined. This is the house of Mercury – the planet will not be far away in
a BIRTH-CHART. If it is in the sixth house with the Sun, work in the general
field of communication will be rewarding.

The Sun in the SEVENTH HOUSE

The emphasis on the partner is particularly strong with the Sun in the
seventh house – to the extent indeed that the personality of this person may
be completely subsumed in that of the other. There is little doubt that there
will *be* a partner, for the need for one is compellingly strong. The placing of

Venus is important (this is the Venus house); if it is in the seventh house
with the Sun commitment to a partner may be made even more overwhelming by an imbalance in the personality, so that a sense of independence may
be altogether absent – and worse, will not be missed. If the Sun happens to
be in opposition ASPECT to the ASCENDANT, the problem will be considerably exacerbated, to the extent that the absence of the partner, even
temporarily, will be almost unbearable.

The Sun in the EIGHTH HOUSE

'Transformation' is a major theme of this house, and there is a desire and
need for self-knowledge, which may well transform the individual as he or
she grows older and learns more. Great emotional intensity will be
conferred by the Sun from this house, and powers of intuition are there to
be employed, and should be. Self-expression must be used, and sex is one
of the areas which will be an excellent outlet. Sex will indeed be important
to these people, to the extent of obsession in some cases; but there is a
strong connection between the astrological indications of sex and money,
and an obsession with finance is not out of the question. This may take the
shape, should the positive influence of the Sun be affected by negative
aspects, of unreasonable optimism about money and investments.

The Sun in the NINTH HOUSE

The house is sometimes known as 'the house of dreams', and this is
reflected in the chance that someone with the Sun in the ninth may come
close to seeing fantasy as reality; practicality should be applied in order that
the individual may channel natural intelligence in a positive direction –
intellectual growth, for instance, the broadening of horizons. Further
education is to be encouraged, and the development and expansion of the
mind. The individual will work hard for this, and the rewards will be great;
not so great however as to compensate for missed pleasures – the chase
after intellectual development should not be all-embracing, or distance
these people from friends who are less interested in the life of the intellect.

The Sun in the TENTH HOUSE

Those in whose BIRTH-CHART the Sun inhabits the tenth house will be
determined to make themselves known, to make material progress, and to

see themselves as powerful and influential. This is an emotional need which will be satisfied in one way or another. Their enthusiasm will hopefully be infectious enough to make it unnecessary to be unduly autocratic; friendly persuasion should be successful in most cases. If the Sun is in a FIRE SIGN it will burn fiercely, and if its heat is properly applied – to burn without scorching – these individuals should be big achievers; from a WATER SIGN intuition will be strong; an EARTH SIGN will increase practicality, and an AIR SIGN a lively communicative intellect.

The Sun in the ELEVENTH HOUSE

Someone with the Sun influencing for them from the eleventh house will be at their best working with others. There is a real need to be involved with a social group of some sort – not merely a group of friends, but a group working for a common cause, perhaps a charity. The creative power of the Sun can be used to great effect in strengthening a community purpose – but it can also edge a person into seeing him- or herself as the natural leader whose powers of leadership must immediately be recognized. This can lead to problems of communication, especially when a newcomer to a group attempts to assume control. In enthusiasm for the group, there may be an instinctive reluctance to get close to any individual; this too can lead to problems. A way out is to compartmentalize, so that while working with a group towards some goal, the individual can also nourish more personal friendships.

The Sun in the TWELFTH HOUSE

Those with this placing of the Sun are at their best working behind the scenes and in a familiar environment, distanced as much as possible from anything or anyone who may disturb the peace and tranquillity which is needed if the work is to have positive results. Any attempt to persuade this person to be more extrovert, to work in any position which is in a spotlight, is doomed to failure. In extreme cases, even a partner may be seen – perhaps after the first few years – as a commitment which is in the end unnecessary. This view may come as a result of self-examination, for the motto 'Know yourself' may well have been written for someone with the Sun in the twelfth house.

* * *

sunrise chart Some astrologers set a chart for the moment of sunrise when the day but not the time of birth of a subject is known.

Sun ruler *see* PERSONAL PLANETS

Sun-sign astrology Sun-sign astrology – in which the zodiac sign occupied by the Sun at the time of birth is the sole factor used to describe a person – began effectively in 1930 with a newspaper column in the English *Sunday Express*. The astrologer R H NAYLOR was commissioned by the editor to write an article examining the BIRTH-CHART of Princess Margaret, who had been born on 21 August. This provoked considerable interest, and Naylor was invited to write a series of articles. In the first of the series, published on 5 October 1930, Naylor wrote that British aircraft were likely to be in danger. On the day of publication it was announced that the airship R-101, en route to India with a distinguished group of passengers, had crashed in France. Not unnaturally, the newspaper capitalized on Naylor's apparent prediction, he was given much increased space, and soon became the first nationally-known astrologer. Naylor realized quickly that he must find a way of involving all his readers. Since everyone knew the date of their birthday, he simply published a list of the dates when the Sun passed through each zodiac sign, and wrote twelve paragraphs, one for each of them. Within a very short time, people were asking each other 'What's your sign?', and there began the overwhelming public interest in astrology which created a number of astrologer millionaires.

Sun-signs, the One's Sun-sign (sometimes called 'star-sign') is the section of the ecliptic through which the Sun is passing at the time of one's birth. This is for convenience called by the name of the constellation which occupied that space over 2,000 years ago, though the sign no longer completely matches its original zodiac sign (*see* PRECESSION). Now seen by the general public as the probably the most important astrological consideration, this is only true since the invention of SUN-SIGN ASTROLOGY in 1930; traditionally the ASCENDANT or RISING-SIGN was considered the most significant of the two. The Sun-sign was thought to portray the hidden personality – that part of one's personality known, if at all, only by one's partner or most intimate friends, while the Ascendant showed the outward and obvious personality traits. For Sun-sign indications *see* under the relevant sign, i.e. ARIES, TAURUS, CANCER, etc.

superior planets The so-called 'superior planets' are those that orbit the Sun at distances greater than that of Earth – i.e., Mars, Jupiter, Saturn Uranus, Neptune, Pluto and Chiron. The term has nothing to do with their astrological significance.

swift in motion A planet which is moving faster than its MEAN MOTION.

synastry The comparison of two or more HOROSCOPES with a view to considering the compatibility or otherwise of the subjects.

synchronicity A term coined by the psychologist C G Jung to describe the inexplicable occurrence of two similar events at the same time, but apparently unconnected. Most astrologers would not accept his thesis that this is the result of an 'acausal connecting principle', but it has been accepted by those who have a problem with and are concerned by the difficulty of discovering any kind of scientific explanation for astrology.

synodic month The time between two full Moons – i.e., 29.5606 days. And *see* CALENDAR.

– T –

table of houses Tables showing the signs and degrees for house CUSPS, used to calculate and draw up a HOROSCOPE.

talisman (or amulet) An object kept on the body (usually suspended on a chain) that is believed to have supernatural powers to bring good fortune. The most common modern talismans are crucifixes, but in the past they were often astrological – made of the metal associated with a zodiac sign or planet strongly associated with the individual, and often engraved with more astrological information – and made at a propitious time.

tarot Connections have been made between astrology and the tarot. These are at best nebulous, and there are numerous connections between particular cards and particular signs and planets, none of which appear to have been made as a result of research, and several of which appear to be obtuse (for instance the connection of the Juggler with Taurus, and of the Sun with Gemini).

Taurus ♉

The second sign of the zodiac. SUN-SIGN dates: 21 April– 21May.

It should be remembered when reading of the characteristics of the Sun-signs that these will always be affected by the effects of the rising-sign, the planets in various other signs and houses, and the relationships the planets make to each other.

General characteristics

A need for security and routine, a conviction that the Sun will rise tomorrow and that life will as inevitably follow the same pattern day after day, is more important for someone with the Sun in Taurus than for any other Sun-sign person. They are inevitably from time to time disappointed, but will do their best to ensure that, for instance, their work offers routine rather than uncertainty or surprises, and that a regular pay-cheque is deposited in the bank (rather than relying on irregular payments). Emotional security is as important to them: which can mean that they rely too much on a partner's total commitment to them and their daily life – they can become possessive, seeing any deviation from the known domestic routine as a danger. Reliable and stable, unlikely to give a partner grounds for uncertainty or anxiety, they tend to be plodders – trustworthy but deliberate, painstaking but somewhat slow, both at work and (for instance) in personal relationships, where an element of excitement may be lacking. Though passionate, Taureans offer sensual and considerate lovemaking rather than exhilarating and stimulating sexuality. Once again, routine may be a somewhat disappointing and monotonous keyword.

The growing child

A Taurean baby is likely to be attractive even among the most attractive peers – and is likely to retain his or her good looks (Taureans are claimed to be the best-looking of Sun-sign people). Usually contented, the babies are likely to show patience and good behaviour through infancy, to be tractable and on the whole cheerful within the routines of childhood. Their appetites will be more than healthy, and baby chubbiness will all too easily become obesity if the diet is not watched – Taurean children will eat anything, and the fact that they can easily be bribed into good behaviour by the promise of chocolate or other favoured food may tempt parents to be too indulgent in this area. At school they will be methodical and well organized, and will use their charisma to keep their teachers well onside – occasionally lazy, they will only have to exercise their abundant charm to deflect criticism. They will develop at their own pace, refusing to be rushed, and will make steady rather than spectacular progress. In adolescence their easy relationship with the world will continue, with the conviction that a smile will get them out of any tight corner – as will indeed often be the case.

Education

Both at school and in further education the Taurean will fit well into a tightly structured environment, keeping rigorously to the set routine of

lessons and lectures, and plodding steadily through the curricula, unspectac-
ularly perhaps, but with a steady determination which will lead them if not
to brilliant success at least to a very respectable command of whatever disciplines they are studying. They may tend to eschew the social side of
school and university life, which can lead to a sort of isolation, in which the
one world of which they are thoroughly aware is that of the classroom or
lecture-room and the room in which they do their private study. If they look
for relaxation during these years it is likely to be with similarly-minded
groups of people. Most Sun-sign Taureans appreciate and love music
(which they may indeed choose to study); music clubs or choirs will
therefore be attractive. They are also usually attracted to pottery,
embroidery, sculpture, which may be areas both of study and relaxation.

Friendship, romance and sex

People with a Taurean Sun-sign might be said to 'know how to live' – they
enjoy life and are eager to ensure that their friends do the same. Their
friendship is reliable and lifelong, they are dependable and full of infectious
good-will. The only problem may be with possessiveness – they sometimes
seem unable to understand that their friends may have *other* friends, and at
worst can become jealous and resentful. This is true in their romantic lives:
the idea that a girlfriend or boyfriend in the early stages of a relationship
may be unwilling to say goodbye to former friends, is anathema to them,
and at worst can lead to a premature collapse of a promising affair.
However, once committed, a partner will unquestionably be given a good
time – Taureans positively enjoy spending money on those they love, and
good food and wine and luxurious presents will be taken as read. Sexually
they are also generous, and just as they are reputed to be the best-looking
among the signs, so they are claimed as excellent, considerate, sensual
lovers. Yet once again possessiveness can raise its head, as can unjustifiable
jealousy, and unless these can be restrained the most promising relationships can be doomed before the sheets are turned down.

Permanent partnership and family

Everything in the preceding paragraph can be applied to a permanent relationship: possessiveness, jealousy, the absence of any conception that the
partner does not belong heart and soul to the Taurean, can doom the most

promising partnership. The Taurean's love of routine can seem stifling to a partner, as can what may seem a rather too intense commitment to making money (however obviously this is meant to make the family thoroughly secure). However, the positive elements of the Sun-sign are also emphasized: the generosity of spirit as well as purse, the shared enjoyment of life. A Taurean will want his or her child to feel totally secure within the family, and have the means to take advantage of any opportunities which are offered. They will impose strict discipline, often without explanation – laying down a law the only apparent justification for which will be that 'I say so'. On the other hand, sometimes self-indulgent themselves, they may give way far too easily to requests for fattening foods – and spoil their children by providing the latest current electronic gadget, obliquely showing off to other parents.

Occupation

A Sun-sign Taurean above all needs security, so will not be happy in a career which is not as secure as conditions will allow – that is, with a company which seems well established and prosperous. Self-employment, with the financial uncertainty that that usually entails, would not be a happy condition. The natural Taurean flair for making money will be well served by a job in a bank, large corporation, financial investment company – though even there they may have to condition themselves to take the occasional risk, mainly, however, with other people's money. Again, a desirable condition of employment is regularity – regular timekeeping, a regular climb up the promotion ladder; a Taurean who catches the same train every working day to the same destination to sit at the same desk next to the same colleagues and deal with familiar conditions of work, will be on the whole a happy Taurean. An exception to the general antipathy to self-employment is the pleasure and pride a Taurean can take in building up his or her own business, necessarily well funded, well backed and financed, and ideally with a rather assertive partner willing to cope with public relations and marketing.

Health

The Taurean metabolism is generally speaking slow, and this (together with their taste for good food and wine) exacerbates a natural tendency to put on weight; once this has happened, it is often difficult to lose it – they tend to be happily self-indulgent and disinclined to reject the after-dinner mints. Fresh fruit and vegetables are not always to taste, but are requisites if the Taurean is to stay healthy. A steady diet and an equally steady exercise routine are highly desirable if exhaustion and lethargy are not to take hold; and the exercise should aim to speed up the metabolism – so dance classes, aerobics, exercise which persuades them to move faster and with more energy are to be encouraged. At the gym, exercise machines will appeal because they enable the Taurean to work at his or her own steady pace, without having to compete with more vigorous types. Saunas and regular massage will be effective in expelling toxicity. The Taurean body area is the neck and throat (a cold will almost inevitably start with a sore throat and end with a cough). The thyroid gland is also ruled by Taurus, and if the already leisurely metabolism seems to slow spectacularly, especially with age, this should certainly be checked for its efficiency.

Finance

Taureans seem to have a natural understanding of finance and how to manage money. This does not mean that they are great jugglers on the stock exchanges of the world – they take few chances; what they are interested in is building a secure package of investments which will bring a steady growth of capital – they are most unhappy should there be a threat to the security of their cash reserves. A Taurean's best financial scheme probably involves a savings scheme geared to a large insurance company or building society, rather than leaving funds in the hands of advisers over whom he or she has no control. If this sounds like the attitude of a miser, this is far from the truth; for Taureans, money is to be enjoyed – and indeed among the less secure investments which might be considered are the restaurant or hotel business, where there are chances of discounts on weekends away, or excellent meals or wines. When a considerable amount of money is spent it is likely to be on the home environment – not only on buildings and furnishings but on perhaps a collection of paintings or other *objets d'art*, which will give pleasure as well as being a good investment. The Taurean should always keep in mind the question whether he or she is putting material possessions ahead of human relationships.

Growing Older

The Taurean, with a naturally slow metabolism and a reluctance to rush about, may find as he or she ages that rushing about becomes not merely undesirable but impossible, as the lack of regular exercise results in stiffening limbs. It will also become even more difficult to shed excess weight – all a good argument for keeping in shape in earlier years. If there has been a reasonable income throughout life, the Taurean will probably have been careful enough to have built up a reserve of funds with which to bolster state pensions, and should not find that retirement is accompanied by too much financial difficulty. (It will probably be the case that even in extreme old age there will be a reluctance to cut into capital; the realization that 'you can't take it with you' is quite difficult for a Taurean to grasp.) As for occupying the stretches of time that will become available in retirement, many Taureans are content to expand their lifetime hobbies, which may include activities such as embroidery or model-making – pleasures that require patience and meticulous attention to detail. Here too are the natural gardeners of the zodiac, many of whom enjoy making their own wine or beer. Away from home, amateur acting can attract – and when heavier games are no longer possible, Taurean bowlers are often seen on the greens.

Taurus as rising-sign

The Taurean need for security will be even more heavily stressed when Taurus is the RISING-SIGN, and will relate both to finance and the emotions. There will be a strong sense of ambition, and an emphasis on material possessions, particularly security of income and the safety and growth of investments – when anything is bought (a house, furniture, art works) there will be careful consideration of the degree to which its value may appreciate. With Taurus rising there will be a strong need for sexual expression, and considerable demands will be made on the partner. Commitment to that partner will be firm, sincere and deep – but possessiveness may mar the relationship, together with possible (often unfounded) jealousy.

Traditional associations

- Ruling Planet – Venus
- Triplicity/Element – earth
- Quadruplicity/Quality – fixed

- Colour – pink
- Gemstone – sapphire, sometimes emerald
- Metal – copper
- Flowers – rose, poppy, foxglove
- Trees – ash, cypress, apple, vines
- Herbs and Spices – cloves, sorrel, spearmint
- Foodstuffs – wheat, berry fruits, apples, pears, grapes
- Animals – cattle
- Countries – Ireland, Switzerland, Iran, Israel, Japan
- Cities – Dublin, Honolulu, Lucerne, Mantua, Leipzig
- US States – Louisiana, Maryland, Minnesota

* * *

temperaments The four temperaments were associated with the HUMOURS in early medicine and hence with astrology. The choleric, melancholic, phlegmatic and sanguine temperaments (linked to phlegm, black bile, yellow bile and blood – the humours) were linked to certain signs:

- Phlegmatic signs – Cancer, Scorpio and Pisces
- Melancholic signs – Taurus, Virgo and Capricorn
- Choleric signs – Aries, Leo and Sagittarius
- Sanguine signs – Gemini, Libra and Aquarius

See also ELEMENTS.

temples An archaic traditional name for the HOUSES.

tenth house The house of Capricorn and Saturn concerns itself with one's ambitions and aspirations, with worldly progress and social status – also with authority and power and the way in which one copes with these. If a PERSONAL PLANET is placed in this house, it will be a strong indication of a need for personal involvement in a career. The family and a sense of tradition is also focused here. Traditionally there was always an association with the father, and the part he may play in shaping the early career. Career changes will often be indicated here, especially those that may increase an individual's status and involve additional responsibility and increased prestige. In MUNDANE astrology, the association is with those who run political parties, judges, presidents and heads of state – but also popular culture. *NB* in many systems of HOUSE DIVISION the CUSP of the tenth house is always on the MC. This is not so, however, with the EQUAL HOUSE system. *See also* MIDHEAVEN.

Tetrabiblos, The An astrological text by Claudius PTOLEMY – the title translated simply as 'four books'. He treats the subject in a highly scientific way. His theories are based on the proposition that the four ELEMENTS are the basis of everything known in the universe as he comprehended it. His was a severely pragmatic view of astrology, rejecting any idea of the planets as gods. He had already stated, in his astronomical work, the *Almagest*, the importance of accurate observation of the heavens and of planetary positions, and it is in that book that he goes into the matter of calculating a HOROSCOPE. He discusses in *The Tetrabiblos* the possible effects of the fixed stars, assigns particular signs to particular countries, and discusses MEDICAL ASTROLOGY on the grounds that the planets have effects in particular parts of the body. He emphasizes the importance of the moment of CONCEPTION, but realizes that it is impossible to specify this. He speculates on the possibility of discovering the probable length of life, and writes of the seven AGES OF MAN. Discussing the problem of free will, he points out that although the planets appear to indicate future events, the complexities of the theory make it impossible to predict these accurately.

    The Tetrabiblos – after over 2,000 years – is in print and available in excellent English translation both in book form and on the world wide web.

tetragonous An archaic name for the SQUARE ASPECT.

third house The house of Gemini and Mercury, sometimes called the house of brothers and sisters, is the area of the chart concerned with relatives other than the parents and children – brothers, sisters, uncles, aunts, cousins – also perhaps the children of relatives or friends. It can show how a child will relate to school life, and relates to day-to-day travel such as commuting (it is also sometimes called the house of short journeys). A subject's mental attitude, communication skills and memory are the responsibility of the third house, and it can also reflect his or her reaction to environment – i.e. town or country, bustle or quiet, noise or silence. It rules the lungs and arms. In MUNDANE ASTROLOGY it is related to the communication system of a country or city, to means of transport, and to public opinion.

'thirteenth sign', the *see* OPHIUCHUS

Thrasyllus, Tiberius Claudius (d. AD36) When the Emperor Tiberius was in exile from Rome in 5BC he encountered on the island of Rhodes a Greek grammarian, the editor of the works of Democritus and PLATO (he published one of the earliest editions of Plato's complete works). He was the author of a treatise, *The Pinax,* in which he quotes from PETOSIRIS, NECHEPSO and HERMES – the first reliably dated mention of Hermes to have survived.

However, it is as the most influential astrologer of Imperial Rome that he is now remembered. Tiberius had previously sought out various astrologers and consulted them about his future, having them executed after the consultations for fear lest they should betray his horoscope to his enemies. Thrasyllus might well have suffered the same fate – indeed Tiberius was actually planning to throw him over a precipice, but first asked him how he saw his own horoscope for the day. As the historian Suetonius puts it:

> *Thrasyllus, after measuring the positions and distances of the stars, hesitated, then showed alarm. The more he looked, the greater his astonishment and fright. Then he cried that a critical and perhaps fatal emergency was upon him. Tiberius clasped him, commending his divination of peril, and promising that he would escape it. Thrasyllus was admitted among his closest friends, his pronouncements were regarded as oracular.*
> *[Suetonius, Augustus, 98]*

When Augustus summoned Tiberius back to Rome and, as Thrasyllus had predicted, proclaimed him his heir, Tiberius took Thrasyllus back with him, and conferred upon him the valuable gift of Roman citizenship. Upon Augustus's death, Tiberius, now Emperor, continued to consult Thrasyllus, and during his nine years reign the astrologer was never far from his side. It was a dangerous time for astrologers, and Thrasyllus was clearly a master politician – when the ambitious praetor Sejanus consulted him about the affair he was having with the wife of the Emperor's son, Drusus, he managed to maintain good relations not only with him but with Tiberius, supporting Sejanus in the battle for the succession which had arisen between him and Agrippina, Augustus' granddaughter, who wanted the throne for her children. Thrasyllus survived the fall of Sejanus, and continued to advise the Emperor. It is said that towards the end of Tiberius's life, when he saw enemies all around him and became a crazed killer of anyone he suspected, Thrasyllus was instrumental in rescuing many of the condemned, by assuring Tiberius that he would survive them all.

   Thrasyllus's daughter married the knight L Ennius in AD 15, and his granddaughter by that marriage married Naevius Sutorius Macro, the knight who was Tiberius's regent at the end of the Emperor's life.

topocentric house system An extremely complex modern system of HOUSE DIVISION said to have been devised after comparing events in the lives of subjects and relating them to a system devised to illustrate them.

transit A PLANET's movement through a SIGN or HOUSE.

transpersonal planets Uranus, Neptune and Pluto, so-called because their ORBITS are too long to affect individuals.

Transpluto A HYPOTHETICAL PLANET.

tredecile *see* SESQUIQUINTILE

Trent, A J *see* GARNETT, RICHARD

trigon A traditional name for a TRIPLICITY, or sometimes a 'TRINE'.

trine The planets are in trine ASPECT when they are 120° apart. An ORB of 8° is allowed. A trine is a positive aspect.

triplicities *see* ELEMENTS

tropical signs *see* SOLSTICES

tropical zodiac The tropical zodiac begins at the point where the ECLIPTIC and the EQUATOR intersect at the northern VERNAL EQUINOX – at 0° Aries. And *see* SIDEREAL ZODIAC.

tropic of Cancer *see* SOLSTICES

tropic of Capricorn *see* SOLSTICES

T-square When two planets are in OPPOSITION with a third halfway between them (i.e., at their MIDPOINT) they are said to form a T-square, regarded as an energizing aspect which can be a positive or negative factor in a HOROSCOPE, depending on the nature of the planets involved and their SIGN positions.

twelfth house The house of Pisces and Neptune, the twelfth house is associated with the ideas of seclusion, escapism and faith. It is traditionally linked to hospitals and prisons (it was once known as the house of bondage) but in modern times it has been found to be powerfully associated with the unconscious, and should be studied when discussing the root of psychological problems. There is here an association with another traditional name, The house of one's own undoing – which seems to suggest psychological problems rooted in the personality. The ELEVENTH HOUSE will show how to approach and come to terms with such problems, but it is the twelfth that will describe their fundamental nature. This is particularly the case if a planet is placed within 10° of the ASCENDANT, a strong indication that the concerns of that planet are repressed and need to be externalized. Planets TRANSITTING this or PROGRESSIONS to planets placed in it may have an inhibiting effect, but can encourage reflection and serious thought in connection with important issues. Sacrifice is a matter of the twelfth house, and can be a theme when the house is in focus.

– U –

Ummanu Soothsayers who advised the kings of Assyria in the 5th and 6th centuries BC, using various omens which included events in the sky: conjunctions of planets, comets, eclipses. The royal library of Ashurbanipal (669–640BC) contained thousands of texts recording these omens. They took such forms as:

> *The planets Jupiter and Venus were visible during the eclipse until it cleared. This is propitious for your Majesty and evil for the lands in the West.*

unaspected planets Planets which are completely unaspected, receiving no major ASPECTS from another planet, are extremely rare – especially if fairly narrow ORBS are allowed. A few astrologers claim that they should be completely ignored; more assert that an unaspected planet is an extremely strong focal point in a HOROSCOPE, pointing to an important area of the personality, but one which is not integrated with the life of the individual.

Urania One of the nine Muses of Greek mythology, personifying the highest aspirations of art and intellect, who became the muse of ASTROLOGY and ASTRONOMY in the days when the two terms were interchangeable. She presided over all celestial forces, and was one of the arbiters of fate.

Uranian astrology An unconventional system of astrology first taught in Hamburg by Alfred Witte, said to have evolved it by applying his theories to events during the battles of the First World War. These theories involve the use of HYPOTHETICAL PLANETS (invented with the help of Friedrich Sieggruen) and rely largely on MIDPOINTS. Uranian astrology became popular especially in the USA in the 1970s, but is not widely used at the present time.

Uranus ♅

The first of three 'modern' planets, and the seventh major planet of the solar system, Uranus rules Aquarius (traditionally ruled by Saturn). Uranus was discovered in 1781 by William Herschel, whose name it briefly bore. It orbits the Sun every 84 years, taking approximately 7 years to pass through each zodiac sign, during which it exerts the same influence in the HOROSCOPES of everyone born during that period. Unless the sign in which it is placed is also occupied by the Sun or Moon, or is the ASCENDANT, it will tend merely to colour the other characteristics revealed in the horoscope. For instance, if ambition is heavily emphasized due to the influence of other planets, Uranus will show the degree of that influence, or to some extent how it emerges in the character of the subject. The planet may also provoke changes in life, but on the whole it has a GENERATION INFLUENCE rather than specially affecting an individual.

One individual effect, however, manifests when Uranus makes specific angles to the position it occupied at the moment of birth. Perhaps its most important influence occurs when it has travelled half-way round the zodiac, and is exactly 180° from its natal position. This happens when the individual concerned is about 40 years old, and Uranus occupies its POLAR SIGN. The *Uranus half-return* can be used to help activate new interest, to change and sharpen one's image; it sometimes signals what could be called a new lease of life – perhaps the mid-life crisis. The *full return*, when one is 84, can be equally interesting; individuals at this age have been observed to perform exceptional feats such as parachute drops and deep-sea dives.

Uranus and the zodiac signs

Uranus in ARIES

Energy and drive will be a part of the character, together with a pioneering spirit; these will inform and strengthen ambition and assist the subject to deal with a position of power, if a quality of leadership shows itself elsewhere in the HOROSCOPE. A sensitive person will be enlivened by this placing of Uranus, and the emotional level will be boosted. With Cancer, Libra or Capricorn strongly emphasized, Uranus may provoke tension.

Uranus in TAURUS

There may be a conflict between conservative, formal behaviour and sudden incursions into eccentricity and unconventionality. Work may be uneven. A certain spice will be lent to the character of those with Taurus emphasized by Sun, Moon or RISING-SIGN placement, and Virgos and Capricorns should find their approach to life enlivened. Uranus will help those who work creatively by steadying their flow of ideas and helping them consider fine detail.

Uranus in GEMINI

Any versatile and original individual will find these qualities sharpened and emphasized by Uranus working from Gemini. This influence can be positively used, especially if the dominating signs in the HOROSCOPE are Gemini, Libra or Aquarius. While the influence will not be entirely free of tension, particularly where Sagittarians or Virgos are concerned, Uranus works well from Gemini, where it is in sympathetic mood, making people lively, alert and outspoken.

Uranus in CANCER

Those with Cancer as SUN-SIGN or RISING-SIGN will undoubtedly be prone to worry, and find it extremely difficult to relax – Uranus will do nothing to weaken these traits. But at least people with Uranus in Cancer will be imaginative enough to find out ways of dealing with these characteristics, probably through expressing their imagination creatively. There could be a conflict between wanting to express their own personalities and concern for family opinion, and this could be a source of difficulty. The planet will work best for Scorpios and Pisceans.

Uranus in LEO

There are strong links between Uranus and power, and when the planet is in Leo a liking for – a positive *need* for – power will emerge, especially if Leo is emphasized in other ways. An interest in politics is very likely here, and the creative forces of Uranus will also emerge. Stubbornness will be characteristic, especially if Taurus, Scorpio or Aquarius are emphasized. The planet will enliven Aries and Sagittarians.

Uranus in VIRGO

If the individual is a worrier and prone to tension, Uranus will be no help at all – indeed, may assist these proclivities to emerge. The individual will be discriminating, but tend to act erratically, especially if Virgo is emphasized in other ways. Taureans and Capricorns will find life easier, for Uranus will increase their originality and help them lose their devotion to convention, which can hold them back. This group of people as a whole may be specially concerned with ecology and conservation.

Uranus in LIBRA

If Libra is already accented, a need to see fair play and a concern for justice will be particularly marked; it will also emerge strongly with anyone in whose HOROSCOPE the planet has this position. The tension inherent in Uranus is mitigated when it is in this sign, though it may catch up with those whose dominant signs are Aries, Cancer or Capricorn. It is an excellent placing for Aquarians and Geminians, who will be more ready than usually to listen to and accept the opinions of others, and even act on them – in their own way.

Uranus in SCORPIO

Those with Scorpio as an already dominant sign will very probably be among the leaders of their generation when Uranus is also in that sign. They will want to move mountains, and some may very well succeed. With everyone else the planet will add intensity and a sense of purpose, which will emerge most strongly with Capricorns and Pisceans, giving them an additional energy source to tap. The planet will add confidence to those who are generally somewhat shy.

Uranus in SAGITTARIUS

If the individual is intellectually sharp, the planet will add fire and enthusiasm to their need for challenge, and will add the ability to evolve new concepts. The humanitarian aspects of the Uranus influence will certainly manifest, as will increased originality of expression – especially if Sagittarius is a dominating sign. The planet will also help Ariens and Leos in this way; everyone with Uranus in Sagittarius will be able to make use of its capacity to strengthen enthusiasm and forward planning.

Uranus in CAPRICORN

Two opposing characteristics may quarrel with each other from time to time, a tendency to support new and unconventional ideas and attitudes meeting head-on a tendency to cling to the traditional and well tried. It is possible to get the best of both these worlds, if not always with great ease. A balance must be sought. The see-saw tendency is most likely to emerge with Capricorns or Aquarians, and possibly with Ariens, Cancerians and Librans; Taureans and Virgos will benefit most from having Uranus in Capricorn.

Uranus in AQUARIUS

The influence of Uranus is at its strongest in Aquarius, the sign that it rules. Aquarians who have this placing of Uranus will express an above-average number of the characteristics of their Sun-sign. Eccentricity and unpredictability will also emerge – but on the positive side, so will true friendliness and a humanitarian spirit. For all other Sun-sign individuals an element of Aquarianism will emerge in their personalities (*see* AQUARIUS).

Uranus in PISCES

Pisces is a sign noted for kindliness and charity, and those with Uranus in Pisces will bring the humanitarian elements of the planet to the fore. These tendencies will not dominate the personality completely, but there will certainly be a basic sympathy for those working to improve the lot of the less fortunate. The tension implied by Uranus will come into contact with the emotional forces of Pisces, and if they are recognized and channelled constructively they can work well. Pisceans and Virgos will feel this influence strongly; Cancerians and Scorpios will benefit most.

Uranus and the houses

Uranus in the FIRST HOUSE

Independence and originality will be marked with Uranus in the first house – but a streak of perversity and unpredictability may also show itself. The influence of the ASCENDANT will be emphasized; consider the influence of the sign in which Uranus is placed, which will also form part of the character.

Uranus in the SECOND HOUSE
There will be a somewhat cavalier attitude to money, with investments made without due consideration, and sometimes proving disastrous. If financial problems arise, the problem will have been the result of the subject's own decisions.

Uranus in the THIRD HOUSE
The education may progress in fits and starts, but brilliance and originality will be seen, and a free-ranging mind should be allowed to develop. Restriction would cramp an intelligence which needs a free rein if it is to be stimulated.

Uranus in the FOURTH HOUSE
A certain perversity will be discernable, with moodiness and unpredictability. A desire for a stable home life will conflict with a need for freedom from responsibility. Original ideas should not be set aside, but be properly developed.

Uranus in the FIFTH HOUSE
This is a positive placing of a sometimes troubling planet, and it should encourage originality and brilliance of mind, together with a positive, enthusiastic attitude to love affairs and a disregard of emotional risks. A tendency to take risks should be noted.

Uranus in the SIXTH HOUSE
Strain and tension – perhaps the result of one of the positive effects of Uranus in this house, where it encourages intellectual adventurousness and brilliance – may have a negative effect on the health because of an inability to relax. The diet should be watched and a steady routine cultivated.

Uranus in the SEVENTH HOUSE
Someone with Uranus in the seventh house may hesitate to commit to a permanent relationship, despite a romantic outlook which will contribute to his or her powers of sexual attraction. Will romance overcome the desire for independence, or will the wish to remain free predominate?

Uranus in the EIGHTH HOUSE

A carefree attitude to finance may need to be reined in, for there will be a tendency to swing from a disregard for money to a keen appreciation of the pleasures it can bring; a somewhat similar attitude to sex can lead to periods of cool and distant sensuality, giving way at other times to keen and responsive appetite.

Uranus in the NINTH HOUSE

Possible scientific or literary flair spiced with originality and enthusiasm are characteristic of this placing of Uranus. A need for excitement, new and different experiences can be satisfied by travel – when negative TRANSITS to the planet should be avoided if there are not to be complications and delays.

Uranus in the TENTH HOUSE

Sudden changes of direction in the career are possible, and are sometimes accepted despite the fact that much previous experience will then be wasted. An attraction to politics is possible, and there can be a distinct appetite for power, and for a career that will involve excitement and/or glamour.

Uranus in the ELEVENTH HOUSE

The need for a broad social life will bring the subject into contact with numerous acquaintances who may never become real friends, for a friendly character is accompanied by a disinclination to become too close to all but a very few others. Unpredictability will be a feature, but a real talent for hard work on behalf of others.

Uranus in the TWELFTH HOUSE

An emotional need and desire to care for others is joined by cool logic which can inhibit close personal relationships. This can make for excellent work in nursing or the medical profession in general, but the idea of sharing life with a permanent partner may not be realized.

* * *

– V –

Varley, John (1778–1842) A brilliant water-colour artist, friend of William Blake, Varley was also a keen astrologer who every morning would work out the TRANSITS for the day. He never worked professionally, and was somewhat depressed when he became far better-known as an astrologer than as an artist. While he made no charge for the horoscopes he worked out for his sitters, he did publish a book in which he commented on the connection between personal appearance and the zodiac signs (*A Treatise on Zodiacal Physiognomy*, 1828) in which he included numerous engravings of faces matched with the relevant signs. He appears to have been extremely accurate in some predictions, and among those he impressed was John Ruskin, events in whose past life he apparently detailed with great accuracy. When he caught a chill by sitting on damp grass while sketching, he remarked to his son, 'I shall not get better – all the aspects are too strong against me to recover'. He died shortly afterwards.

Vedic astrology Otherwise Jyotish or Jyotisha, Vedic astrology is based on the ancient Indian holistic tradition, and aims to assist people to understand their karma, or the way in which good actions give rise to good effects, bad ones to bad effects, thus causing a chain of successive transmigrations, the circumstances of each life being explained by actions in a previous one. Vedic astrology relies on the SIDEREAL ZODIAC rather than the TROPICAL ZODIAC used by Western astrologers.

Venus ♀

Venus is the second major planet in order from the Sun, and the one that comes closest to the Earth. It orbits the Sun every 225 days. It RULES Taurus and Libra, is in DETRIMENT in Scorpio and Aries; it is EXALTED in Pisces and in FALL in Virgo. Because, like Mercury, it is never far from the Sun in the sky, in a HOROSCOPE it can only fall either in the same sign as the Sun, or in one of the two signs on either side of it: i.e., if the Sun is in Gemini, Venus can only fall either in Gemini, in Taurus or Aries, or in Cancer or Leo. Its strikingly clear, bright light made it surely one of the first closely observed planets, and in myth as well as astrology it has always been associated with purity and love – love in its noncarnal sense – with personal relationships, and with the feminine side of a subject's nature. It encourages gentleness, friendship, and pleasant social intercourse; it can, however, make for carelessness, indecision, romanticism and dependence.

Venus and the zodiac signs

Venus in ARIES

This position of Venus can contribute almost overwhelming charm and, knowing that they possess this quality, people with Venus in this sign may tend to rely on it to a worrying extent, putting their own needs in a relationship first, and tending to steamroller partners into granting their every whim. The planet is in a lively and passionate mood in this sign, and there will be a distinct tendency to fall in love at first sight, and to go all out to win the affection of a possible partner. Once in a relationship the enthusiasm of these characters, not only for sex but for romance, can make them wonderful partners, provided they keep their selfishness in check and make allowances for the other person's tastes. They will find this easier if their Sun-sign is Pisces, for the tender caring side of that sign will make an admirable balance. With the Sun in Aquarius or Gemini the emotions will be additionally warmed, and a possible slight detachment will be less marked. With the Sun sharing Aries with Venus the tendency to dash into a relationship will be emphasized, while a Taurean Sun will add an enthusiasm for sex which will keep partner involved for however long the liaison lasts.

Venus in TAURUS

Venus rules Taurus and is in an uncompromising mood in this sign. However, there will be a note of caution, and no tendency to rush into a relationship, despite heightened desire and an agreeably warm, sensual personality. Love for a partner or family will be powerful, but also perhaps overpossessive, and shown by showering the loved ones with almost too many gifts. A need to express love will join with a desire really to enjoy the partnership, and this will be shown in romantic wooing even after the liaison is firm. With Taurus as a Sun-sign possessiveness will be emphasized; the Sun in Pisces or Cancer will heighten the positive expression of emotion, while also steadying it. If the Sun is in Aries the typical emphasis of the sign will be somewhat softened, while the lively flirtatiousness of a Geminian Sun will be given sincerity and depth.

Venus in GEMINI

In a relationship, those with Venus in Gemini will need friendship, liveliness, good intellectual rapport, and a partner pleased to enjoy light-hearted flirtation and sheer fun – quite apart from an interest in a varied and lively sex life. It is more likely than not that someone with Venus in Gemini, whether male or female, will be tempted to have more than one relationship at a time – and may give way to that temptation. They have the ability to cover their tracks, and can sometime get away with the kind of farcical rushing about and manoeuvring that other people would find far too complicated and far too exhausting. With Aries or Leo as Sun-sign light-hearted enjoyment of sex and a naturally passionate character make this situation even more likely: these people hate being tied down. A Sun-sign Taurean will be far less possessive than otherwise, and the sensitive Cancerian will be less sensitive (though maybe a little nervous). If Venus is in Gemini with the Sun, all the flirtatiousness and duality will be addition-ally emphasized.

Venus in CANCER

The caring, affectionate qualities of Cancer are enhanced when Venus is in the sign; the downside of the placing is that the Cancerian tendency to worry is equally emphasized, and the concern will be directed at the partner. However, that will be a small price to pay for all the genuine affection and concern. A high level of emotion will need to be expressed in every sense of the word 'love', and this will emerge whatever the Sun-sign. If the Sun is in Taurus it will tend to be low-level, at least on the outside, but smouldering and intense beneath a possibly cool exterior. Possessiveness could be a real problem. Those with Gemini or Virgo Sun-signs will benefit: the lightheart-edness of the first will be counterbalanced, and the modesty and withdrawal

of the second will be offset. With a Leo Sun-sign those with Venus
in Cancer will be less inclined to lay down the law in every area of
a partnership; but the passion and drama of the personality will if anything be emphasized.

Venus in LEO

The partners of people with Venus in Leo will certainly know that they
are loved: emotion will at no stage be kept under wraps. Whatever money
the individual has will be freely spent in wooing a prospective partner
and entertaining one who has been captured. Generosity will not be
confined to money, but will extend to emotion, both romantic and sexual.
Depending, as usual, to some degree on the placing of the Sun and the
rising-sign, those with Venus in Leo will almost top the list of those who
expend startling amounts of emotion and money on their partners. It goes
without saying that they need an enthusiastic response – a lover who does
not receive what is offered with the same enthusiasm shown by the giver,
will not last long. This is not someone to whom one should say: 'But really,
can you afford it?' Nor should one back away from the excitement and
passion shown. If Venus shares Leo with the Sun, the results will be
startling and everything said above should be printed in red ink. With
Gemini or Virgo as Sun-signs everything will be even more colourful and
inventive and warm. With the Sun in Libra, some attempt should really be
made to curb the exuberance a little.

Venus in VIRGO

Critical, not particularly emotional, and encouraging discrimination, rationality and modesty, Virgo is not a sign in which Venus can be expected to be
particularly happy, and such is the case. Those with Venus in Virgo tend to
be shy, have little confidence in their own powers of attraction, and find it
difficult to approach anyone to whom they are themselves attracted. They
need friendship, and enjoy it; but if sex rears its head too early or too enthusiastically they can be frightened off. Even if things move slowly, a fairly
low emotional level together with a possible lack of enthusiasm for sex can
provide problems. Hopefully, the Sun- or rising-sign will offer some help –
for instance if the Sun is in Cancer or Leo, there will be less of a problem
with shyness; and with a Scorpio Sun-sign this placing of Venus can be a

positive help, cooling the sometimes overpassionate approach suggested by that Sun-sign. Not a good placing of Venus for Librans, however, who are romantics and themselves often somewhat shy. With a Virgo Sun-sign a real effort must be made to relax into a relationship.

Venus in LIBRA

Venus rules Libra, so its effect from that sign is stronger than otherwise. The planet is in a tender, romantic and considerate mood, and will pass these qualities on to anyone with this placing of Venus – who in addition will be extremely diplomatic and kindly. The need to be in a relationship is heightened, and it is possible that these individuals may commit themselves rather more speedily than is entirely wise: as is often the case with Sun-sign Librans, this provides a lesson which is learned the hard way. These people have a high appreciation of beauty, and may well not only enjoy but work in the field of the fine arts. Creative ability – perhaps in music or design – will be expressed with elegance and refinement. If Libra is also the Sun-sign, the psychological motivation of the subject will be expressed within the relationship and will centre on the partner. Venus will be extremely helpful to Sun-sign Virgoans, helping to bolster their confidence and weaken their self-consciousness when relating to other people. The Sun-sign Scorpio will be less heavily passionate, gentler, more sensitive, while the extravagant Leo will be slightly less free with money and emotion. A passionate Sagittarian will be more understanding and loving.

Venus in SCORPIO

Traditionally, Venus is said not to be at her best in Scorpio, and certainly the effect of the planet can be to make Scorpio passion even more passionate and a touch turgid. A deep intensity of emotion that needs full expression will demand an equal response from a partner, and be disappointed if it is not forthcoming. This can make for claustrophobia, and the partner may feel he or she needs more freedom and less cloying emotion than is expressed. There will more than likely be elements of jealousy and posses- siveness, both of which are likely to be fatal to a relationship, however hard the individual works for it. Individuals willing to take this under account, think twice before accusing a partner of unfaithfulness, and allow them to do their own thing, can, however, get much from this placing of Venus.

Those with a Virgo or Capricorn Sun-sign will not find this easy; they must try to adapt. The Scorpio way of loving will be emphasized when Libra is the Sun-sign, and a passionate addiction to sexual pleasure will be added to this usually less ardent sign. This will be true too with Scorpio and Sagittarian Sun-signs, and since these are by nature already passionate, the firework displays should be vivid and colourful.

Venus in SAGITTARIUS

A bright, breezy, casual attitude to love will be characteristic when Venus is placed in Sagittarius. These people will need a high degree of sexual satisfaction, and a partner must be ready to meet blow with blow; boredom in bed will simply not be tolerated, and one must remember that Sagittarius is not only versatile but also a dual sign. Apply these characteristics to the sex life and no imagination is needed as to the effect. However, the partner will also need to be on the same intellectual level as the one with Venus in Sagittarius. Restlessness could be a problem, not only in the love life, but at work, and in both these spheres can be equally damaging. From Sagittarius Venus works well for someone with a Libra Sun-sign, helping them to look less severely on their partner when flaws are discovered. The rather cool Capricorn and Aquarian will have their emotional level increased. Those with a Sagittarian Sun-sign must be careful not to take their partners for granted. A Sun-sign Scorpio will find fun in any relationship, and will be less completely focused on sex.

Venus in CAPRICORN

A slightly cool attitude to love is compensated by enormous fidelity and a caring quality second to none. These people will want to do everything for their partners' comfort and wellbeing. A sense of pride ensures that they will want to show their partners off – and those partners should take care that they are worth showing off, for Capricorn demands a sense of style and wants the partner to be considered as handsome and carefully chosen as a fine antique. Not perhaps the most lovable attitude; but with some luck the positions of other planets will soften it somewhat – there is unlikely to be a great deal of help here from Venus, not in a very strong position in Capricorn, though emphasizing a degree of consideration and care. When Scorpio is the Sun-sign Venus will help control and channel the emotions, and add an uncharacteristic ability to hold back at times. Those with the Sun in Sagittarius will be surprisingly formal in their approach to a possible partner, though this will not survive long once a real acquaintanceship has sprung up. A Capricorn Sun-sign encourages a solitary life, even within a relationship – and this may also be true of an Aquarian. Piscean emotion will be steadied.

Venus in AQUARIUS

A marvellously glamorous position for Venus leads the planet to bestow real star quality and powers of attraction. With this, however, comes a certain feeling of distance and remoteness, so that however enthusiastic the love life it may be difficult to attain the feeling of total closeness which most people need in a relationship. Venus is not strongly emotional or affectionate when in Aquarius, though it works wonderfully well in friendship, and there is a streak of kindness which will show itself whenever consolation or consideration or practical help are needed. With the Sun in Capricorn, while Venus can be cooler in this sign than elsewhere, she contributes an unconventional attitude which can be intriguing and interesting in equal measure. Those with an Aquarian Sun-sign will need to consider very carefully what they need from a relationship before they commit themselves, and with a Piscean Sun-sign there is an equal need for detachment, for considering the situation as unemotionally as possible before commitment.

Venus in PISCES

Warm sensitivity and strong emotions are directed firmly towards the partner when Venus is in Pisces. There may however be some feelings of inadequacy which are compensated by ever increasing attention to the comfort and needs of the partner. There will also almost certainly be a higher than average tendency to worry about him or her. These people really need to know their worth and persuade themselves that they are in an equal partnership where they are as essential as the other person, and quite as valuable; Venus will then work very well for them from this sign, whatever sign the Sun is in. As to that, however, this is a particularly good placing of Venus for a Sun-sign Capricorn, increasing the emotional level and decreasing the chance that the attitude to sex is too uptight. Venus will also work to cool the somewhat distant quality of Aquarius, though there

are certain tensions between the Sun-sign and Venus-sign qualities.
With the Sun also in Pisces there will be a tendency to overdo the emotional
response; the brashness of Aries will be toned down, and a greater
sensitivity encouraged. Venus works well for Sun-sign Taureans, helping
to counter possessiveness.

Venus and the houses

Venus in the FIRST HOUSE

A languid charm and a need to love and be loved will be important characteristics of those with Venus in the first house. Grace of movement is linked
to a leisurely disregard of any need for exercise – even perhaps a dislike of
it; and laziness in this respect may also be seen in other areas of life.
Relaxed conversation will be a pleasure, and a need for harmony will
usually ensure that there is little place for argument or disruption. A loving
permanent relationship will resolve any problems which might arise from a
tendency to resentfulness.

Venus in the SECOND HOUSE

This is the house of Venus, and at home here the planet exerts a strong
influence. A love of beauty will extend to a concern for the subject's own
impression upon the world: he or she will want to present themselves as
well as possible. There will be great pleasure in collecting and owning
beautiful things, and possessions will be important – care must be taken that
loved ones are not themselves regarded as possessions. Generosity will be a
characteristic, but sometimes may be used to impress.

Venus in the THIRD HOUSE

A love of family will mean that there is real closeness and sympathy
between family members; the ability to communicate with them should
extend outwards, so that relationships with others outside the family are
almost equally easy and good. A healthy social life will be appreciated, and
a relaxed and easy personality will be popular. Intellectual challenge will be
welcome, however difficult the problem or research to be done; work will
be carefully and meticulously done, with excellent use made of every
available research tool.

Venus in the FOURTH HOUSE

A tendency to spoil children will almost inevitably mean that parting from them, when they decide to leave home, will be traumatic. Expensive gifts and free help with money will not necessarily have the desired result, and recognition of their independence is the only reliable solution. The subject him- or herself may have had a closer than average relationship with the mother – even to the extent that there may have been equal trauma when the time came for themselves to leave home. Pride will be taken in the physical home, which will be as comfortable and beautiful as the income can support.

Venus in the FIFTH HOUSE

The love life will be highly romantic, and there may be a strong tempta-tion to put the loved one on a pedestal, with consequent difficulty when he or she proves not to be absolutely perfect. A love of comfort and luxury will be strong; how far it can be indulged will depend largely on the sign Venus inhabits. The arts will be appreciated and supported, and there may well be creative potential, especially in the field of fashion design or paint-ing. A fascination with finance can be worrying, for there is a strong tendency to gamble.

Venus in the SIXTH HOUSE

A love of good food and wine together with a somewhat slow metabolism may be translated into weight gain, with some difficulty in taking suffi-ciently strong action to control it. It will be worth checking the health of the thyroid gland. Work will be done at the subject's own pace, which will not be particularly speedy; procrastination may feature. Untidy or slovenly working conditions will not be tolerated – unless the end result is remarkably pleasing. In personal relations with others, good manners and politeness will be at a premium: lapses in either will be strongly criticized.

Venus in the SEVENTH HOUSE

A loving permanent relationship will be a strong ambition, and to achieve it there is the possibility of premature commitment The importance of not rushing in may not be recognized until too late. Within a partnership, there will have to be recognition that those with Venus in the seventh house may come to rely so much on a partner that their own personality is flooded and eventually submerged by that of the other. The fact that this will be the result of love, of adoration, does not make it any less of a problem. Friendship must be an element, and it must be possible to work together for the good of the partnership.

Venus in the EIGHTH HOUSE

A rich and rewarding sex life is likely, and from the eighth house Venus works to increase passion – to such an extent that jealousy should be watched for. There will be a high degree of insight and sympathy with the partner, and if Venus is in a WATER SIGN a high level of intuition, which can usually be trusted. Traditionally, this placing of Venus makes for a shrewd business sense and a flair for investment; and there should be a distinct talent for being able to analyse problems – whether the subject's own or those of a friend or colleague.

Venus in the NINTH HOUSE

Those with Venus in the ninth house are likely to be philosophical and relaxed about life, and their ambition will be to live quietly, untroubled by the world and its problems. They will also be eager to see as much of that world as possible, and travel will be at the head of their list of ambitions – they will tend to fall in love with foreign countries (possibly because of a romantic conception of them rather than reality); and similar personal romance may be found abroad, with people of other nations – indeed there is a tendency for those with this placing of Venus to marry people from overseas.

Venus in the TENTH HOUSE

Taking great pride in their work, people with Venus in the tenth house will do best working with others; they will not find it difficult to get on with colleagues, but may find it difficult if forced to work alone (for instance, if promoted to a solitary position of influence and power). Work, a career, will be emotionally important, and they will need to feel thoroughly involved with any task they undertake; money is important to them, but should not be *all*-important.

Venus in the ELEVENTH HOUSE

For a number of reasons, working with others is desirable. Those
with Venus in this house will enjoy attracting the attention and admiration of colleagues, and will set out to please them – quite apart from
enjoying working with them to further the aims of the group. Social
life is important, and under normal situations they will have a wide circle of
friends and an even larger circle of acquaintances, who will enjoy being
entertained by them, for they will have a distinct flair for organizing
parties and social events.

Venus in the TWELFTH HOUSE

Inhibition and shyness can complicate the love life of those with Venus in
the twelfth house; they will tend to be highly secretive about this aspect of
their life, and find difficulty in expressing their feelings. A tendency to
shrink from contact with others, especially if emotions begin to show
themselves, can lead to the development of a private fantasy life which may
become a substitute for a more outward, healthier expression of their
emotions. Under stress, comfort-eating – and drinking – can become a
problem. Sexuality can sometimes be replaced by religiosity.

* * *

vernal equinox In the northern hemisphere, the beginning of the
astrological year, when the Sun crosses the CELESTIAL EQUATOR from south
to north, at the first degree of Aries. In the southern hemisphere this is the
autumn equinox.

vernal point The point on the ECLIPTIC where the Sun is placed at the
moment of the VERNAL EQUINOX – 1° Aries.

vertex A discredited theory said to represent the 'inner life of the
ASCENDANT', this was arrived at by calculating the degree of the Ascendant
as though the subject were born in the opposite hemisphere.

Vesta The second largest of the ASTEROIDS. Vesta, the virgin goddess
(originally the Greek Hestia) was invoked to protect the home. Many

astrologers therefore assert that the asteroid represents domesticity and the qualities in life one most treasures – though others claim that it encourages attention to physical fitness – exercise, a balanced diet and a sensible attitude to alcohol and other indulgences. It is associated with natural remedies and alternative medicine. It strengthens a woman's attitude to her own sexuality, whether positive or negative; it is often associated with virginity and the idealization of the sexual impulse. This can become extreme in either direction, leading on the one hand to restraint and even abstinence, on the other to the utmost promiscuity.

Vettius Valens (fl. AD150–180) Vettius Valens (who probably worked in Alexandria) published over 130 BIRTH-CHARTS from Antioch, in Syria, dating from 37 to 188BC – the largest collection to have survived – in his *Anthologia*, a major teaching manual. This collection of the horoscopes of famous people seems to have been made specifically for his own students, in much the same way as similar records of birth-charts of famous contemporaries are collected by 21st-century astrologers eager to compare one to the other, for the purpose of confirming their views of what astrological indications suggest particular personality traits. Vettius Valens deals with NATAL and HORARY ASTROLOGY as comprehensively as was possible in his time. He regarded astrology to a large extent as a 'mystery' – the names of NECHEPSO and PETOSIRIS often occur – and at one stage requires his students to take an oath not to reveal his secrets to anyone outside the astrological fraternity.

via combusta (or 'the Burning Way') Ancient astrologers considered that if the Moon was set at birth against a cluster of fixed stars in the early degrees of Scorpio, it was as severely affected as if it was eclipsed. In modern astrology the via combusta is measured from 15° Libra to 15° Scorpio, and if the Moon is within these points the whole chart is considered void and uninterpretable. This is important in HORARY ASTROLOGY, for it means that nothing can be done about the problem or situation.

Virgo ♍

The sixth sign of the zodiac. SUN-SIGN period 24 August–22 September.

It should always be remembered when reading of the characteristics of the Sun-signs that these will always be affected by the effects of the rising-sign, the planets in various other signs and houses, and the relationships the planets make to each other.

General characteristics

A sense of continual activity is what, above all, signals a Virgo Sun-sign personality. Those with this emphasis are as busy when relaxing as when they are engaged in the most intense work – though all the bustle is not necessarily as productive as might be hoped, for Virgos have relatively little talent for organization, and a lot of effort can go to waste. With a strong sense of duty, they work well and faithfully for others, and with great attention to detail – sometimes amounting to niggling. With a high level of nervous energy, they can suffer from tension when faced with difficult problems or situations. This can manifest itself in headaches or migraines, best cured by relying on the Virgo talent for meticulousness – they will work out in detail the elements of a problem and apply their strong critical sense to working out a solution. Inherent modesty can dampen their enthusiasm when courting a possible partner, for those to whom they are attracted are almost always seen as 'too good' for them. Lack of a strong interest in sex can be a problem in a permanent relationship, as can their strong critical sense, for continual criticism too freely expressed can weaken the strongest bond.

The growing child

Neat and clean, Virgoan children will usually be willing and eager to help out with household tasks, and from the earliest age will need to be kept busy. Bored Virgoan children are all too likely to invent activity for themselves, which will not always be productive. Finding them 'something to do' will always be important. At the same time it will be necessary to ensure that energy is not wasted. There is bound to be a certain amount of fleeting from one task to another, but this need not be discouraged as long as consistency of effort is encouraged. From a very early age these children will be capable of working painstakingly – if not fussily – on a task which engages their interest, and those activities which need dexterity of mind or hands will be particularly popular. Any tension or worry will probably show itself first at the table, in a reluctance to eat, and in minor digestive upsets. A Virgoan child who complains of a stomach ache will usually confess, when questioned, to having been upset in some way, perhaps by another child.

Education

Young Virgoans will work hard at school, not only because they have a natural interest in acquiring knowledge, but to please their teachers or lecturers. This will not necessarily, especially in the early years, make them popular with fellow students, who may regard them not only as 'swots' but as overeager to curry favour. There may well indeed be a tendency to work too hard to please their teachers, and even to become unpaid servants of their seniors. Tending to be shy, relationships with their peers will probably not be easy at first, but some Virgos have excellent powers of leadership, and encouraged in the right way can from an early age be capable of assuming command in all sorts of situations. As far as study itself is concerned, they should do well, particularly in literary and allied subjects. Their notebooks and the notes themselves will be as neat and tidy as their own persons, everything beautifully organized; later, essays will be painstakingly researched and arguments impeccably set out. As long as they don't allow themselves to be distracted by small detail, those with this Sun-sign should build an excellent scholastic CV.

Friendship, romance and sex

Practical and active, Sun-sign Virgos will organize a friendship almost too well, and their boundless energy can be wearing. Being naturally critical, they will not be slow to venture an opinion when they think their friends have let them down in some way – so friendships may become strained. Romantically, they are retiring, reluctant to accept compliments as genuine – but their modesty is charming, and they often have an inner desire to be thoroughly romanced. When they love they do so faithfully, truly and lastingly. Those with a Virgo Sun-sign can adjust well to a celibate life (Virgo is after all the sign of virginity), and they need coaxing if they are to express their love openly, for it will be unusual if there is not a degree of inhibition which works against their showing their feelings – especially sexually. It is more likely than not to be the case that they will not be openly sensual, and may even see sex as a necessary evil ('Lie back and think of England'). Other areas of the full BIRTH-CHART – especially the positions of Venus and Mars – may well of course mitigate this, and it should not be taken for granted. In a permanent relationship the chief danger, all this aside, may be the tendency to be overcritical and to nag.

Permanent partnership and family

If we can take it for granted that a solution can be found that will solve the problem of their possible sexual inhibition, (and anyone with the Sun in Virgo should consider very carefully whether this is a problem to which they need to attend) a Virgoan partner has much to offer. He or she will work extremely hard for the comfort of partner and family. Care must be taken to keep the Virgo critical sense under control, at least as far as its open expression is concerned: a continual flow of disapproval and dispar-agement can wear away the most loving affection. If criticism is freely expressed, it should be accompanied by appreciation (not to say self-criticism). A Virgoan parent will see to it that a child is fully occupied, and will encourage reading and writing from a very early age. There will be no question of unlimited access to television or the world-wide web. There is an element of the teacher in most Virgos, which makes it easy for them to inspire their children. Once again, and as always, the tendency to be over-critical must be governed; it can seriously damage a child's perception of him- or herself.

Occupation

A man or woman with a Virgo Sun-sign will make the ideal secretary or PA. Meticulous attention to detail and a relish for organizing other people's lives suggests that they are likely to be extremely competent at making sure that every entry in a diary is in its proper place, that an employer's working life is planned to the last minute. This does not of course mean that there is no talent for becoming something more than a secretary – but encourage-ment and a bolstering of self-confidence will be needed if this is to be the case. There may be some rough edges to smooth when it comes to relationships with colleagues, however, and especially employees – there is likely to be a continual flow of criticism, unbalanced by an equal quantity of praise. This critical sense can be well deployed in journalism or professional criticism, though the talent for teaching is also worth exploration, and a career in politics may prove rewarding. The outdoor life is important to most Virgoans, so unless the career takes them into the open air, some spare-time activity should be devised that will do so.

Health

The stomach is the area of the body associated with Virgo, and when anxiety and tension build, the first outward signs are likely to be a reluctance to eat, or a problem with diet. Headaches and migraine can then develop, which will exacerbate the situation, so that even more symptoms appear, such as skin problems and allergies. Fortunately Virgoans are good at self-analysis, and can usually be relied upon to recognize what is causing the tension, and to assess the problem and deal with it. At the best of times diet is important to them; they react well to whole foods and a vegetarian diet. Physical exercise is particularly important, and fortunately their love of the outdoors makes it easy for them to enjoy it – walking, jogging, cycling, tennis and outdoor games in general, which burn up not only physical but nervous energy. Varying the form the exercise takes is excellent for them, avoiding the boredom which can otherwise become a problem. Younger Virgos will enjoy gymnastics or athletics, and have the mental stamina to stick at the necessary vigorous training.

Finance

Sun-sign Virgos will be at their most meticulous when working out what to do with their money – especially when thinking about possible investments. Every detail of a possible speculation will be collected and sifted, and every authority consulted. They tend to favour investments that offer a steady, even slow growth of capital, though sometimes a temporary fit of boredom may encourage them to go for something a little more exciting – in which case it will be important to obtain professional advice from a broker or bank manager. More usually they will show great care with the money they have been able to set aside, and are unlikely to take real risks with it. Always needing to be kept busy and at work, it is by no means impossible that a

second, spare-time business will appeal; if this is set up, Virgo will
work as hard and thoroughly as in their main career, and consequently
success is likely. When thinking about such a possibility, they should concentrate on one particular area, and one that really interests them – and not
only as a means of extra income. With a characteristically modest lifestyle,
Virgos are not usually overeager to become seriously rich, but an interest in
business and finance can be valuable not only financially but as a means
of self-expression.

Growing older

Virgos often look forward to retirement as offering the time in which
to cultivate the hobby or hobbies which have had to take a back seat
during their working lives. This is almost certain to include gardening,
which has probably been a life-time interest – a practical one if they have
been able to maintain a garden. Not being particularly devoted to money as
such, they are unlikely to regret or worry about any diminution of income
which retirement brings – and indeed their care for the investment of any
money they have been able to save may mean that there are few financial
problems to come. They will keep busy as long as they remain active, and
while even when business worries have ceased they will always find
something to worry about, the occasions on which tension becomes a real
problem may be far fewer. They will continue to exercise regularly
(gardening will certainly help with this), and the continual activity characteristic of the sign should mean that having learned over a lifetime what diet
is best for then, they should have as trouble-free an old age, medically, as
those of any other sign.

Virgo as rising-sign

The practical and logical side of Virgo will be strongly emphasized when
that sign is rising in the HOROSCOPE, but will be expressed only after serious
constructive thought. There is a much greater chance that emotions will be
openly expressed when Virgo is rising than when it is the Sun-sign, and
they are likely to be warm and tender and well to the fore in a permanent
relationship. (This is due to the effect of the POLAR SIGN, Pisces, which has a
strong relationship on partnership for those with Virgo rising.) This will
bring a special, unique quality to a permanent relationship, which will

probably be recognized only by the couple themselves, and will be specially valuable. Mercury will ensure that the need to communicate is also greater with these folk than for those with a Virgo Sun-sign, and there will be considerably more liveliness and fun between friends.

Traditional associations
- Ruling Planet – Mercury
- Triplicity/Element – earth
- Quadruplicity/Quality – mutable
- Colours – navy blue, dark brown, green
- Gemstone – sardonyx
- Metal – mercury or nickel
- Flowers – all bright-coloured small flowers, such as the anemone
- Trees – all nut-bearing trees (shared with Gemini)
- Herbs and Spices – those with bright yellow or blue flowers or colouring
- Foodstuffs – vegetables grown under the earth
- Animals – all domestic pets
- Countries – Greece, the West Indies, Turkey, Brazil, Costa Rica, N Korea, Singapore, New Zealand
- Cities – Boston, Heidelberg, Los Angeles, Paris, Athens
- US State – California

* * *

virtues and vices Medieval astrologers linked the seven virtues and seven vices to the seven then observed PLANETS and the days of the week associated with them; these often appear symbolically in the art of the period. Hope and indolence were linked to the Sun and to Sunday, chastity and envy to the Moon and Monday, wisdom and gluttony to Mercury and Tuesday, love and lust to Venus and Wednesday, courage and wrath to Mars and Thursday, faith and pride to Jupiter and Friday, and prudence and covetousness to Saturn and Saturday.

Vitruvius (fl.1st century BC) Marcus Vitruvius Pollio was a Roman architect and engineer, and an elegant writer on architecture. He also wrote in support of astrology, claiming that the work of BEROSUS and the Chaldeans made it perfectly clear that the Sun, Moon and planets had an observable effect on human life.

void of course When a planet passes through one of the SIGNS of a HOROSCOPE without coming into aspect with any other planet, it is said to be void of course.

Vulcan A HYPOTHETICAL PLANET which is interpreted in different ways by different astrologers.

– W –

Walker, Patric (1931–95) The most successful SUN-SIGN newspaper and magazine columnist of his time, Walker became interested in astrology in the 1960s, prior to which he had been a show-business journalist. He started writing a column for *Nova* at the end of the 1960s, and in 1974 succeeded to the columns written by the earlier astrologer 'Celeste'. His columns were syndicated worldwide and he became extremely wealthy. At one moment he would claim that he had been carefully trained in astrology (though he would never say by whom), and at another that he really had no knowledge at all, and would be incapable of drawing up an accurate BIRTH-CHART. This did not prevent him from becoming an adviser to a large number of fashionable show-business personalities.

Warner, William John (1866–1936) Irish astrologer, palmist and numerologist who adopted the names Cheiro and Count Louis Hamon. The most famous 'society palmist' of his time, he first worked in England before moving to America, impressing people as various as Mark Twain, Oscar Wilde, Thomas Edison and William Gladstone. It is said that in Hollywood he saw as many as 30 clients a day. His interest in astrology was marginal. He wrote some screenplays and published books on palmistry and numerology, and a novel, *The Hand of Fate*.

water signs Cancer, Scorpio and Pisces. *See* ELEMENTS.

weather forecasting *see* METEOROLOGY

Whalley, John (1653–1724) Born in Ireland, Whalley was at first a shoemaker, but gradually established himself in Dublin as an astrologer, issuing almanacs. He became so well known that he was consulted by the King's officers in an attempt to discover the whereabouts of the Duke of Monmouth. As a Protestant he was unpopular with the Catholics, and at one time was put in the pillory; he escaped to England, where he kept a coffee-house. Back in Ireland by the 1690s he continued to publish his almanacs, *Advice from the Stars*, and having somersaulted from his previous position specifically catered for a Roman Catholic readership. As a practising astrologer he seems to have specialized in decumbitures – charts drawn up for the moment when an illness begins, with the intention of foretelling its duration. In 1701 he published his translation of PTOLEMY's *The Tetrabiblos* – the first in English. After his death, his favourite apprentice, Isaac Butler, continued to publish his almanacs.

Wharton, Sir George (1617–81) The son of a blacksmith, Wharton studied astronomy and mathematics at Oxford, and began issuing almanacs in 1641 under the name of Naworth. On the outbreak of the Civil War he raised a troop of horse for the King, but after the Royalist defeat returned to Oxford to study astrology. Astrological warfare broke out between him and his rivals on the Parliamentary side, William LILLY, John PARTRIDGE and John BOOKER, who busily denounced each other in their almanacs. During the Interregnum he was arrested and imprisoned at Newgate, escaped, and was re-imprisoned; condemned to be hanged he was saved by the intervention of Lilly. After the Restoration, he was made a baronet in recognition of his services to the Royalist cause; he published no more almanacs, but put out several collections of witty poetry.

Wing, Vincent (1619–88) Having taught himself Latin, Greek and mathematics, Wing began to publish astrological books in the 1640s, but was best known for his *Astronomia Britannica* (1652), a complete system of Copernican astronomy. For many years he issued annual sets of remarkably accurate ephemerides, and at the same time published an annual almanac, *Olympia Domata*, which sold 50,000 copies a year, and was said to have forecast his own death, making his will a fortnight earlier. He maintained a regular correspondence with contemporary astrologers, both Royalist and Parliamentarian, and edited George Atwell's *An Apology, or, Defence of the Divine Art of Natural Astrology* (1660).

Witte, Alfred (1878–1941) An influential figure in German astrology during the 1920s and early 1930s, founder of the Hamburg School of Astrology, Witte was devoted to the use of MIDPOINTS before this was common. In the 1920s he devised a new system of planetary RULERSHIPS and took an individual view of the use of the HOUSES. He insisted on the existence of a number of HYPOTHETICAL PLANETS, and URANIAN astrologers still use some trans-Neptunian 'planets' whose existence has yet to be verified. When the Nazi government turned against astrology, his books (including *The Rulebook for Planetary Pictures*) was banned and burned. He committed suicide when threatened with arrest by the Gestapo.

Wohl, Ludwig ('Louis') de (1903–61) Born in Berlin and partly Jewish, de Wohl was an unsuccessful novelist and journalist until in 1930 he met Baron Harald Keun von Hoogerwoerd, an astrologer who interested de Wohl in the subject. Within a short time the latter had taught himself enough to begin to practise. In 1935 he arrived in Britain as a refugee, and in 1940, according to his autobiographical book, *The Stars of War and Peace* (1947), approached M Virgil Tilea, of the Rumanian diplomatic service in London, and suggested that the Allies would do well to engage the services of an astrologer who would tell them what HITLER's astrologer was telling him – for, he claimed, the Führer was utterly dependent on astrology (but *see* KRAFFT). After a meeting with Lord Halifax, Secretary of State for Foreign Affairs, he found himself employed by the Special Operations Executive, and appeared in public wearing the uniform of a captain in the British Army (though he held no such rank). No-one appears to have taken any notice of the astrological reports he submitted to the War Cabinet, though he was sent to New York in 1941 with the intention that he persuade American astrologers to collaborate in writing black propaganda against the Third Reich. Working for the well-known propagandist Sefton Delmer, de Wohl produced translations of NOSTRADAMUS which promised an Allied victory; these were dropped as leaflets over Germany. Shortly afterwards, he ceased to work for Britain propaganda, and his life until his death in 1961 remains obscure.

Wolsey, Cardinal Thomas (ca.1475–1530) English prelate and statesman, Wolsey employed the astrologer John Robins to calculate the horoscope of King Henry VIII in order to enable him better to understand the King's character and predict and satisfy his wishes. He used astrology for other purposes, such as timing the start of journeys or the dispatch of embassies.

Woodruff, Maurice (1920–85) An English astrologer and extremely successful psychic whose career as a clairvoyant overtook his practice of astrology. He claimed to have innumerable well-known actors and society people among his clients, including the actor Peter Sellers.

Wulff, Wilhelm (b. 1893) A German astrologer forced by the SS to work for Heinrich Himmler and other Nazi officers. After Hess' defection (*see* KRAFFT) Wulff was arrested and spend four months in a concentration camp. He wrote about his association with Himmler in *Zodiac and Swastika* (1973).

– Z –

Zadkiel *see* MORRISON, RICHARD JAMES and PEARCE, A J

Zain, C C *see* BENJAMINE

zenith The point of the sky immediately overhead.

zodiac The zodiac is a circle drawn through the part of the sky including the path of the Sun, Moon and planets as they appear to move around the Earth. The Earth as it rotates around the Sun is tilted at an angle of 23° 27' to the horizontal, so half of the zodiac lies to the north of the celestial equator and half to the south. Sometime between the 7th and 5th centuries BC, the apparent path of the Sun around the 360°circle of the ECLIPTIC was divided into twelve sections, each of 30°. This division, which happened independently in Babylon, Egypt and China, originated as a measuring device and approximated to the length of the year, which brings the sky back to the same point after 365.2422 days. The twelve divisions form what is known as the zodiac (the name, seems first to have been used by the ancient Greeks to describe the sculptured figures of animals). The Egyptian and Babylonian astrologers used the SIDEREAL zodiac of the fixed stars.

A particular CONSTELLATION lay behind each of the sections, and each section became named for that constellation – Aries, Taurus, Gemini, Cancer and so on. This had the advantage that by the 5th century BC the astronomer-astrologers of ancient Babylonia could accurately map the progress of a planet through the heavens by referring to the zodiac signs, instead of only roughly estimating their positions.

Some constellations take up a great deal more space in the circle than others, while some overlap each other, but the ancients managed to overcome the problem of reducing the twelve zodiac signs to equal sizes. It was decided from the earliest times that the names of the constellations were to be used simply *as* names, describing equal sections of the circle in the order in which they occurred. While a particular constellation may occupy more or less space in the circle of the ecliptic, the *sign* occupies, strictly, 30°.

In the West, the zodiac begins on 20, 21 or 22 March each year, at the vernal equinox – the point at which the Sun appears to cross the equator from south to north at the spring equinox of the northern hemisphere. The equinox never occurs in exactly the same spot two years in succession but, due to the oscillation of the Earth's axis, slowly rotates around the sky, taking some 25,800 years to complete the circle. This fact, first discovered by HIPPARCHUS in 120BC, means that the constellations as seen today do not coincide with their positions 3,000 years ago. This fact much preoccupies critics of astrology. But *see* PRECESSION.

There are, then, actually two zodiacs, the TROPICAL or moving zodiac, measured from the first point of Aries, and the fixed or SIDEREAL zodiac, measured from the fixed stars, which moves forward relative to the calendar by one day every 72 years. 'Sidereal' means 'of the stars', 'tropical' means that the tropical zodiac is measured from the four turning-points of the Sun, when it crosses the equator to the north (in March) or the south (in September), and the points at which it reaches its greatest distance from the equator in either direction.

The device of the twelve sections of the zodiac clearly first originated as a measuring device. How they became associated with the humans, beasts and other symbols of the constellations can never be known, and indeed speculation is difficult since while one or two of the star patterns very roughly suggest the symbols which were attached to them – notably perhaps Gemini and Scorpio – the others appear completely random until the figures are drawn over them. It is equally impossible to discover when the idea originated that the position of the Sun seen against the patterns of the sky could have something to say about the character of a man or woman born at a specific time, or could be used to predict the future. It seems a strong possibility that it grew out of the general idea proposed by PLATO – that the soul (for which we could today substitute the unconscious) chose instinctively to follow one of the twelve zodiacal gods.

What is not difficult to fathom is how the zodiac and the movement of the planets around it became used as a system of prognostication: it merely joined other, almost innumerable PREDICTION systems.

Emphasis on the zodiac as a result of the oversimplification of astrology in the 1930s (a result of the invention of SUN-SIGN ASTROLOGY in the popular press) for a time did considerable harm to the idea of astrology as a complex system relying on a great number of factors other than the zodiac sign occupied by the Sun. While the naming of sections of the ecliptic after the zodiac figures remains a great convenience, it must always be remembered that these symbols in themselves mean little or nothing other than as convenient labels. *See* DENDERAH ZODIAC.

Zodiac Man, The Traditionally, the twelve signs of the zodiac have been associated with various areas of the body. Thomas Creech (1659–1700) recorded this in verse:

> *Now learn what signs the several limbs obey,*
> *Whose powers they feel and whose obedience pay.*
> *The Ram defends the neck, the head the Bull;*
> *The arms bright Twins, are subject to your rule;*
> *In the shoulders Leo; and the Crab's obeyed*
> *In the breast; and in the guts the modest Maid;*
> *In the buttocks Libra; Scorpio warms desires*
> *In secret parts, and spreads unruly fires;*
> *The thighs the Centaur; and the Goat commands*
> *The knees, and binds them up with double bands;*
> *The parted legs in moist Aquarius meet;*
> *And Pisces gives protection to the feet.*

Such verses were not always accurate: the true governance is as follows:

- Aries – the head
- Taurus – the neck and throat
- Gemini – the shoulders, arms and hands
- Cancer – the chest and breasts
- Leo – the heart and spine
- Virgo – the stomach and bowels
- Libra – the kidneys
- Scorpio – the genitals
- Sagittarius – the hips, thighs and liver

- Capricorn – the knees and shins (also the skin, teeth and bones)
- Aquarius – the ankles (and circulation)
- Pisces – the feet

MANILIUS is the first writer we know to have listed the correspondences between areas of the body and the signs. These were used in MEDICAL ASTROLOGY, the main rule relating to bleeding, or phlebotomy – which for centuries was a cure-all. It was considered fatal to bleed any part of the body at the time when the Moon occupied the sign which ruled that part.

BIBLIOGRAPHY

Among the books that have been helpful in compiling this encyclopedia the following have been most useful:

Adam, C G M, *Fresh Sidelights on Astrology* (Modern Astrology, London, 1916)

Addey, J M, *Astrology Reborn* (American Federation of Astrologers Inc., Bournemouth, 1973)

Allen, D C, *The Star-Crossed Renaissance* (Duke University Press, Carolina, 1941)

Allen, R H, *Star Names* (Dover Publications, New York, 1963)

Ashmole, E, *Notes and Correspondence* (ed. Josten, C H, Oxford, 1949)

Bailey, A, *Esoteric Astrology* (Lucis, London, 1951)

Barclay, O, *Horary Astrology Rediscovered* (Whitford Press, West Chester, 1990)

Barton, T, *Ancient Astrology* (Routledge, London, 1994)

Bonatus, G, *The Astrologers' Guide, or Anima Astrologiæ* (ed. Serjeant, W C E, Society of Metaphysicians Ltd; Facsimile of 1886 Ed edition (1 Aug 1986) London, 1986)

Bradley, D A, *Profession and Birthdate* (The Llewellyn Foundation, Los Angeles, 1950)

Brady, B, *The Eagle and the Lark* (Red Wheel/Weiser, York Beach, 1992)

Brinsley, J, *Ludus Literarius* (ed. Campagnac, E T, The University Press, Liverpool, 1917)

Burmyn, L, *Planets in Combination* (ACS Publications, San Diego, 1987)

Capp, B, *Astrology and the Popular Press* (Faber and Faber, London, 1979)

Carelli, A, *The 360 degrees of the Zodiac* (American Federation of Astrologers, Washington, 1951)

Carter, C E O, *An Encyclopaedia of Psychological Astrology* (W Foulsham & Co London, 1926)
The Principles of Astrology (Theosophical Publishing House, London, 1925)
Astrological Aspects (Fowler, London, 1969)

Christian, P, *The History and Practice of Magic* (tr. Kirkup, J and Shaw, J; Lyle Stuart, New York, 1963)

Clow, B H, *Chiron* (Llewellyn Publications, Minnesota, 1987)

Cornell, H L, *Encyclopaedia of Medical Astrology* (Astrology Classics) York, 2005)

Cumont, F V M, *Astrology and Religion among the Greeks and Romans* (Dover Publications Inc, New York, 1912)

Curry, P, *Prophecy and Power* (Polity Press, London, 1989)
A Confusion of Prophets (Collins & Brown, London, 1992)

Davis, M, *Astrolocality Astrology* (Wessex Astrologer Ltd, Bournemouth, 1999)

Davison, R C, *The Technique of Prediction* (Fowler, London, 1972)

Dean, G, and Mather, A (ed.), *Recent Advances in Natal Astrology* (Camelot Press, London, 1977)

Devore, N, *Encyclopaedia of Astrology* (New York, 1947)

Dygges, L, *A Prognostication, etc.* (Thomas Gemini, London, 1555)

Eade, J C, *The Forgotten Sky* (Oxford University Press, Oxford, 1984)

Ebertin, R, *The Combination of Stellar Influences* (American Federation of Astrologers London, 1972)

Elwell, D, *Cosmic Loom* (Thorsons, London, 1987)

Evans, J, *Magical Jewels of the middle ages and the renaissance, particularly in England* (The Clarendon Press, Oxford, 1922)

Fagan, C, *Astrological Origins* (Llewellyn Publications, Minnesota, 1971)

Filbey, J, and P, *Astronomy for Astrologers* (Aquarian Press, Wellingborough, 1984)

Garin, E, *Astrology in the Renaissance* (Arkana, London, 1990)

Gauquelin, M, *The Cosmic Clocks* (H. Regnery Co, London, 1967)
Cosmic Influences on HumanBehaviour (Garnstone Press Ltd, London, 1974)

Gettings, F, *The Arkana Dictionary of Astrology* (Arkana, London, 1990)

Gleadow, R, *The Origins of the Zodiac* (Jonathan Cape, London, 1968)

Hall, P, *Astrological Keywords* (Owen, London, 1959)

Hamblin, D, *Harmonic Charts* (HarperCollins, Wellingborough, 1983)

Herbst, B, *Houses of the Horoscope* (ACS Publications Inc., San Diego, 1988)

Hone, M E, *The Modern Textbook of Astrology* (Fowler, London, 1951)

Howe, E, *Urania's Children* (Kimber, London, 1967)

Illingworth, V (ed.), *A Dictionary of Astronomy* (Macmillan, London,1979)

Jayne, C A, *The Unknown Planets* (New York, 1974)

Jones, M E, *The Sabian Symbols in Astrology* (Sabian Publishing Society, New York, 1953)

Kitson, A, (ed.), *History and Astrology* (Mandala, London, 1989)

Koestler, A, *The Sleepwalkers* (Hutchinson, London, 1959)

Leo, Alan, various works (*see* text)

Leventhal, H, *In the Shadow of the Enlightenment* (New York University Press, New York, 1976)

Lewis, J, *Astro*cart*ography* (Equinox, San Francisco, 1976)

Lilly, W, *Christian Astrology* (Partridge and Blunden, London, 1647)

Lindsay, J, *Origins of Astrology* (Muller, London, 1971)

Lineman, R, *Eclipse Interpretation Manual* (American Federation of Astrologers Tempe, 1991)

Lyndoe, E, *Plan with the Planets* (1st Herbert Jenkins London, 1949)

McCafferey, E, *Astrology, its history and influence in the Western World* (University Microfilms New York, 1973)

Manilius, *Astronomica* (tr. Goold, G P; Heinemann, London, 1927)

Matthews, E C, *Fixed Stars and Degrees of the Zodiac* (Sign Book Co, Bloomington, 1968)

Nelson, J H, *Cosmic Patterns* (American Federation of Astrologers Inc Washington, 1974)

Pagan, I M, *Pioneer to Poet* (The Theosophical Publishing Society, London, 1911)

Parker, D, *Astrology in the Modern World* (Taplinger, London, 1970)

Ptolemy, *Tetrabiblos* (tr. Robbins, F R, Heinemann, London, 1940)

Reinhart, M, *Chiron and the healing journey* (Arkana, London, 1989)

Robson, V E, *Astrology and Human Sex Life* (Foulsham, London, 1963)
    The Fixed Stars and Constellations in Astrology (HarperCollins, London, 1969)

Rudhyar, D, *The Astrology of Personality* (Doubleday, New York, 1970)

Sepharial, *New Dictionary of Astrology* (Foulsham, London, 1921)

Sibley, E, *An Illustration of the Celestial Science of Astrology* (Kessinger Publishing, London, 2004)

Tester, J, *A History of Western Astrology* (Boydell, New York, 1988)

Thomas, K, *Religion and the Decline of Magic* (Penguin, London, 1971)

Thierens, A E, *The Elements of Esoteric Astrology* (Kessinger Publishing Co, London, 1931)

Thorndike, L, *A History of Magic and Experimental Science* (New York, 1941)

Traister, B H, *The Notorious Astrological Physician of London: works and days of Simon Forman* (University of Chicago Press, Chicago, 2001)

Ungar, A, and Huber, L, *The Horary Reference Book* (Acs Pubns, San Diego, 1984)

Whitfield, P, *Astrology: a history* (British Library Publishing Division, London, 2001)

Wohl, L de, *Secret Service of the Sky* (The Cresset Press, London, 1938)

Wood, C, *Chaucer and the Country of the Stars* (Princeton University Press, Princeton, 1970)

Woolley, B, *The Queen's Conjurer: the science and magic of Dr Dee* (Henry Holt & Company, London, 2001)
    The Herbalist: Nicholas Culpeper (HarperCollins Publishers, London, 2004)

Wulff, W, *Zodiac and Swastika* (Barker, New York, 1973)

'Zadkiel', *An Introduction to Astrology* (R T Cross, London, 1831)

NOTE: While every care has been taken to ensure the accuracy of the information in this book, the publisher and authors will, if informed, correct any errors or omissions in future editions.